CLASSIC STORIES
OF
WORLD WAR I

An Hachette UK Company
www.hachette.co.uk

This volume first published in Great Britain in 1989 by
Octopus Publishing Group Ltd
Carmelite House, 50 Victoria Embankment, London EC4Y 0DZ
www.octopusbooks.co.uk

This edition published in 2018 by Cassell, an imprint of
Octopus Publishing Group Ltd

Acknowledgments for each story or excerpt can be found on page 256.

ISBN 978-0-7537-3308-0

A CIP catalogue record for this book is available from the British Library

Printed and bound in China

10 9 8 7 6 5 4 3 2 1

For the Cassell edition
Publisher: Lucy Pessell
Designer: Lisa Layton
Editor: Sarah Vaughan
Production Controller: Katie Jarvis

CLASSIC STORIES
OF
WORLD WAR I

CASSELL
ILLUSTRATED

Contents

The Tale

Joseph Conrad

Outside the large single window the crepuscular light was dying out slowly in a great square gleam without color, framed rigidly in the gathering shades of the room.

It was a long room. The irresistible tide of the night ran into the most distant part of it, where the whispering of a man's voice, passionately interrupted and passionately renewed, seemed to plead against the answering murmurs of infinite sadness.

At last no answering murmur came. His movement when he rose slowly from his knees by the side of the deep, shadowy couch holding the shadowy suggestion of a reclining woman, revealed him tall under the low ceiling, and sombre all over except for the crude discord of the white collar under the shape of his head and the faint, minute spark of a brass button here and there on his uniform.

He stood over her a moment masculine and mysterious in his immobility before he sat down on a chair near by. He could see only the faint oval of her upturned face and, extended on her black dress, her pale hands, a moment before abandoned to his kisses and now as if too weary to move.

He dared not make a sound, shrinking as a man would do from the prosaic necessities of existence. As usual, it was the woman who had the courage. Her voice was heard first—almost conventional—while her being vibrated yet with conflicting emotions.

"Tell me something," she said.

The darkness hid his surprise and then his smile. Had he not just said to her everything worth saying in the world—and that not for the first time!

"What am I to tell you?" he asked, in a voice creditably steady. He was beginning to feel grateful to her for that something final in her tone which had eased the strain.

"Why not tell me a tale?"

"A tale!" He was really amazed.

"Yes. Why not?"

These words came with a slight petulance, the hint of a loved woman's capricious will, which is capricious only because it feels itself to be a law, embarrassing sometimes and always difficult to elude.

"Why not?" he repeated, with a slightly mocking accent, as though he had been asked to give her the moon. But now he was feeling a little angry with her for that feminine mobility that slips out of an emotion as easily as out of a splendid gown.

He heard her say a little unsteadily, with a sort of fluttering intonation which made him think suddenly of a butterfly's flight:

"You used to tell—your—your simple and—and professional—tales very well at one time. Or well enough to interest me. You had a—a sort of art—in the days—the days before the war."

"Really?" he said, with involuntary gloom. "But now, you see, the war is going on," he continued in such a dead, equable tone that she felt a slight chill fall over her shoulders. And yet she persisted. For there's nothing more unswerving in the world than a woman's caprice.

"It could be a tale not of this world," she explained.

"You want a tale of the other, the better world?" he asked, with a matter-of-fact surprise. "You must evoke for that task those who have already gone there."

"No. I don't mean that. I mean another—some other—world. In the universe—not in heaven."

"I am relieved. But you forget that I have only a five days' leave."

"Yes. And I've also taken a five days' leave from—from my duties."

"I like that word."

"What word?"

"Duty."

"It is horrible—sometimes."

"Oh, that's because you think it's narrow. But it isn't. It contains infinities, and—and so———"

"What is this jargon?"

He disregarded the interjected scorn. "An infinity of absolution, for instance," he continued. "But as to this 'another world'—who's going to look for it and for the tale that is in it?"

"You," she said, with a strange, almost rough, sweetness of assertion.

He made a shadowy movement of assent in his chair, the irony of which not even the gathered darkness could render mysterious.

"As you will. In that world, then, there was once upon a time a Commanding Officer and a Northman. Put in the capitals, please, because they had no other names. It was a world of seas and continents and islands———"

"Like the earth," she murmured bitterly.

"Yes. What else could you expect from sending a man made of our common, tormented clay on a voyage of discovery? What else could he find? What else could you understand or care for, or feel the existence of even? There was comedy in it and slaughter."

"Always like the earth," she murmured. "Always. And since I could find in the universe only what was deeply rooted in the fibres of my being there was love in it too. But we won't talk of that."

"No. We won't," she said, in a neutral tone which concealed perfectly her relief—or her disappointment. Then after a pause she added: "It's going to be a comic story."

"Well—" he paused too. "Yes. In a way. In a very grim way. It will be human, and, as you know, comedy is but a matter of the visual angle. And it won't be a noisy story. All the long guns in it will be dumb—as dumb as so many telescopes."

"Ah, there are guns in it, then! And may I ask—where?"

"Afloat. You remember that the world of which we speak had its seas. A war was going on in it. It was a funny world and terribly in earnest. Its war was being carried on over the land, over the water, under the water, up in the air, and even under the ground. And many young men in it, mostly in wardrooms and mess-rooms used to say to each other—pardon the unparliamentary word—they used to say, 'It's a damned bad war, but it's better than no war at all.' Sounds flippant, doesn't it?"

He heard a nervous, impatient sigh in the depths of the couch while he went on without pause:

"And yet there is more in it than meets the eye. I mean more wisdom. Flippancy, like comedy, is but a matter of visual first-impression. That world was not very wise. But there was in it a certain amount of common working sagacity. That, however, was mostly worked by the neutrals in diverse ways, public and private, which had to be watched; watched by acute minds and also by actual sharp eyes. They had to be very sharp indeed, too, I can assure you."

"I can imagine," she murmured, appreciatively.

"What is there that you can't imagine?" he pronounced soberly. "You have the world in you. But let us go back to our Commanding Officer, who, of course, commanded a ship of a sort. My tales if often professional (as you remarked just now) have never been technical. So I'll just tell you that the ship was of a very ornamental sort once, with lots of grace and elegance and luxury about her. Yes, once! She was like a pretty woman who had suddenly put on a suit of sackcloth and stuck revolvers in her belt. But she floated lightly, she moved nimbly, she was quite good enough."

"That was the opinion of the Commanding Officer?" said the voice from the couch.

"It was. He used to be sent out with her along certain coasts to see—what he could see. Just that. And sometimes he had some preliminary information to help him, and sometimes he had not. And it was all one, really. It was about as useful as information trying to convey the locality and intentions of a cloud, of a phantom taking shape here and there and impossible to seize, would have been.

"It was in the early days of the War. What at first used to amaze the Commanding Officer was the unchanged face of the waters, with its familiar expression, neither more friendly nor more hostile. On fine days the sun strikes sparks upon the blue; here and there a peaceful smudge of smoke hangs in the distance, and it is impossible to believe that the familiar clear horizon traces the limit of one great circular ambush."

"Yes, it is impossible to believe, till some day you see a ship not your own ship (that isn't so impressive), but some ship in company blow up all of a sudden and plop under almost before you know what had happened to her. Then you begin to believe. Henceforth you go out for the work to see—what you can see, and you keep on at it with the conviction that some day you will die from something you have not seen. One envies the soldiers at the end of the day, wiping the sweat and blood from their faces, counting the dead fallen to their hands, looking at the devastated field, the torn earth that seems to suffer and bleed with them. One does, really. The final brutality of it—the taste of primitive passion—the ferocious frankness of the blow struck with one's hand—the direct call and the straight response. Well, the sea gave you nothing of that, and seemed to pretend that there was nothing the matter with the world."

She interrupted, stirring a little.

"Oh yes. Sincerity—frankness—passion—three words of your gospel. Don't I know them!"

"Think! Isn't it ours—believed in common?" he asked anxiously, yet without expecting an answer, and went on at once. "Such were the feelings of the Commanding Officer. When the night came trailing over the sea, hiding what looked like the hypocrisy of an old friend, it was a relief. The night blinds you frankly and there are circumstances when the sunlight may grow as odious to one as falsehood itself. Night is all right.

"At night the Commanding Officer could let his thoughts get away—I won't tell you where. Somewhere where there was no choice but between truth and death. But thick weather, though it blinded one, brought no such relief. Mist is deceitful, the dead luminosity of the fog is irritating. It seems that you *ought* to see.

"One gloomy, nasty day the ship was steaming along her beat in sight of a rocky, dangerous coast that stood out intensely black like an Indian-ink drawing on grey paper. Presently the Second-in-Command spoke to his chief. He thought he saw something on the water, to seaward. Small wreckage, perhaps.

"'But there shouldn't be any wreckage here, sir,' he remarked.

"'No,' said the Commanding Officer. 'The last reported submarined ships were sunk a long way to the westward. But one never knows. There may have been others since then not reported nor seen. Gone with all hands.'

"That was how it began. The ship's course was altered to pass the object close; for it was necessary to have a good look at what one could see. Close, but without touching; for it was not advisable to come in contact with objects of any form whatever floating casually about. Close, but without stopping or even diminishing speed; for in those times it was not prudent to linger on any particular spot, even for a moment. I may tell you at once that the object was not dangerous in itself. No use in describing it. It may have been nothing more remarkable than, say, a barrel of a certain shape and color. But it was significant.

"The smooth bow-wave hove it up as if for a closer inspection, and then the ship, brought again to her course, turned her back on it with indifference, while twenty pairs of eyes on her deck stared in all directions trying to see—what they could see.

"The Commanding Officer and his Second-in-Command discussed the object with understanding. It appeared to them to be not so much a proof of the sagacity as of the activity of certain neutrals. This activity had in many cases taken the form of replenishing the stores of certain submarines at sea. This was generally believed, if not absolutely known. But the very nature of things in those early days pointed that way. The object, looked at closely and turned away from with apparent indifference, put it beyond doubt that something of the sort had been done somewhere in the neighborhood.

"The object in itself was more than suspect. But the fact of its being left in evidence roused other suspicions. Was it the result of some deep and devilish purpose? As to that all speculation soon appeared to be a vain thing. Finally, the two officers came to the conclusion that it was left there most likely by accident, complicated possibly by some unforeseen necessity; such, perhaps, as the sudden need to get away quickly from the spot, or something of that kind.

"Their discussion had been carried on in curt, weighty phrases, separated by long, thoughtful silences. And all the time their eyes roamed about the horizon in an everlasting, almost mechanical effort of vigilance. The younger man summed up grimly:

"'Well, it's evidence. That's what this is. Evidence of what we were pretty certain of before. And plain too.'

"'And much good it will do to us,' retorted the Commanding Officer. 'The parties are miles away, the submarine, devil only knows where, ready to kill; and the noble neutral slipping away to the eastward, ready to lie!'

"The Second-in-Command laughed a little at the time. But he guessed that the neutral wouldn't even have to lie very much. Fellows like that, unless caught in the very act, felt themselves pretty safe. They could afford to chuckle. That fellow was probably chuckling to himself. It's very possible he had been before at the game and didn't care a rap for the bit of evidence left behind. It was a game in which practice made one bold and successful too.

"And again he laughed faintly. But his Commanding Officer was in revolt against the murderous stealthiness of methods and the atrocious callousness of complicities that seemed to taint the very source of men's deep emotions and noblest activities; to corrupt their imagination which builds up the final conceptions of life and death. He suffered———"

The voice from the sofa interrupted the narrator.

"How well I can understand that in him!"

He bent forward slightly.

"Yes. I too. Everything should be open in love and war. Open as the day, since both are the call of an ideal which it is so easy, so terribly easy, to degrade in the name of Victory."

He paused; then went on: "I don't know that the Commanding Officer delved so deep as that into his feelings. But he did suffer from them—a sort of disenchanted sadness. It is possible, even, that he suspected himself of folly. Man is various. But he had no time for much introspection, because from the southwest a wall of fog had advanced upon his ship. Great convolutions of vapours flew over, swirling about masts and funnel, which looked as if they were beginning to melt. Then they vanished.

"The ship was stopped, all sounds ceased, and the very fog became motionless, growing denser and as if solid in its amazing dumb immobility. The men at their stations lost sight of each other. Footsteps sounded stealthy; rare voices, impersonal and remote, died out with resonance. A blind white stillness took possession of the world.

"It looked, too, as if it would last for days. I don't mean to say that the fog did not vary a little in its density. Now and then it would thin out mysteriously, revealing to the men a more or less ghostly presentment of their ship. Several times the shadow of the coast itself swam darkly before their eyes through the fluctuating opaque brightness of the great white cloud clinging to the water.

"Taking advantage of these moments, the ship had been moved cautiously nearer the shore. It was useless to remain out in such thick weather. Her officers knew every nook and cranny of the coast along their beat. They thought that she would be much better in a certain cove. It wasn't a large place, just ample room for a ship to swing at her anchor. She would have an easier time of it till the fog lifted up.

"Slowly, with infinite caution and patience, they crept closer and closer, seeing no more of the cliffs than an evanescent dark loom with a narrow border of angry foam at its foot. At the moment of anchoring the fog was so thick that for all they could see they might have been a thousand miles out in the open sea. Yet the shelter of the land could be felt. There was a peculiar quality in the stillness of the air. Very faint, very elusive, the wash of the ripple against the encircling land reached their ears, with mysterious sudden pauses.

"The anchor dropped, the leads were laid in. The Commanding Officer went below into his cabin. But he had not been there very long when a voice outside his door requested his presence on deck. He thought to himself: 'What is it now?' He felt some impatience at being called out again to face the wearisome fog.

"He found that it had thinned again a little and had taken on a gloomy hue from the dark cliffs which had no form, no outline, but asserted themselves as a curtain of shadows all round the ship, except in one bright spot, which was the entrance from the open sea. Several officers were looking that way from the bridge. The Second-in-Command met him with the breathlessly whispered information that there was another ship in the cove.

"She had been made out by several pairs of eyes only a couple of minutes before. She was lying at anchor very near the entrance—a mere vague blot on the fog's brightness. And the Commanding Officer by staring in the direction pointed out to him by eager hands ended by distinguishing it at last himself. Indubitably a vessel of some sort.

"'It's a wonder we didn't run slap into her when coming in,' observed the Second-in-Command.

"'Send a boat on board before she vanishes,' said the Commanding Officer.

He surmised that this was a coaster. It could hardly be anything else. But another thought came into his head suddenly. 'It is a wonder,' he said to his Second-in-Command, who had rejoined him after sending the boat away.

"By that time both of them had been struck by the fact that the ship so suddenly discovered had not manifested her presence by ringing her bell.

"'We came in very quietly, that's true,' concluded the younger officer. 'But they must have heard our leadsmen at least. We couldn't have passed her more than fifty yards off. The closest shave! They may even have made us out, since they were aware of something coming in. And the strange thing is that we never heard a sound from her. The fellows on board must have been holding their breath.'

"'Aye,' said the Commanding Officer thoughtfully.

"In due course the boarding-boat returned, appearing suddenly alongside, as though she had burrowed her way under the fog. The officer in charge came up to make his report, but the Commanding Officer didn't give him time to begin. He cried from a distance:

"'Coaster, isn't she?'

"'No, sir. A stranger—a neutral,' was the answer.

"'No. Really! Well, tell us all about it. What is she doing here?'

"The young man stated then that he had been told a long and complicated story of engine troubles. But it was plausible enough from a strictly professional point of view and it had the usual features: disablement, dangerous drifting along the shore, weather more or less thick for days, fear of a gale, ultimately a resolve to go in and anchor anywhere on the coast, and so on. Fairly plausible.

"'Engines still disabled?' inquired the Commanding Officer.

"'No, sir. She has steam on them.'

"The Commanding Officer took his Second aside. 'By Jove!' he said, 'you were right! They were holding their breaths as we passed them. They were.'

"But the Second-in-Command had his doubts now.

"'A fog like this does muffle small sounds, sir,' he remarked. 'And what could his object be, after all?'

"'To sneak out unnoticed,' answered the Commanding Officer.

"'Then why didn't he? He might have done it, you know. Not exactly unnoticed, perhaps. I don't suppose he could have slipped his cable without making some noise. Still, in a minute or so he would have been lost to view—clean gone before we had made him out fairly. Yet he didn't.'

"They looked at each other. The Commanding Officer shook his head. Such suspicions as the one which had entered his head are not defended easily. He did not even state it openly. The boarding officer finished his report. The cargo of the ship was of a harmless and useful character. She was bound to an English port. Papers and everything in perfect order. Nothing suspicious to be detected anywhere.

"Then, passing to the men, he reported the crew on deck as the usual lot. Engineers of the well-known type, and very full of their achievement in repairing the engines. The mate surly. The master rather a fine specimen of a Northman, civil enough, but appeared to have been drinking. Seemed to be recovering from a regular bout of it.

"'I told him I couldn't give him permission to proceed. He said he wouldn't dare to move his ship her own length out in such weather as this, permission or no permission. I left a man on board, though.'

"'Quite right.'

"The Commanding Officer, after communing with his suspicions for a time, called his Second aside.

"'What if she were the very ship which had been feeding some infernal submarine or other?' he said in an undertone.

"The other started. Then, with conviction:

"'She would get off scot-free. You couldn't prove it, sir.'

"'I want to look into it myself.'

"'From the report we've heard I am afraid you couldn't even make a case for reasonable suspicion, sir.'

"'I'll go on board all the same.'

"He had made up his mind. Curiosity is the great motive power of hatred and love. What did he expect to find? He could not have told anybody—not even himself.

"What he really expected to find there was the atmosphere, the atmosphere of gratuitous treachery, which in his view nothing could excuse; for he thought that even a passion of unrighteousness for its own sake could not excuse that. But could he detect it? Sniff it? Taste it? Receive some mysterious communication which would turn his invincible suspicions into a certitude strong enough to provoke action with all its risks?

"The master met him on the after-deck, looming up in the fog amongst the blurred shapes of the usual ship's fittings. He was a robust Northman, bearded, and in the force of his age. A round leather cap fitted his head closely. His hands were rammed deep into the pockets of his short leather jacket. He kept them there while he explained that at sea he lived in the chart-room, and led the way there, striding carelessly. Just before reaching the door under the bridge he staggered a little, recovered himself, flung it open, and stood aside, leaning his shoulder as if involuntarily against the side of the house, and staring vaguely into the fog-filled space. But he followed the Commanding Officer at once, flung the door to, snapped on the electric light, and hastened to thrust his hands back into his pockets, as though afraid of being seized by them either in friendship or in hostility.

"The place was stuffy and hot. The usual chart-rack overhead was full, and the chart on the table was kept unrolled by an empty cup standing on a saucer half-full of some spilt dark liquid. A slightly nibbled biscuit reposed on the chronometer case. There were two settees, and one of them had been made up into a bed with a pillow and some blankets, which were now very much tumbled. The Northman let himself fall on it, his hands still in his pockets.

"'Well, here I am,' he said, with a curious air of being surprised at the sound of his own voice.

"The Commanding Officer from the other settee observed the handsome, flushed face. Drops of fog hung on the yellow beard and moustaches of the Northman. The much darker eyebrows ran together in a puzzled frown, and suddenly he jumped up.

"'What I mean is that I don't know where I am. I really don't,' he burst out, with extreme earnestness. 'Hang it all I got turned around somehow. The fog has been after me for a week. More than a week. And then my engines broke down. I will tell you how it was.'

"He burst out into loquacity. It was not hurried, but it was insistent. It was not continuous for all that. It was broken by the most queer, thoughtful pauses. Each of these pauses lasted no more than a couple of seconds, and each had the profundity of an endless meditation. When he began again nothing betrayed in him the slightest consciousness of these intervals. There was the same fixed glance, the same unchanged earnestness of tone. He didn't know. Indeed, more than one of these pauses occurred in the middle of a sentence.

"The Commanding Officer listened to the tale. It struck him as more plausible than simple truth is in the habit of being. But that, perhaps, was prejudice. All the time the Northman was speaking the Commanding Officer had been aware of an inward voice, a grave murmur in the depth of his very own self, telling another tale, as if on purpose to keep alive in him his indignation and his anger with that baseness of greed or of mere outlook which lies often at the root of simple ideas.

"It was the story that had been already told to the boarding officer an hour or so before. The Commanding Officer nodded slightly at the Northman from time to time. The latter came to an end and turned his eyes away. He added, as an afterthought:

"'Wasn't it enough to drive a man out of his mind with worry? And it's my first voyage to this part, too. And the ship's my own. Your officer has seen the papers. She isn't much, as you can see for yourself. Just an old cargo-boat. Bare living for my family.'

"He raised a big arm to point at a row of photographs plastering the bulkhead. The movement was ponderous, as if the arm had been made of lead. The Commanding Officer said, carelessly:

"'You will be making a fortune yet for your family with this old ship.'

"'Yes, if I don't lose her,' said the Northman gloomily.

"'I mean—out of this war,' added the Commanding Officer.

"The Northman stared at him in a curiously unseeing and at the same time interested manner, as only eyes of a particular blue shade can stare.

"'And you wouldn't be angry at it,' he said, 'Would you? You are too much of a gentleman. We didn't bring this on you. And suppose we sat down and cried. What good would that be? Let those cry who made the trouble,' he concluded with energy. 'Time's money, you say. Well—*this* time *is* money. Oh! isn't it!'

"The Commanding Officer tried to keep under the feeling of immense disgust. He said to himself that it was unreasonable. Men were like that—moral cannibals feeding on each other's misfortunes. He said aloud:

"'You have made it perfectly plain how it is that you are here. Your log-book confirms you very minutely. Of course, a log-book may be cooked. Nothing easier.'

"The Northman never moved a muscle. He was gazing at the floor; he seemed not to have heard. He raised his head after a while.

"'But you can't suspect me of anything,' he muttered, negligently.

"The Commanding Officer thought: 'Why should he say this?'

"Immediately afterwards the man before him added: 'My cargo is for an English port.'

"His voice had turned husky for the moment. The Commanding Officer reflected: 'That's true. There can be nothing. I can't suspect him. Yet why was he lying with steam up in this fog and then, hearing us come in, why didn't he give some sign of life? Why? Could it be anything else but a guilty conscience? He could tell by the leadsmen that this was a man-of-war.'

"Yes—why? The Commanding Officer went on thinking: 'Suppose I ask him and then watch his face. He will betray himself in some way. It's perfectly plain that the fellow *has* been drinking. Yes, he has been drinking; but he will have a lie ready all the same.' The Commanding Officer was one of those men who are made morally and almost physically uncomfortable by the mere thought of having to beat down a lie. He shrank from the act in scorn and disgust, which was invincible because more temperamental than moral.

"So he went out on deck instead and had the crew mustered formally for his inspection. He found them very much what the report of the boarding officer had led him to expect. And from their answers to his questions he could discover no flaw in the logbook story.

"He dismissed them. His impression of them was a picked lot; have been promised a fistful of money each if this came off; all slightly anxious, but not frightened. Not a single one of them likely to give the show away. They don't feel in danger of their life. They know England and English ways too well!

"He felt alarmed at catching himself thinking as if his vaguest suspicions were turning into a certitude. For, indeed, there was no shadow of reason for his interferences. There was nothing to give away.

"He returned to the chart-room. The Northman had lingered behind there; and something subtly different in his bearing, more bold in his blue, glassy stare, induced the Commanding Officer to conclude that the fellow had snatched at the opportunity to take another swig at the bottle he must have had concealed somewhere.

"He noticed, too, that the Northman on meeting his eyes put on an elaborately surprised expression. At least, it seemed elaborated. Nothing could be trusted. And the Englishman felt himself with astonishing conviction faced by an enormous lie, solid like a wall, with no way round to get at the truth, whose ugly murderous face he seemed to see peeping over at him with a cynical grin.

"'I dare say,' he began suddenly, 'you are wondering at my proceedings, though I am not detaining you, am I? You wouldn't dare to move in this fog?'

"'I don't know where I am,' the Northman ejaculated earnestly. 'I really don't.'

"He looked around as if the very chart-room fittings were strange to him. The Commanding Officer asked him whether he had not seen any unusual objects floating about while he was at sea.

"'Objects! What objects? We were groping blind in the fog for days.'

"'We had a few clear intervals,' said the Commanding Officer. 'And I'll tell you what we have seen and the conclusion I've come to about it.'

"He told him in a few words. He heard the sound of a sharp breath indrawn through closed teeth. The Northman with his hand on the table stood absolutely motionless and dumb. He stood as if thunderstruck. Then he produced a fatuous smile.

"Or at least so it appeared to the Commanding Officer. Was this significant, or of no meaning whatever? He didn't know, he couldn't tell. All the truth had departed out of the world as if drawn in, absorbed in this monstrous villainy this man was—or was not—guilty of.

"'Shooting's too good for people that conceive neutrality in this pretty way,' remarked the Commanding Officer, after a silence.

"'Yes, yes, yes,' the Northman assented, hurriedly—then added an unexpected and dreamy-voiced 'Perhaps.'

"Was he pretending to be drunk, or only trying to appear sober? His glance was straight, but it was somewhat glazed. His lips outlined themselves firmly under his yellow moustache. But they twitched. Did they twitch? And why was he drooping like this in his attitude?

"'There's no perhaps about it,' pronounced the Commanding Officer sternly.

"The Northman had straightened himself. And unexpectedly he looked stern too.

"'No. But what about the tempters? Better kill that lot off. There's about four, five, six million of them,' he said grimly; but in a moment changed into a whining key. 'But I had better hold my tongue. You have some suspicions.'

"'No, I've no suspicions,' declared the Commanding Officer.

"He never faltered. At that moment he had the certitude. The air of the chart-room was thick with guilt and falsehood braving the discovery, defying simple right, common decency, all humanity of feeling, every scruple of conduct.

"The Northman drew a long breath. 'Well we know that you English are gentlemen. But let us speak the truth. Why should we love you so very much? You haven't done anything to be loved. We don't love the other people, of course. They haven't done anything for that either. A fellow comes along with a bag of gold…I haven't been in Rotterdam my last voyage for nothing.'

"'You may be able to tell something interesting, then, to our people when you come into port,' interjected the officer.

"'I might. But you keep some people in your pay at Rotterdam. Let them report. I am a neutral—am I not?…Have you ever seen a poor man on one side and a bag of gold on the other? Of course, I couldn't be tempted. I haven't the nerve for it. Really I haven't. It's nothing to me. I am just talking openly for once.'

"'Yes. And I am listening to you,' said the Commanding Officer quietly.

"The Northman leaned forward over the table. 'Now that I know you have no suspicions, I talk. You don't know what a poor man is. I do. I am poor myself. This old ship, she isn't much, and she is mortgaged too. Bare living, no more. Of course, I wouldn't have the nerve. But a man who has nerve! See. The stuff he takes aboard looks like any other cargo—packages, barrels, tins, copper tubes—what not. He doesn't see it work. It isn't real to him. But he sees the gold. That's real. Of course, nothing could induce me. I suffer from an internal disease. I would either go crazy from anxiety—or—or—take to drink, or something. The risk is too great. Why—ruin!'

"'It should be death.' The Commanding Officer got up, after this curt declaration, which the other received with a hard stare oddly combined with an uncertain smile. The Officer's gorge rose at the atmosphere of murderous complicity which surrounded him, denser, more impenetrable, more acrid than the fog outside.

"'It's nothing to me,' murmured the Northman, swaying visibly.

"'Of course not,' assented the Commanding Officer, with a great effort to keep his voice calm and low. The certitude was strong within him. 'But I am going to clear all you fellows off this coast at once. And I will begin with you. You must leave in half an hour.'

"By that time the Officer was walking along the deck with the Northman at his elbow.

"'What! In this fog?' the latter cried out huskily.

"'Yes, you will have to go in this fog.'

"'But I don't know where I am. I really don't.'

"The Commanding Officer turned round. A sort of fury possessed him. The eyes of the two men met. Those of the Northman expressed a profound amazement.

"'Oh, you don't know how to get out,' the Commanding Officer spoke with composure, but his heart was beating with anger and dread. 'I will give you your course. Steer south-by-east-half-east for about four miles and then you will be clear to haul to the eastward for your port. The weather will clear up before very long.'

"'Must I? What could induce me? I haven't the nerve.'

"'And yet you must go. Unless you want to———'

"'I don't want to,' panted the Northman. 'I've had enough of it.'

"The Commanding Officer got over the side. The Northman remained still as if rooted to the deck. Before his boat reached his ship the Commanding Officer heard the steamer beginning to pick up her anchor. Then, shadowy in the fog, she steamed out on the given course.

"'Yes,' he said to his officers, 'I let him go.'"

The narrator bent forwards towards the couch, where no movement betrayed the presence of a living person.

"Listen," he said forcibly. "That course would lead the Northman straight on a deadly ledge of rock. And the Commanding Officer gave it to him. He steamed out—ran on it—and went down. So he had spoken the truth. He did not know where he was. But it proves nothing. Nothing either way. It may have been the only truth in all his story. And yet…He seems to have been driven out by a menacing stare—nothing more."

He abandoned all pretence.

"Yes, I gave that course to him. It seemed to me a supreme test. I believe—no, I don't believe. I don't know. At the time I was certain. They all went down; and I don't know whether I have done stern retribution—or murder; whether I have added to the corpses that litter the bed of the unreadable sea, the bodies of men completely innocent or basely guilty. I don't know. I shall never know."

He rose. The woman on the couch got up and threw her arms round his neck. Her eyes put two gleams in the deep shadow of the room. She knew his passion for truth, his horror of deceit, his humanity.

"Oh, my poor, poor—"

"I shall never know," he repeated sternly, disengaging himself, pressed her hands to his lips, and went out.

The Traitor

(from *Ashenden*)

W. Somerset Maugham

NOTE: Ashenden, a British Secret Service Agent, has received orders to go into Switzerland on a mission from his chief R.

Having taken a room at the hotel at which he had been instructed to stay, Ashenden went out; it was a lovely day, early in August, and the sun shone in an unclouded sky. He had not been to Lucerne since he was a boy, and but vaguely remembered a covered bridge, a great stone lion, and a church in which he had sat, bored yet impressed, while they played an organ; and now, wandering along a shady quay (and the lake looked just as tawdry and unreal as it looked on the picture postcards), he tried not so much to find his way about a half-forgotten scene as to reform in his mind some recollection of the shy and eager lad, so impatient for life (which he saw not in the present of his adolescence but only in the future of his manhood), who so long ago had wandered there. But it seemed to him that the most vivid of his memories was not of himself but of the crowd; he seemed to remember sun and heat and people; the train was crowded and so was the hotel; the lake steamers were packed, and on the quays and in the streets you threaded your way among the throng of holiday makers. They were fat and old and ugly and odd, and they stank. Now, in war-time, Lucerne was as deserted as it must have been before the world at large discovered that Switzerland was the playground of Europe. Most of the hotels were closed, the streets were empty, the rowing boats for hire rocked idly at the water's edge and there was none to take them, and in the avenues by the lake the only persons to be seen were serious Swiss taking their neutrality, like a dachshund, for a walk with them. Ashenden felt exhilarated by the solitude, and, sitting down on a bench that faced the water, surrendered himself deliberately to the sensation. It was true that the lake was absurd, the water was too blue, the mountains too snowy, and its beauty, hitting you in the face, exasperated rather than thrilled; but all the same, there was something pleasing in the prospect, an artless candor, like one of Mendelssohn's "Songs Without Words," that made Ashenden smile with complacency. Lucerne reminded him of wax flowers under glass cases and cuckoo clocks and fancy work in Berlin wool. So long, at all events, as the fine weather lasted he was prepared to enjoy himself. He did not see why he should not at least try to combine pleasure to himself with profit to his country. He was traveling with a brand-new passport in his pocket, under a borrowed name, and this gave him an agreeable sense of owning a new personality. He was often slightly tired of himself, and it diverted him for a while to be merely a creature of R.'s facile invention. The experience he had just enjoyed appealed to his acute sense of the absurd. R., it is true, had not seen the fun of it: what humor R. possessed was of a sardonic turn, and he had no facility for taking in good part a joke at his own expense. To do that you must be able to look at yourself from the outside and be at the same time spectator and actor in the pleasant comedy of life. R. was a soldier, and regarded introspection as unhealthy, un-English, and unpatriotic. Ashenden got up and strolled slowly to his hotel. It was a small German hotel of the second class, spotlessly clean, and his bedroom had a nice view; it was furnished with brightly varnished pitch-pine, and though on a cold, wet day it would have been wretched, in that warm and sunny weather it was gay and pleasant. There were tables in the hall, and he sat down at one of these and ordered a bottle of beer. The landlady was curious to know why in that dead season he had come to stay, and he was glad to satisfy her curiosity. He told her that he had recently recovered from an attack of typhoid, and had come to Lucerne to get back his strength. He was employed in the Censorship Department, and was taking the opportunity to brush up his rusty German. He asked her if she could recommend to him a German teacher. The landlady was a blond and blowsy Swiss, good humored and talkative, so that Ashenden felt pretty sure that she would repeat in the proper quarter the information he gave her. It was his turn now to ask a few questions. She was voluble on the subject of the War, on account of which the hotel, in that month so full that rooms had to be found for visitors in neighboring houses, was nearly empty. A few people came in from outside to eat their meals *en pension*, but she had only two lots of resident guests. One was an old Irish couple who lived in Vevey and passed their summers in Lucerne, and the other was an Englishman and his wife. She was a German, and they were obliged on that account to live in a neutral country. Ashenden took care to show little curiosity about them he recognized in the description Grantley Caypor—but of her own accord she told him that they spent most of the day walking about the mountains. Herr Caypor was a botanist and much interested in the flora of the country. His lady was a very nice woman, and she felt her position keenly. Ah, well, the War could not last forever. The landlady bustled away and Ashenden went upstairs.

Dinner was at seven, and, wishing to be in the dining-room before anyone else, so that he could take stock of his fellow-guests as they entered, he went down as soon as he heard the bell. It was a very plain, stiff, whitewashed room, with chairs of the same shiny pitch-pine as in his bedroom, and on the walls were oleographs of Swiss lakes. On each little table was a bunch of flowers. It was all neat and clean and presaged a bad dinner. Ashenden would have liked to make up for it by ordering a bottle of the best Rhine wine to be found in the hotel, but did not venture to draw attention to himself by extravagance (he saw on two or three tables half-empty bottles of table hock, which made him surmise that his fellow guests drank thriftily), and so contented himself with ordering a pint of lager. Presently one or two persons came in, single men with some occupation in Lucerne and obviously Swiss, and sat down each at his little table and untied the napkins that at the end of luncheon they had neatly tied up. They propped newspapers against their water-jugs and read while they somewhat noisily ate their soup. Then entered a very tall, bent man, with white hair and a drooping white moustache, accompanied by a little old white-haired lady in black. These were certainly the Irish Colonel and his wife of whom the landlady had spoken. They took their seats, and the Colonel poured out a thimbleful of wine for his wife and a thimbleful for himself. They waited in silence for their dinner to be served to them by the buxom, hearty maid.

At last the persons arrived for whom Ashenden had been waiting. He was doing his best to read a German book, and it was only by an exercise of self-control that he allowed himself only for one instant to raise his eyes as they came in. His glance showed him a man of about forty-five with short, dark hair, somewhat grizzled, of middle height but corpulent, with a broad, red, clean-shaven face. He wore a shirt open at the neck, with a wide collar and a grey suit. He walked ahead of his wife, and of her Ashenden only caught the impression of a German woman, self-effaced and dusty. Grantley Caypor sat down and began in a loud voice explaining to the waitress that they had taken an immense walk. They had been up some mountain the name of which meant nothing to Ashenden, but which excited in the maid expressions of astonishment and enthusiasm. Then Caypor, still in fluent German, but with a marked English accent, said that they were so late they had not even gone up to wash, but had just rinsed their hands outside. He had a resonant voice and a jovial manner.

"Serve me quick; we're starving with hunger, and bring beer—bring three bottles. *Lieber Gott*, what a thirst I have!"

He seemed to be a man of exuberant vitality. He brought into that dull, over-clean dining-room the breath of life, and everyone in it appeared on a sudden more alert. He began to talk to his wife in English, and everything he said could be heard by all; but presently she interrupted him with a remark made in an undertone. Caypor stopped, and Ashenden felt that his eyes were turned in his direction. Mrs. Caypor had noticed the arrival of a stranger and had drawn her husband's attention to it. Ashenden turned the page of the book he was pretending to read, but he felt that Caypor's gaze was fixed intently upon him. When he addressed his wife again it was in so low a tone that Ashenden could not even tell what language he used; but when the maid brought them their soup Caypor, his voice still low, asked her a question. It was plain that he was enquiring who Ashenden was. Ashenden could catch of the maid's reply but the one word *lander*.

One or two people finished their dinner and went out picking their teeth. The old Irish Colonel and his old wife rose from their table, and he stood aside to let her pass. They had eaten their meal without exchanging a word. She walked slowly to the door; but the Colonel stopped to say a word to a Swiss who might have been a local attorney, and when she reached it she stood there, bowed and with a sheep-like look, patiently waiting for her husband to come and open it for her. Ashenden realized that she had never opened a door herself. She did not know how to. In a minute the Colonel, with his old, old gait, came to the door and opened it; she passed out and he followed. The little incident offered a key to their whole lives, and from it Ashenden began to reconstruct their histories, circumstances, and characters; but he pulled himself up: he could not allow himself the luxury of creation. He finished his dinner.

When he went into the hall he saw tied to the leg of a table a bull-terrier, and, in passing, mechanically put down his hand to fondle the dog's drooping, soft ears. The landlady was standing at the foot of the stairs.

"Whose is this lovely beast?" asked Ashenden.

"He belongs to Herr Caypor. Fritzi he is called. Herr Caypor says he has a longer pedigree than the King of England."

Fritzi rubbed himself against Ashenden's leg, and with his nose sought the palm of his hand. Ashenden went upstairs to fetch his hat, and when he came down saw Caypor standing at the entrance of the hotel talking with the landlady. From the sudden silence and their constrained manner he guessed that Caypor had been making inquiries about him. When he passed between them into the street, out of the corner of his eye he saw Caypor give him a suspicious stare. That frank, jovial red face bore then a look of shifty cunning.

Ashenden strolled along till he found a tavern where he could have his coffee in the open, and, to compensate himself for the bottle of beer that his sense of duty had urged him to drink at dinner, ordered the best brandy the house provided. He was pleased at last to have come face to face with the man of whom he had heard so much, and in a day or two hoped to become acquainted with him. It is never very difficult to get to know anyone who has a dog. But he was in no hurry; he would let things take their course. With the object he had in view he could not afford to be hasty.

Ashenden reviewed the circumstances. Grantley Caypor was an Englishman, born, according to his passport, in Birmingham, and he was forty-two years of age. His wife, to whom he had been married for eleven years, was of German birth and parentage. That was public knowledge. Information about his antecedents was contained in a private document. He had started life, according to this, in a lawyer's office in Birmingham and then had drifted into journalism. He had been connected with an English paper in Cairo and with another in Shanghai. There he got into trouble for attempting to get money by false pretences and was sentenced to a short term of imprisonment. All trace of him was lost for two years after his release, when he reappeared in a shipping office in Marseilles. From there, still in the shipping business, he went to Hamburg, where he married, and to London. In London he set up for himself in the export business, but after some time failed and was made a bankrupt. He returned to journalism. At the outbreak of war he was once more in the shipping business, and in August, 1914, was living quietly with his German wife at Southampton. In the beginning of the following year he told his employers that, owing to the nationality of his wife, his position was intolerable; they had no fault to find with him, and, recognizing that he was in an awkward fix, granted his request that he should be transferred to Genoa. Here he remained till Italy entered the War, but then gave notice, and with his papers in perfect order crossed the border and took up his residence in Switzerland.

All this indicated a man of doubtful honesty and unsettled disposition, with no background and of no financial standing; but the facts were of no importance to anyone till it was discovered that Caypor, certainly from the beginning of the War and perhaps sooner, was in the service of the German Intelligence Department. He had a salary of forty pounds a month. But, though dangerous and wily, no steps would have been taken to deal with him if he had contented himself with transmitting such news as he was able to get in Switzerland. He could do no great harm there, and it might even be possible to make use of him to convey information that it was desirable to let the enemy have. He had no notion that anything was known of him. His letters, and he received a good many, were closely censored; there were few codes that the people who dealt with such matters could not in the end decipher, and it might be that sooner or later through him it would be possible to lay hands on the organization that still flourished in England. But then he did something that drew R.'s attention to him. Had he known it, none could have blamed him for shaking in his shoes: R. was not a very nice man to get on the wrong side of. Caypor scraped acquaintance in Zurich with a young Spaniard, Gomez by name, who had lately entered the British Secret Service, by his nationality inspired him with confidence, and managed to worm out of him the fact that he was engaged in espionage. Probably the Spaniard, with a very human desire to seem important, had done no more than talk mysteriously; but on Caypor's information he was watched when he went to Germany, and one day caught just as he was posting a letter in a code that was eventually deciphered. He was tried, convicted, and shot. It was bad enough to lose a useful and disinterested agent, but it entailed besides the changing of a safe and simple code. R. was not pleased. But R. was not the man to let any desire of revenge stand in the way of his main object, and it occurred to him that if Caypor was merely betraying his country for money it might be possible to get him to take more money to betray his employers. The fact that he had succeeded in delivering into their hands an agent of the Allies must seem to them an earnest of his good faith. He might be very useful. But R. had no notion what kind of man Caypor was; he had lived his shabby, furtive life obscurely, and the only photograph that existed of him was one taken for a passport. Ashenden's instructions were to get acquainted with Caypor and see whether there was any chance that he would work honestly for the British. If he thought there was, he was entitled to sound him, and if his suggestions were met with favour to make certain propositions. It was a task that needed tact and a knowledge of men. If, on the other hand, Ashenden came to the conclusion that Caypor could not be bought, he was to watch and report his movements. The information he had obtained from Gustav was vague but important; there was only one point in it that was interesting, and this was that the head of the German Intelligence Department in Berne was growing restive at Caypor's lack of activity. Caypor was asking for a higher salary, and Major von P. had told him that he must earn it. It might be that he was urging him to go to England. If he could be induced to cross the frontier Ashenden's work was done.

"How the devil do you expect *me* to persuade him to put his head in a noose?" asked Ashenden.

"It won't be a noose, it'll be a firing squad," said R.

"Caypor's clever."

"Well, be cleverer, damn your eyes!"

Ashenden made up his mind that he would take no steps to make Caypor's acquaintance, but allow the first advances to be made by him. If he was being pressed for results it must surely occur to him that it would be worthwhile to get into conversation with an Englishman who was employed in the Censorship Department. Ashenden was prepared with a supply of information that it could not in the least benefit the Central Powers to possess. With a false name and a false passport he had little fear that Caypor would guess that he was a British agent.

Ashenden did not have to wait long. Next day he was sitting in the doorway of the hotel, drinking a cup of coffee and already half asleep after a substantial *mittagessen*, when the Caypors came out of the dining-room. Mrs. Caypor went upstairs and Caypor released his dog. The dog bounded along and in a friendly fashion leaped up against Ashenden.

"Come here, Fritzi," cried Caypor, and then to Ashenden: "I'm so sorry. But he's quite gentle."

"Oh, that's all right. He won't hurt me."

Caypor stopped at the doorway.

"He's a bull-terrier. You don't often see them on the Continent."

He seemed while he spoke to be taking Ashenden's measure; he called to the maid: "A coffee, please, fräulein. You've just arrived, haven't you?"

"Yes, I came yesterday."

"Really? I didn't see you in the dining-room last night. Are you making a stay?"

"I don't know. I've been ill, and I've come here to recuperate."

The maid came with the coffee, and, seeing Caypor talking to Ashenden, put the tray on the table at which he was sitting. Caypor gave a laugh of faint embarrassment.

"I don't want to force myself upon you. I don't know why the maid put my coffee on your table."

"Please sit down," said Ashenden.

"It's very good of you. I've lived so long on the Continent that I'm always forgetting that my countrymen are apt to look upon it as confounded cheek if you talk to them. Are you English, by the way, or American?"

"English," said Ashenden.

Ashenden was by nature a very shy person, and he had in vain tried to cure himself of a failing that at his age was unseemly, but on occasion he knew how to make effective use of it. He explained now, in a hesitating and awkward manner, the facts that he had the day before told the landlady and that he was convinced she had already passed on to Caypor.

"You couldn't have come to a better place than Lucerne. It's an oasis of peace in this war-weary world. When you're here you might almost forget that there is such a thing as a war going on. That is why I've come here. I'm a journalist by profession."

"I couldn't help wondering if you wrote," said Ashenden, with an eagerly timid smile.

It was clear that he had not learnt that "oasis of peace in a war-weary world" at the shipping office.

"You see, I married a German lady," said Caypor gravely.

"Oh, really?"

"I don't think anyone could be more patriotic than I am. I'm English through and through, and I don't mind telling you that in my opinion the British Empire is the greatest instrument for good that the world has ever seen; but having a German wife I naturally see a good deal of the reverse of the medal. You don't have to tell me that the Germans have faults, but, frankly, I'm not prepared to admit that they're devils incarnate. At the beginning of the war my poor wife had a very rough time in England, and I for one couldn't have blamed her if she'd felt rather bitter about it. Everyone thought she was a spy. It'll make you laugh when you know her. She's the typical German *hausfrau*, who cares for nothing but her house and her husband and our only child Fritzi." Caypor fondled his dog and gave a little laugh. "Yes, Fritzi, you are our child, aren't you? Naturally, it made my position very awkward. I was connected with some very important papers, and my editors weren't quite comfortable about it. Well, to cut a long story short I thought the most dignified course was to resign and come to a neutral country till the storm blew over. My wife and I never discuss the War, though I'm bound to tell you that it's more on my account than hers. She's much more tolerant than I am, and she's more willing to look upon this terrible business from my point of view than I am from hers."

"That is strange," said Ashenden. "As a rule women are so much more rabid than men."

"My wife is a very remarkable person. I should like to introduce you to her. By the way, I don't know if you know my name. Grantley Caypor."

"My name is Somerville," said Ashenden.

He told him then of the work he had been doing in the Censorship Department, and he fancied that into Caypor's eyes came a certain intentness. Presently he told him that he was looking for someone to give him conversation lessons in German, so that he might rub up his rusty knowledge of the language; and as he spoke a notion flashed across his mind. He gave Caypor a look, and saw that the same notion had come to him. It had occurred to them at the same instant that it would be a very good plan for Ashenden's teacher to be Mrs. Caypor.

"I asked our landlady if she could find me someone, and she said she thought she could. I must ask her again. It ought not to be very hard to find a man who is prepared to come and talk German to me for an hour a day."

"I wouldn't take anyone on the landlady's recommendation." said Caypor. "After all, you want someone with a good North German accent, and she only talks Swiss. I'll ask my wife if she knows anyone. My wife's a very highly educated woman, and you could trust her recommendation."

"That's very kind of you."

Ashenden observed Grantley Caypor at his ease. He noticed how the small, grey-green eyes, which last night he had not been able to see, contradicted the red, good-humored frankness of the face. They were quick and shifty, but when the mind behind them was seized by an unexpected notion they were suddenly still. It gave one a peculiar feeling of the working of the brain. They were not eyes that inspired confidence; Caypor did that with his jolly, good-natured smile, the openness of his broad, weather-beaten face, his comfortable obesity, and the cheeriness of his loud, deep voice. He was doing his best now to be agreeable. While Ashenden talked to him, a little shyly still but gaining confidence from that breezy, cordial manner, capable of putting anyone at his ease, it intrigued him to remember that the man was a common spy. It gave a tang to his conversation to reflect that he had been ready to sell his country for no more than forty pounds a month. Ashenden had known Gomez, the young Spaniard, whom Caypor had betrayed. He was a high-spirited youth, with a love of adventure, and he had undertaken his dangerous mission not for the money he earned by it but from a passion for romance. It amused him to outwit the clumsy German, and it appealed to his sense of the absurd to play a part in a shilling shocker. It was not very nice to think of him now, six feet underground in a prison yard. He was young and he had a certain grace of gesture. Ashenden wondered whether Caypor had felt a qualm when he delivered him up to destruction.

"I suppose you know a little German?" asked Caypor, interested in the stranger.

"Oh yes, I was a student in Germany, and I used to talk it fluently; but that is long ago, and I have forgotten. I can still read it comfortably."

"Oh yes, I noticed you were reading a German book last night."

Fool! It was only a little while since he had told Ashenden that he had not seen him at dinner. He wondered whether Caypor had observed the slip. How difficult it was never to make one! Ashenden must be on his guard; the thing that made him most nervous was the thought that he might not answer readily enough to his assumed name of Somerville. Of course, there was always the chance that Caypor had made the slip on purpose to see by Ashenden's face whether he noticed anything. Caypor got up.

"There is my wife. We go for a walk up one of the mountains every afternoon. I can tell you some charming walks. The flowers even now are lovely."

"I'm afraid I must wait till I'm a bit stronger," said Ashenden with a little sigh.

He had naturally a pale face and never looked as robust as he was. Mrs. Caypor came downstairs and her husband joined her. They walked down the road, Fritzi bounding round them, and Ashenden saw that Caypor immediately began to speak with volubility. He was evidently telling his wife the results of his interview with Ashenden. Ashenden looked at the sun shining so gaily on the lake; the shadow of a breeze fluttered the green leaves of the trees; everything invited to a stroll. He got up, went to his room, and, throwing himself on his bed, had a very pleasant sleep.

He went into dinner that evening as the Caypors were finishing, for he had wandered melancholy about Lucerne in the hope of finding a cocktail that would enable him to face the potato salad that he foresaw, and on their way out of the dining-room Caypor stopped and asked him if he would drink coffee with them. When Ashenden joined them in the hall, Caypor got up and introduced him to his wife. She bowed stiffly, and no answering smile came to her face to respond to Ashenden's civil greeting. It was not hard to see that her attitude was definitely hostile. It put Ashenden at his ease. She was a plainish woman, nearing forty, with a muddy skin and vague features; her drab hair was arranged in a plait round her head like that of Napoleon's Queen of Prussia, and she was squarely built, plump rather than fat, and solid. But she did not look stupid; she looked, on the contrary, a woman of character, and Ashenden, who had lived enough in Germany to recognize the type, was ready to believe that though capable of doing the housework, cooking the dinner, and climbing a mountain, she might be also prodigiously well-informed. She wore a white blouse that showed a sunburned neck, a black skirt, and heavy walking boots. Caypor, addressing her in English, told her in his jovial way, as though she did not know it already, what Ashenden had told him about himself. She listened grimly.

"I think you told me you understood German," said Caypor, his big red face wreathed in polite smiles but his little eyes darting about restlessly.

"Yes, I was for some time a student in Heidelberg."

"Really?" said Mrs. Caypor in English, an expression of faint interest for a moment chasing away the sullenness from her face. "I know Heidelberg very well. I was at school there for one year."

Her English was correct but throaty, and the mouthing emphasis she gave her words was disagreeable. Ashenden was diffuse in praise of the old university town and the beauty of the neighborhood. She heard him, from the standpoint of her Teutonic superiority, with toleration rather than with enthusiasm.

"It is well known that the valley of the Neckar is one of the beauty places of the whole world," she said.

"I have not told you, my dear," said Caypor then, "that Mr. Somerville is looking for someone to give him conversation lessons while he is here. I told him that perhaps you could suggest a teacher."

"No, I know no one whom I could conscientiously recommend," she answered. "The Swiss accent is hateful beyond words. It could do Mr. Somerville only harm to converse with a Swiss."

"If I were in your place, Mr. Somerville, I would try and persuade my wife to give you lessons. She is, if I may say so, a very cultivated and highly educated woman."

"*Ach*, Grantley, I have not the time. I have my own work to do."

Ashenden saw that he was being given his opportunity. The trap was prepared, and all he had to do was to fall in. He turned to Mrs. Caypor with a manner that he tried to make shy, deprecating, and modest.

"Of course, it would be too wonderful if you would give me lessons. I should look upon it as a real privilege. Naturally, I wouldn't want to interfere with your work. I am just here to get well, with nothing in the world to do, and I would suit my time entirely to your convenience."

He felt a flash of satisfaction pass from one to the other, and in Mrs. Caypor's blue eyes he fancied that he saw a dark glow.

"Of course, it would be a purely business arrangement," said Caypor. "There's no reason that my good wife shouldn't earn a little pin-money. Would you think ten francs an hour too much?"

"No," said Ashenden, "I should think myself lucky to get a first-rate teacher for that."

"What do you say, my dear? Surely you can spare an hour, and you would be doing this gentleman a kindness. He would learn that all Germans are not the devilish fiends that they think them in England."

On Mrs. Caypor's brow was an uneasy frown, and Ashenden could not but think with apprehension of that hour's conversation a day that he was going to exchange with her. Heaven only knew how he would have to rack his brain for subjects of discourse with that heavy and morose woman. Now she made a visible effort.

"I shall be very pleased to give Mr. Somerville conversation lessons."

"I congratulate you, Mr. Somerville," said Caypor noisily. "You're in for a treat. When will you start—tomorrow at eleven?"

"That would suit me very well if it suits Mrs. Caypor."

"Yes, that is as good an hour as another," she answered.

Ashenden left them to discuss the happy outcome of their diplomacy. But when, punctually at eleven next morning, he heard a knock at his door (for it had been arranged that Mrs. Caypor should give him his lesson in his room), it was not without trepidation that he opened it. It behoved him to be frank, a trifle indiscreet, but obviously wary of a German woman, sufficiently intelligent and impulsive. Mrs. Caypor's face was dark and sulky. She plainly hated having anything to do with him. But they sat down, and she began, somewhat peremptorily, to ask him questions about his knowledge of German literature. She corrected his mistakes with exactness, and when he put before her some difficulty in German construction, she explained it with clearness and precision. It was obvious that though she hated giving him a lesson, she meant to give it conscientiously. She seemed to have not only an aptitude for teaching but a love of it, and as the hour went on she began to speak with greater earnestness. It was already only by an effort that she remembered that he was a brutal Englishman. Ashenden, noticing the unconscious struggle within her, found himself not a little entertained; and it was with truth that, when later in the day Caypor asked him how the lesson had gone, he answered that it was highly satisfactory. Mrs. Caypor was an excellent teacher and a most interesting person.

"I told you so. She's the most remarkable woman I know."

And Ashenden had a feeling that when in his hearty, laughing way Caypor said this he was for the first time entirely sincere.

In a day or two Ashenden guessed that Mrs. Caypor was giving him lessons only in order to enable Caypor to arrive at a closer intimacy with him, for she confined herself strictly to matters of literature, music, and painting; and when Ashenden, by way of experiment, brought the conversation round to the War, she cut him short.

"I think that is a topic that we had better avoid, Herr Somerville," she said.

She continued to give her lessons with the greatest thoroughness, and he had his money's worth; but every day she came with the same sullen face, and it was only in the interest of teaching that she lost for a moment her instinctive dislike of him. Ashenden exercised in turn, but in vain, all his wiles. He was ingratiating, ingenious, humble, grateful, flattering, simple, and timid. She remained coldly hostile. She was a fanatic. Her patriotism was aggressive but disinterested, and, obsessed with the notion of the superiority of all things German, she loathed England with a virulent hatred because in that country she saw the chief obstacle to their diffusion. Her ideal was a German world, in which the rest of the nations, under a hegemony greater than that of Rome, should enjoy the benefits of German science and German art and German culture. There was in the conception a magnificent impudence that appealed to Ashenden's sense of humor. She was no fool. She had read much in several languages, and she could talk of the books she had read with good sense. She had a knowledge of modern painting and modern music that not a little impressed Ashenden. It was amusing once to hear her before luncheon play one of those silvery little pieces of Debussy; she played it disdainfully because it was French and so light, but with an angry appreciation of its grace and gaiety. When Ashenden congratulated her she shrugged her shoulders.

"The decadent music of a decadent nation," she said. Then, with powerful hands, she struck the first resounding chords of a sonata by Beethoven; but she stopped. "I cannot play, I am out of practice; and you English, what do you know of music? You have not produced a composer since Purcell."

"What do you think of that statement?" Ashenden asked Caypor, who was standing near.

"I confess its truth. The little I know of music my wife taught me. I wish you could hear her play when she is in practice." He put his fat hand, with its square, stumpy fingers on her shoulder.

"She can wring your heart-strings with pure beauty."

"*Dummer Kerl* (Stupid fellow)," she said in a soft voice; and Ashenden saw her mouth for a moment quiver, but she quickly recovered. "You English, you cannot paint, you cannot model, you cannot write music."

"Some of us can at times write pleasing verses," said Ashenden with good humor, for it was not his business to be put out, and—he did not know why—two lines occurring to him, he said them:

> "Whither, O splendid ship, thy white sails crowding,
>
> Leaning across the bosom of the urgent West?"

"Yes," said Mrs. Caypor, with a strange gesture, "you can write poetry. I wonder why?"

And to Ashenden's surprise she went on, in her guttural English, to recite the next two lines of the poem he had quoted.

"Come, Grantley, *mittagessen* is ready; let us go into the dining-room."

They left Ashenden reflective.

Ashenden admired goodness, but was not outraged by wickedness. People sometimes thought him heartless because he was more often interested in others than attached to them, and even in the few to whom he was attached his eyes saw with equal clearness the merits and the defects. When he liked people it was not because he was blind to their faults—he did not mind their faults—but accepted them with a tolerant shrug of the shoulders, or because he ascribed to them excellencies that they did not possess; and since he judged his friends with candor they never disappointed him, and he seldom lost one. He asked from none more than he could give. He was able to pursue his study of the Caypors without prejudice and without passion. Mrs. Caypor seemed to him more of a piece, and therefore the easier of the two to understand; she obviously detested him. Though it was so necessary for her to be civil to him, her antipathy was strong enough to wring from her now and then an expression of rudeness; and had she been safely able to do so she would have killed him without a qualm. But in the pressure of Caypor's chubby hand on his wife's shoulder and in the fugitive trembling of her lips, Ashenden had divined that this unprepossessing woman and that mean, fat man were joined together by a deep and sincere love. It was touching. Ashenden assembled the observations that he had been making for the past few days, and little things that he had noticed but to which he had attached no significance returned to him. It seemed to him that Mrs. Caypor loved her husband because she was of a stronger character than he and because she felt his dependence on her; she loved him for his admiration of her, and you might guess that till she met him, this dumpy, plain woman with her dullness, good sense, and want of humor could not have much enjoyed the admiration of men. She enjoyed his heartiness and his noisy jokes, and his high spirits stirred her sluggish blood; he was a great big bouncing boy, and he would never be anything else, and she felt like a mother towards him. She had made him what he was, and he was her man and she was his woman, and she loved him, notwithstanding his weakness (for with her clear head she must always have been conscious of that); she loved him, *ach, was,* as Isolde loved Tristan. But then there was the espionage. Even Ashenden, with all his tolerance for human frailty, could not but feel that to betray your country for money is not a very pretty proceeding. Of course, she knew of it—indeed, it was probably through her that Caypor had first been approached; he would never have undertaken such work if she had not urged him to it. She loved him, and she was an honest and an upright woman. By what devious means had she persuaded herself to force her husband to adopt so base and dishonourable a calling? Ashenden lost himself in a labyrinth of conjecture as he tried to piece together the actions of her mind.

Grantley Caypor was another story. There was little to admire in him, but at that moment Ashenden was not looking for an object of admiration; but there was much that was singular and much that was unexpected in that gross and vulgar fellow. Ashenden watched with entertainment the suave manner in which the spy tried to inveigle him in his toils. It was a couple of days after his first lesson that Caypor after dinner, his wife having gone upstairs, threw himself heavily into a chair by Ashenden's side. His faithful Fritzi came up to him and put his long muzzle with its black nose on his knee.

"He has no brain," said Caypor, "but a heart of gold. Look at those little pink eyes. Did you ever see anything so stupid? And what an ugly face, but what incredible charm!"

"Have you had him long?" asked Ashenden.

"I got him in 1914, just before the outbreak of war. By the way, what do you think of the news today? Of course, my wife and I never discuss the War. You can't think what a relief to me it is to find a fellow-countryman to whom I can open my heart."

He handed Ashenden a cheap Swiss cigar, and Ashenden making a rueful sacrifice to duty and accepted it.

"Of course, they haven't got a chance, the Germans," said Caypor, "not a dog's chance. I knew they were beaten the moment we came in."

His manner was earnest, sincere, and confidential. Ashenden made a commonplace rejoinder.

"It's the greatest grief of my life that, owing to my wife's nationality, I was unable to do any war work. I tried to enlist the day war broke out, but they wouldn't have me on account of my age; but I don't mind telling you, if the War goes on much longer, wife or no wife, I'm going to do something. With my knowledge of languages I ought to be of some service in the Censorship Department. That's where you were, wasn't it?"

That was the mark at which he had been aiming, and in answer now to his well-directed questions Ashenden gave him the information that he had already prepared. Caypor drew his chair a little nearer and dropped his voice.

"I'm sure you wouldn't tell me anything that anyone shouldn't know, but after all, these Swiss are absolutely pro-German, and we don't want to give anyone the chance of overhearing."

Then he went on another tack. He told Ashenden a number of things that were of a certain secrecy.

"I wouldn't tell this to anybody else, you know, but I have one or two friends who are in pretty influential positions, and they know they can trust me."

Thus encouraged, Ashenden was a little more deliberately indiscreet, and when they parted both had reason to be satisfied. Ashenden guessed that Caypor's typewriter would be kept busy next morning and that that extremely energetic Major in Berne would shortly receive a most interesting report.

One evening, going upstairs after dinner, Ashenden passed an open bathroom. He caught sight of the Caypors.

"Come in," cried Caypor in his cordial way. "We're washing our Fritzi."

The bull-terrier was constantly getting himself very dirty, and it was Caypor's pride to see him clean and white. Ashenden went in. Mrs. Caypor, with her sleeves turned up and a large white apron, was standing at one end of the bath, while Caypor, in a pair of trousers and a singlet, his fat, freckled arms bare, was soaping the wretched hound.

"We have to do it at night," he said, "because the Fitzgeralds use this bath, and they'd have a fit if they knew we washed the dog in it. We wait till they go to bed. Come along, Fritzi; show the gentlemen how beautifully you behave when you have your face scrubbed."

The poor brute, woebegone but faintly wagging his tail to show that however foul was this operation performed on him he bore no malice to the god who did it, was standing in the middle of the bath in six inches of water. He was soaped all over, and Caypor, talking the while, shampooed him with his great fat hands.

"Oh, what a beautiful dog he's going to be when he's as white as the driven snow! His master will be as proud as Punch to walk out with him, and all the little lady dogs will say: 'Good gracious! Who's that beautiful aristocratic-looking bull-terrier, walking as though he owned the whole of Switzerland?' Now stand still while you have your ears washed. You couldn't bear to go out into the street with dirty ears, could you? Like a nasty little Swiss schoolboy? *Noblesse.* Now the black nose. Oh, and all the soap is going into his little pink eyes and they'll smart."

Mrs. Caypor listened to this nonsense with a good-humored, sluggish smile on her broad, plain face, and presently gravely took a towel.

"Now he's going to have a ducking. Upsie-daisy."

Caypor seized the dog by the fore-legs and ducked him once and ducked him twice. There was a struggle, a flurry, and a splashing. Caypor lifted him out of the bath.

"Now go to mother and she'll dry you."

Mrs. Caypor sat down and, taking the dog between her strong legs, rubbed him till the sweat poured off her forehead. And Fritzi a little shaken and breathless, but happy it was all over, with his sweet, stupid face, white and shining.

"Blood will tell," cried Caypor exultantly. "He knows the names of no less than sixty-four of his ancestors, and they were all nobly born."

Ashenden was faintly troubled. He shivered a little as he walked upstairs.

Then, one Sunday, Caypor told him that he and his wife were going on an excursion and would eat their luncheon at some little mountain restaurant; and he suggested that Ashenden, each paying his share, should come with them. After three weeks at Lucerne, Ashenden thought that his strength would permit him to venture the exertion. They started early, Mrs. Caypor businesslike in her walking boots and Tyrolese hat and alpenstock, and Caypor in stockings and plus-fours, looking very British. The situation amused Ashenden, and he was prepared to enjoy his day. But he meant to keep his eyes open; it was not inconceivable that the Caypors had discovered what he was, and it would not do to go too near a precipice. Mrs. Caypor would not hesitate to give him a push, and Caypor, for all his jolliness, was an ugly customer. But on the face of it there was nothing to mar Ashenden's pleasure in the golden morning. The air was fragrant. Caypor was full of conversation. He told funny stories. He was gay and jovial. The sweat rolled off his great red face, and he laughed at himself because he was so fat. To Ashenden's astonishment he showed a peculiar knowledge of the mountain flowers. Once he went out of the way to pick one he saw a little distance from the path and brought it back to his wife. He looked at it tenderly.

"Isn't it lovely?" he cried, and his shifty, grey-green eyes for a moment were as candid as a child's. "It's like a poem by Walter Savage Landor."

"Botany is my husband's favourite science," said Mrs. Caypor. "I laugh at him sometimes. He is devoted to flowers. Often when we have hardly had enough money to pay the butcher he has spent everything in his pocket to bring me a bunch of roses."

"*Qui fleurit sa maison fleurit son cœur,*" said Grantley Caypor.

Ashenden had once or twice seen Caypor, coming in from a walk, offer Mrs. Fitzgerald a nosegay of mountain flowers with an elephantine courtesy that was not entirely displeasing; and what he had just learned added a certain significance to the pretty little action. His passion for flowers was genuine, and when he gave them to the old Irish lady he gave her something he valued. It showed a real kindness of heart. Ashenden had always thought botany a tedious science, but Caypor, talking exuberantly as they walked along, was able to impart to it life and interest. He must have given it a good deal of study.

"I've never written a book," he said. "There are too many books already, and any desire to write I have is satisfied by the more immediately profitable and quite ephemeral composition of an article for a daily paper. But if I stay here much longer I have half a mind to write a book about the wild flowers of Switzerland. Oh, I wish you'd been here a little earlier. They were marvelous. But one wants to be a poet for that, and I'm only a poor newspaper man."

It was curious to observe how he was able to combine real emotion with false fact.

When they reached the inn, with its view of the mountains and the lake, it was good to see the sensual pleasure with which he poured down his throat a bottle of ice-cold beer. You could not but feel sympathy for a man who took so much delight in simple things. They lunched deliciously off scrambled eggs and mountain trout. Even Mrs. Caypor was moved to an unwonted gentleness by her surroundings—the inn was in an agreeably rural spot; it looked like a picture of a Swiss chalet in a book of early nineteenth century travels—and she treated Ashenden with something less than her usual hostility. When they arrived she had burst into loud German exclamations on the beauty of the scene, and now, softened perhaps, too, by food and drink, her eyes, dwelling on the grandeur before her, filled with tears. She stretched out her hand.

"It is dreadful and I am ashamed; notwithstanding this horrible and unjust war I can feel in my heart at the moment nothing but happiness and gratitude."

Caypor took her by the hand and pressed it, and, an unusual thing with him, addressing her in German, called her little pet names. It was absurd, but touching. Ashenden, leaving them to their emotions, strolled through the garden and sat down on a bench that had been prepared for the comfort of the tourist. The view was, of course, spectacular, but it captured you; it was like a piece of music that was obvious and meretricious, but for the moment shattered your self-control.

And as Ashenden lingered idly in that spot he pondered over the mystery of Grantley Caypor's treachery. If he liked strange people he had found in him one who was strange beyond belief. It would be foolish to deny that he had amiable traits. His joviality was not assumed, he was without pretence a hearty fellow, and he had real good nature. He was always ready to do a kindness. Ashenden had often watched him with the old Irish Colonel and his wife, who were the only other residents of the hotel; he would listen good-humoredly to the old man's tedious stories of the Egyptian war, and he was charming with her. Now that Ashenden had arrived at terms of some familiarity with Caypor he found that he regarded him less with repulsion than with curiosity. He did not think that he had become a spy merely for the money; he was a man of modest tastes, and what he had earned in a shipping office must have sufficed to so good a manager as Mrs. Caypor, and after war was declared there was no lack of remunerative work for men over the military age. It might be that he was one of those men who prefer devious ways to straight for some intricate pleasure they get in fooling their fellows; and that he had turned spy, not from hatred of the country that had imprisoned him, not even from love of his wife, but from a desire to score off the big-wigs who never even knew of his existence. It might be that it was vanity that impelled him, a feeling that his talents had not received the recognition they merited, or just a puckish, impish desire to do mischief. He was a crook. It is true that only two cases of dishonesty had been brought home to him, but if he had been caught twice it might be surmised that he had often been dishonest without being caught. What did Mrs. Caypor think of this? They were so united that she must be aware of it. Did it make her ashamed, for her own uprightness surely none could doubt, or did she accept it as an inevitable kink in the man she loved? Did she do all she could to prevent it or did she close her eyes to something she could not help?

How much easier life would be if people were all black or all white, and how much simpler it would be to act in regard to them! Was Caypor a good man who loved evil, or a bad man who loved good? And how could such unreconcilable elements exist side by side and in harmony within the same heart? For one thing was clear: Caypor was disturbed by no gnawing of conscience; he did his mean and despicable work with gusto. He was a traitor who enjoyed his treachery. Though Ashenden had been studying human nature more or less consciously all his life, it seemed to him that he knew as little about it now in middle age as he had done when he was a child. Of course, R. would have said to him: "Why the devil do you waste your time with such nonsense? The man's a dangerous spy, and your business is to lay him by the heels."

That was true enough. Ashenden had decided that it would be useless to attempt to make any arrangement with Caypor. Though doubtless he would have no feeling about betraying his employers, he could certainly not be trusted. His wife's influence was too strong. Besides, notwithstanding what he had from time to time told Ashenden, he was in his heart convinced that the Central Powers must win the War, and he meant to be on the winning side. Well, then Caypor must be laid by the heels, but how he was to effect that Ashenden had no notion. Suddenly he heard a voice.

"There you are. We've been wondering where you had hidden yourself."

He looked round and saw the Caypors strolling towards him. They were walking hand-in-hand.

"So this is what has kept you quiet," said Caypor as his eyes fell on the view. "What a spot!"

Mrs. Caypor clasped her hands.

"*Ach Gott, wie schön!*" she cried. "*Wie schön.* When I look at that blue lake and those snowy mountains I feel inclined, like Goethe's Faust, to cry to the passing moment: Tarry."

"This is better than being in England with the excursions and alarums of war, isn't it?" said Caypor.

"Much," said Ashenden.

"By the way, did you have any difficulty in getting out?"

"No, not the smallest."

"I'm told they make rather a nuisance of themselves at the frontier nowadays."

"I came through without the smallest difficulty. I don't fancy they bother much about the English. I thought the examination of passports was quite perfunctory."

A fleeting glance passed between Caypor and his wife. Ashenden wondered what it meant. It would be strange if Caypor's thoughts were occupied with the chances of a journey to England at the very moment when he was himself reflecting on its possibility. In a little while Mrs. Caypor suggested that they had better be starting back, and they wandered together in the shade of the trees down the mountain paths.

Ashenden was watchful. He could do nothing (and his inactivity irked him) but wait with his eyes open to seize the opportunity that might present itself. A couple of days later an incident occurred that made him certain something was in the wind. In the course of his morning lesson Mrs. Caypor remarked:

"My husband has gone to Geneva today. He had some business to do there."

"Oh," said Ashenden, "will he be gone long?"

"No, only two days."

It is not everyone who can tell a lie, and Ashenden had the feeling, he hardly knew why, that Mrs. Caypor was telling one then. Her manner, perhaps, was not quite as indifferent as you would have expected when she was mentioning a fact that could be of no interest to Ashenden. It flashed across his mind that Caypor had been summoned to Berne to see the redoubtable head of the German Secret Service. When he had the chance he said casually to the waitress:

"A little less work for you to do, fräulein. I hear that Herr Caypor has gone to Berne."

"Yes. But he'll be back tomorrow."

That proved nothing, but it was something to go upon. Ashenden knew in Lucerne a Swiss who was willing on emergency to do odd jobs, and, looking him up, asked him to take a letter to Berne. It might be possible to pick up Caypor and trace his movements. Next day Caypor appeared once more with his wife at the dinner table, but merely nodded to Ashenden, and afterwards both went straight upstairs. They looked troubled. Caypor, as a rule so animated, walked with bowed shoulders, and looked neither to the right nor to the left. Next morning Ashenden received a reply to his letter. Caypor had seen Major von P. It was possible to guess what the Major had said to him. Ashenden well knew how rough he could be; he was a hard man and brutal, clever, and unscrupulous, and he was not accustomed to mince his words. They were tired of paying Caypor a salary to sit still in Lucerne and do nothing; the time was come for him to go to England. Guesswork? Of course it was guesswork, but in that trade it mostly was: you had to deduce the animal from its jaw-bone. Ashenden knew from Gustav that the Germans wanted to send someone to England. He drew a long breath; if Caypor went he would have to get busy. When Mrs. Caypor came in to give him his lesson she was dull and listless. She looked tired, and her mouth was set obstinately; it occurred to Ashenden that the Caypors had spent most of the night talking. He wished he knew what they had said. Did she urge him to go or did she try to dissuade him? Ashenden watched them again at luncheon. Something was the matter, for they hardly spoke to one another, and as a rule they found plenty to talk about. They left the room early, but when Ashenden went out he saw Caypor sitting in the hall by himself.

"Hulloa!" he cried jovially, but surely the effort was patent, "how are you getting on? I've been to Geneva."

"So I heard," said Ashenden.

"Come and have your coffee with me. My poor wife's got a headache. I told her she'd better go and lie down."

In his shifty green eyes was an expression that Ashenden could not read. "The fact is, she's rather worried, poor dear; I'm thinking of going to England."

Ashenden's heart gave a sudden leap against his ribs, but his face remained impassive.

"Oh, are you going for long? We shall miss you."

"To tell you the truth, I'm fed up with doing nothing. The War looks as though it were going on for years, and I can't sit here indefinitely. Besides, I can't afford it. I've got to earn my living. I may have a German wife, but I am an Englishman, hang it all! and I want to do my bit. I could never face my friends again if I just stayed here in ease and comfort till the end of the War and never attempted to do a thing to help the country. My wife takes her German point of view, and I don't mind telling you that she's a bit upset. You know what women are."

Now Ashenden knew what it was that he saw in Caypor's eyes. Fear. It gave him a nasty turn. Caypor didn't want to go to England, he wanted to stay safely in Switzerland; Ashenden knew now what the Major had said to him when he went to see him in Berne. He had got to go or lose his salary. What was it that his wife had said when he told her what had happened? He had wanted her to press him to stay, but it was plain she hadn't done that; perhaps he had not dared to tell her how frightened he was. To her he had always been gay, bold, adventurous, and devil-may-care; and now, the prisoner of his own lies, he had not found it in him to confess himself the mean and sneaking coward he was.

"Are you going to take your wife with you?" asked Ashenden.

"No, she'll stay here."

It had been arranged very neatly. Mrs. Caypor would receive his letters and forward the information they contained to Berne.

"I've been out of England so long that I don't quite know how to set about getting war work. What would you do in my place?"

"I don't know; what sort of work are you thinking of?"

"Well, you know, I imagine I could do the same thing as you did. I wonder if there's anyone in the Censorship Department that you could give me a letter of introduction to."

It was only by a miracle that Ashenden saved himself from showing by a smothered cry or by a broken gesture how startled he was; but not by Caypor's request, by what had just dawned upon him. What an idiot he had been! He had been disturbed by the thought that he was wasting his time at Lucerne; he was doing nothing, and though, in fact, as it turned out, Caypor was going to England, it was due to no cleverness of his. He could take to himself no credit for the result. And now he saw that he had been put in Lucerne, told how to describe himself and given the proper information, so that what actually had occurred should occur. It would be a wonderful thing for the German Secret Service to get an agent into the Censorship Department; and by a happy accident there was Grantley Caypor, the very man for the job, on friendly terms with someone who had worked there. What a bit of luck! Major von P. was a man of culture and, rubbing his hands, he must surely have murmured: *stultum facit fortuna quem vult perdere*. It was a trap of that devilish R., and the grim Major at Berne had fallen into it. Ashenden had done his work just by sitting still and doing nothing. He almost laughed as he thought what a fool R. had made of him.

"I was on very good terms with the chief of my department. I could give you a note to him if you liked."

"That would be just the thing."

"But, of course, I must give the facts. I must say I've met you here and only known you a fortnight."

"Of course. But you'll say what else you can for me, won't you?"

"Oh, certainly."

"I don't know yet if I can get a visa. I'm told they're rather fussy."

"I don't see why. I shall be very sick if they refuse me one when I want to go back."

"I'll go and see how my wife is getting on," said Caypor suddenly, getting up. "When will you let me have that letter?"

"Whenever you like. Are you going at once?"

"As soon as possible."

Caypor left him. Ashenden waited in the hall for a quarter of an hour so that there should appear in him no sign of hurry. Then he went upstairs and prepared various communications. In one he informed R. that Caypor was going to England; in another he made arrangements through Berne that wherever Caypor applied for a visa it should be granted to him without question; and these he despatched forthwith. When he went down to dinner he handed to Caypor a cordial letter of introduction.

Next day but one Caypor left Lucerne.

Ashenden waited. He continued to have his hour's lesson with Mrs. Caypor, and under her conscientious tuition began now to speak German with ease. They talked of Goethe and Winckelmann, of art and life and travel. Fritzi sat quietly by her chair.

"He misses his master," she said, pulling his ears. "He only really cares for him, he suffers me only as belonging to him."

After his lesson Ashenden went every morning to Cook's to ask for his letters. It was here that all communications were addressed to him. He could not move till he received instructions, but R. could be trusted not to leave him idle long; and meanwhile there was nothing for him to do but have patience. Presently he received a letter from the consul in Geneva to say that Caypor had there applied for his visa and had set out for France. Having read this, Ashenden went on for a little stroll by the lake, and on his way back happened to see Mrs. Caypor coming out of Cook's office. He guessed that she was having her letters addressed there too. He went up to her.

"Have you had news of Herr Caypor?" he asked her.

"No," she said. "I suppose I could hardly expect to yet." He walked along by her side. She was disappointed, but not yet anxious; she knew how irregular was the post. But next day during the lesson he could not but see that she was impatient to have done with it. The post was delivered at noon, and at five minutes to she looked at her watch and him. Though Ashenden knew very well that no letter would ever come for her, he had not the heart to keep her on tenterhooks.

"Don't you think that's enough for the day? I'm sure you want to go down to Cook's," he said.

"Thank you. That is very amiable of you."

When a little later he went there himself he found her standing in the middle of the office. Her face was distraught. She addressed him wildly:

"My husband promised to write from Paris. I am sure there is a letter for me, but these stupid people say there's nothing. They're so careless; it's a scandal."

Ashenden did not know what to say. While the clerk was looking through the bundle to see if there was anything for him she came up to the desk again.

"When does the next post come in from France?" she asked.

"Sometimes there are letters about five."

"I'll come then."

She turned and walked rapidly away. Fritzi followed her with his tail between his legs. There was no doubt of it; already the fear had seized her that something was wrong. Next morning she looked dreadful; she could not have closed her eyes all night; and in the lesson she started up from her chair.

"You must excuse me, Herr Somerville, I cannot give you a lesson today. I am not feeling well."

Before Ashenden could say anything she had flung herself nervously from the room, and in the evening he got a note from her to say that she regretted that she must discontinue giving him conversation lessons. She gave no reason. Then Ashenden saw no more of her; she ceased coming in to meals; except to go morning and afternoon to Cook's; she spent apparently the whole day in her room. Ashenden thought of her sitting there hour after hour with that hideous fear gnawing at her heart. Who could help feeling sorry for her? The time hung heavy on his hands too. He read a good deal and wrote a little, he hired a canoe and went for long leisurely paddles on the lake; and at last one morning the clerk at Cook's handed him a letter. It was from R. It had all the appearance of a business communication, but between the lines he read a good deal.

"Dear Sir (it began),
        "The goods, with accompanying letter, despatched by you from Lucerne have been duly delivered. We are obliged to you for executing our instructions with such promptness."

It went on in this strain. R. was exultant. Ashenden guessed that Caypor had been arrested, and by now had paid the penalty of his crime. He shuddered. He remembered a dreadful scene. Dawn. A cold, grey dawn, with a drizzling rain falling. A man, blindfolded, standing against a wall, an officer, very pale, giving an order, a volley, and then a young soldier, one of the firing party, turning round and holding on to his gun for support, vomiting. The officer turned paler still, and he, Ashenden, feeling dreadfully faint. How terrified Caypor must have been! It was awful when the tears ran down their faces. Ashenden shook himself. He went to the ticket-office and, obedient to his orders, bought himself a ticket for Geneva.

As he was waiting for his change Mrs. Caypor came in. He was shocked at the sight of her. She was blowsy and disheveled, and there were heavy rings round her eyes. She was deathly pale. She staggered up to the desk and asked for a letter. The clerk shook his head.

"I'm sorry, madam, there's nothing yet."

"But look, look! Are you sure? Please look again."

The misery in her voice was heartrending. The clerk, with a shrug of the shoulders, took out the letters from a pigeon-hole and sorted them once more.

"No, there's nothing, madam."

She gave a hoarse cry of despair, and her face was distorted with anguish.

"Oh, God! oh, God!" she moaned.

She turned away, the tears streaming from her weary eyes, and for a moment she stood there like a blind man groping and not knowing which way to go. Then a fearful thing happened. Fritzi, the bull-terrier, sat down on his haunches and threw back his head and gave a long, long melancholy howl. Mrs. Caypor looked at him with terror; her eyes seemed really to start from her head. The doubt, the gnawing doubt that had tortured her during those dreadful days of suspense, was a doubt no longer. She knew. She staggered blindly into the street.

In Another Country

(from *Men Without Women*)

Ernest Hemingway

In the fall the War was always there, but we did not go to it any more. It was cold in the fall in Milan and the dark came very early. Then the electric lights came on, and it was pleasant along the streets looking in the windows. There was much game hanging outside the shops, and the snow powdered in the fur of the foxes and the wind blew their tails. The deer hung stiff and heavy and empty, and small birds blew in the wind and the wind turned their feathers. It was a cold fall and the wind came down from the mountains.

We were all at the hospital every afternoon, and there were different ways of walking across the town through the dusk to the hospital. Two of the ways were alongside canals, but they were long. Always, though, you crossed a bridge across a canal to enter the hospital. There was a choice of three bridges. On one of them a woman sold roasted chestnuts. It was warm standing in front of her charcoal fire, and the chestnuts were warm afterward in your pocket. The hospital was very old and very beautiful, and you entered through a gate and walked across a courtyard and out a gate on the other side. There were usually funerals starting from the courtyard. Beyond the old hospital were the new brick pavilions, and there we met every afternoon and were all very polite and interested in what was the matter, and sat in the machines that were to make so much difference.

The doctor came up to the machine where I was sitting and said: "What did you like best to do before the War? Did you practice a sport?"

I said: "Yes, football."

"Good," he said. "You will be able to play football again better than ever."

My knee did not bend and the leg dropped straight from the knee to the ankle without a calf, and the machine was to bend the knee and make it move as in riding a tricycle. But it did not bend yet, and instead the machine lurched when it came to the bending part. The doctor said: "That will all pass. You are a fortunate young man. You will play football again like a champion."

In the next machine was a Major who had a little hand like a baby's. He winked at me when the doctor examined his hand, which was between two leather straps that bounced up and down and flapped the stiff fingers, and said: "And will I too play football, Captain—doctor?" He had been a very great fencer, and before the War the greatest fencer in Italy.

The doctor went to his office in a back room and brought back a photograph which showed a hand that had been withered almost as small as the Major's before it had taken a machine course, and after was a little larger. The Major held the photograph with his good hand and looked at it very carefully. "A wound?" he asked.

"An industrial accident," the doctor said.

"Very interesting, very interesting," the Major said, and handed it back to the doctor.

"You have confidence?"

"No," said the Major.

There were three boys who came each day who were about the same age I was. They were all three from Milan, and one of them was to be a lawyer, and one was to be a painter, and one had intended to be a soldier, and after we were finished with the machines sometimes we walked back together to the Café Cova, which was next door to the Scala. We walked the short way through the communist quarter because we were four together. The people hated us because we were officers, and from a wine-shop someone would call out, "*A basso gli ufficiali!*" as we passed. Another boy who walked with us sometimes and made us five wore a black silk handkerchief across his face because he had no nose then and his face was to be rebuilt. He had gone out to the front from the military academy and been wounded within an hour after he had gone into the front line for the first time. They rebuilt his face, but he came from a very old family and they could never get the nose exactly right. He went to South America and worked in a bank. But this was a long time ago, and then we did not any of us know how it was going to be afterward. We only knew then that there was always the War, but that we were not going to it any more.

We all had the same medals, except the boy with the black silk bandage across his face, and he had not been at the front long enough to get any medals. The tall boy with a very pale face who was to be a lawyer had been a Lieutenant of Arditi and had three medals of the sort we each had only one of. He had lived a very long time with death and was a little detached. We were all a little detached, and there was nothing that held us together except that we met every afternoon at the hospital. Although, as we walked to the Cova through the tough part of town, walking in the dark with light and singing coming out of the wine-shops and sometimes having to walk into the street when the men and women would crowd together on the sidewalk so that we would have had to jostle them to get by, we felt held together by there being something that had happened that they, the people who disliked us, did not understand.

We ourselves all understood the Cova, where it was rich and warm and not too brightly lighted, and noisy and smoky at certain hours, and there were always girls at the tables and the illustrated papers on a rack on the wall. The girls at the Cova were very patriotic, and I found that the most patriotic people in Italy were the café girls—and I believe they are still patriotic.

The boys at first were very polite about my medals and asked me what I had done to get them. I showed them the papers, which were written in very beautiful language, and full of *fratellanza* and *abnegazione*, but which really said, with the adjectives removed, that I had been given the medals because I was an American.

After that their manner changed a little toward me, although I was their friend against outsiders. I was a friend, but I was never really one of them after they had read the citations, because it had been different with them and they had done very different things to get their medals. I had been wounded, it was true; but we all knew that being wounded after all was really an accident. I was never ashamed of the ribbons, though, and sometimes, after the cocktail hour, I would imagine myself having done all the things they had done to get their medals; but walking home at night through the empty streets with the cold wind and all the shops closed, trying to keep near the street lights, I knew that I would never have done such things, and I was very much afraid to die, and often lay in bed at night by myself afraid to die, and wondering how I would be when I went back to the front again.

The three with the medals were like hunting-hawks; and I was not a hawk, although I might seem a hawk to those who had never hunted; they, the three, knew better and so we drifted apart. But I stayed good friends with the boy who had been wounded his first day at the front because he would never know now how he would have turned out; so he could never be accepted either, and I liked him because I thought perhaps he would not have turned out to be a hawk either.

The Major, who had been the great fencer, did not believe in bravery, and spent much time while we sat in the machines correcting my grammar. He had complimented me on how I spoke Italian, and we talked together very easily. One day I had said that Italian seemed such an easy language to me that I could not take a great interest in it; everything was so easy to say. "Ah, yes," the Major said. "Why, then, do you not take up the use of grammar?" So we took up the use of grammar, and soon Italian was such a difficult language that I was afraid to talk to him until I had the grammar straight in my mind.

The Major came very regularly to the hospital. I do not think he ever missed a day, although I am sure he did not believe in the machines. There was a time when none of us believed in the machines, and one day the Major said it was all nonsense. The machines were new then and it was we who were to prove them. "It was an idiotic idea," he said, "a theory, like another." I had not learned my grammar, and he said I was a stupid, impossible disgrace, and he was a fool to have bothered with me. He was a small man and he sat straight up in his chair with his right hand thrust into the machine and looked straight ahead at the wall while the straps thumped up and down with his fingers in them.

"What will you do when the War is over, if it is over?" he asked me. "Speak grammatically!"

"I will go to the States."

"Are you married?"

"No, but I hope to be."

"The more of a fool you are," he said. He seemed very angry.

"A man must not marry."

"Why, Signor Maggiore?"

"Don't call me Signor Maggiore."

"Why must not a man marry?"

"He cannot marry. He cannot marry," he said angrily. "If he is to lose everything, he should not place himself in a position to lose that. He should not place himself in a position to lose. He should find things he cannot lose."

He spoke very angrily and bitterly, and looked straight ahead while he talked.

"But why should he necessarily lose it?"

"He'll lose it," the Major said. He was looking at the wall. Then he looked down at the machine and jerked his little hand out from between the straps and slapped it hard against his thigh. "He'll lose it," he almost shouted. "Don't argue with me!" Then he called to the attendant who ran the machines: "Come and turn this damned thing off."

He went back into the other room for the light treatment and the massage. Then I heard him ask the doctor if he might use his telephone and he shut the door. When he came back into the room I was sitting in another machine. He was wearing his cape and had his cap on, and he came directly toward my machine and put his arm on my shoulder.

"I am so sorry," he said, and patted me on the shoulder with his good hand. "I would not be rude. My wife has just died. You must forgive me."

"Oh—" I said, feeling sick for him. "I am so sorry."

He stood there biting his lower lip. "It is very difficult," he said. "I cannot resign myself."

He looked straight past me and out through the window. Then he began to cry. "I am utterly unable to resign myself," he said, and choked. And then crying, his head up looking at nothing, carrying himself straight and soldierly, with tears on both his cheeks and biting his lips, he walked past the machines and out the door.

The doctor told me that the Major's wife, who was very young and whom he had not married until he was definitely invalided out of the War, had died of pneumonia. She had been sick only a few days. No one expected her to die. The Major did not come to the hospital for three days. Then he came at the usual hour wearing a black band on the sleeve of his uniform. When he came back, there were big framed photographs around the wall of all sorts of wounds before and after they had been cured by the machines. In front of the machine the Major used were three photographs of hands like his that were completely restored. I do not know where the doctor got them. I always understood we were the first to use the machines. The photographs did not make much difference to the Major because he only looked out of the window.

Coming Home

Edith Wharton

I

The young men of our American Relief Corps are beginning to come back from the front with stories.

There was no time to pick them up during the first months—the whole business was too wild and grim. The horror has not decreased, but nerves and sight are beginning to be disciplined to it. In the earlier days, moreover, such fragments of experiences as one got were torn from their setting like bits of flesh scattered by shrapnel. Now things that seemed disjointed are beginning to link themselves together, and the broken bones of history are rising from the battlefields.

I cannot say that, in this respect, all the members of the Relief Corps have made the most of their opportunity. Some are obtuse or perhaps simply inarticulate; others, when going beyond the bald statistics of their job, tend at once to drop into sentiment and cinema scenes; and none but H. Macy Greer has the gift of making the thing told seem as true as if one had seen it. So it is on H. Macy Greer that I depend, and when his motor dashes him back to Paris for supplies, I never fail to hunt him down and coax him to my rooms for dinner and a long cigar.

Greer is a small, hard-muscled youth, with pleasant manners, a sallow face, straight, hemp-colored hair, and grey eyes of unexpected inwardness. He has a voice like thick soup, and speaks with the slovenly drawl of the new generation of Americans, dragging his words along like reluctant dogs on a string, and depriving his narrative of every shade of expression that intelligent intonation gives. But his eyes see so much that they make one see even what his foggy voice obscures.

Some of his tales are dark and dreadful, some are unutterably sad, and some end in a huge laugh of irony. I am not sure how I ought to classify the one I have written down here.

II

On my first dash to the Northern fighting line—Greer told me the other night—I carried supplies to an ambulance, where the surgeon asked me to have a talk with an officer who was badly wounded and fretting for news of his people in the East of France.

45

He was a young Frenchman, a cavalry Lieutenant, trim and slim, with a pleasant smile and obstinate blue eyes that I liked. He looked as if he could hold on tight when it was worth his while. He had had a leg smashed, poor devil, in the first fighting in Flanders, and had been dragging on for weeks in the squalid camp hospital where I found him. He didn't waste any words on himself, but began at once on his family. They were living, when the War broke out, at their country place in the Vosges; his father and mother, his sister, just eighteen, and his brother Alain, two years younger. His father, the Comte de Réchamp, had married late in life and was over seventy; his mother, a good deal younger, was crippled with rheumatism; and there was, besides—to round off the group—a helpless but intensely alive and domineering old grandmother, about whom all the others revolved. You know how French families hang together, and throw out branches that make new roots but keep hold of the central trunk, like that tree—what's it called?—that they give pictures of in books about the East.

Jean de Réchamp—that was my Lieutenant's name—told me his family was a typical case. "We are very *province*," he said. "My people live at Réchamp all the year. We have a house at Nancy—rather a fine old hotel—but my parents go there only once in two or three years, for a few weeks. That is our 'season.'… Imagine the point of view! Or, rather, don't because you can't…" (He had been about the world a good deal and known something of other angles of vision.)

Well, of this helpless, exposed little knot of people he had had no word—simply nothing—since the first of August. He was at home, staying with them, when the War broke out. He was mobilized the first day and had only time to throw his traps into a cart and dash to the station. His depot was on the other side of France, and communication with the East by mail and telegraph was completely interrupted during the first weeks. His regiment was sent at once to the fighting line, and the first news he got came to him in October, from a communique in a Paris paper a month old, saying: "The enemy yesterday retook Réchamp."

After that, dead silence: and the poor devil left in the trenches to digest that "*retook*"!

There are thousands and thousands of just such cases; and men bearing them, and cracking jokes, and hitting out as hard as they can. Jean de Réchamp knew this, and tried to crack jokes too—but he got his leg smashed just afterwards, and ever since he'd been lying on a straw pallet under a horse-blanket, saying to himself: "Réchamp retaken."

"Of course," he explained, with a weary smile, "as long as you can tot up your daily bag in the trenches it is a sort of satisfaction—though I don't quite know why; anyhow, you're so dead beat at night that no dreams come. But lying here staring at the ceiling one goes through the whole business once an hour, at the least: the attack, the slaughter, the ruins…and worse…Haven't I seen and heard things enough on *this* side to know what has been happening on the other? Don't try to sugar the dose. I *like* it bitter."

I was three days in the neighborhood, and I went back every day to see him.

He liked to talk to me because he had a faint hope of my getting news of his family when I returned to Paris. I hadn't much myself, but there was no use telling him so. Besides, things changed from day to day, and when we parted I promised to get word to him as soon as I could find out anything. We both knew, of course, that that wouldn't be till Réchamp was taken a third time—by his own troops; and perhaps, soon after that, I should be able to get there, or near there, and make inquiries myself. To make sure that I should forget nothing, he drew the family photographs from under his pillow, and handed them over: the little witch-grandmother with a face like a withered walnut; the father, a fine broken-looking old boy with a Roman nose and a weak chin; the mother, in crepe, simple, serious, and provincial; the little sister, ditto; and Alain, the young brother just the age the brutes have been carrying off to German prisons—an overgrown, thread-paper boy with too much forehead and eyes, and not a muscle in his body. A charming-looking family, distinguished and amiable; but all, except the grandmother, rather usual. The kind of people who come in sets.

As I packed the photographs I noticed that another lay face down by his pillow. "Is that for me too?" I asked.

He colored and shook his head, and I felt I had blundered. But after a moment he turned the photograph over and held it out.

"It is the young girl I am engaged to. She was at Réchamp visiting my parents when War was declared; but she was to leave the day after I did." He hesitated. "There may have been some difficulty about her going...I should like to be sure she got away...Her name is Yvonne Malo."

He did not offer me the photograph, and I did not need it. That girl had a face of her own! Dark and keen and splendid; a type so different from the others that I found myself staring. If he had not said "*ma fiancée*," I should have understood better. After another pause, he went on: "I will give you her address in Paris. She has no family; she lives alone—she is a musician. Perhaps you may find her there." His color deepened again as he added: "But! know nothing—I have had no news of her, either."

To ease the silence that followed I suggested: "But if she has no family, wouldn't she have been likely to stay with your people? And wouldn't that be the reason of your not hearing from her?"

"Oh no—I don't think she stayed." He seemed about to add, "If she could help it," but shut his lips and slid the picture out of sight.

As soon as I got back to Paris I made inquiries, but without result. The Germans had been pushed back from that particular spot after a fortnight's intermittent occupation; but their lines were near by, across the valley, and Réchamp was still in a net of trenches. No one could get to it, and apparently no news could come from it. For the moment, at any rate, I found it impossible to get in touch with the place.

My inquiries about Mlle. Malo were equally unfruitful. I went to the address Réchamp had given me, somewhere off in Passy, among gardens, in what they call a "square," no doubt because it is oblong—a kind of long, narrow court with rather asthetic studio buildings round it. Mlle. Malo lived in one of them, on the top floor, the *concierge* said, and I looked up and saw a big studio window and a roof-terrace with a dead gourd dangling from a pergola. But she wasn't there, she hadn't been there, and they had no news of her. I wrote to Réchamp of my double failure; he sent me back a line of thanks; and, after that, for a long while I heard no more of him.

By the beginning of November the enemy's hold had begun to loosen in the Argonne and along the Vosges, and one day we were sent off to the east with a couple of ambulances. Of course, we had to have military chauffeurs, and the one attached to my ambulance happened to be a fellow I knew. The day before we started, in talking over our route with him, I said: "I suppose we can manage to get Réchamp now?" He looked puzzled—it was such a little place that he'd forgotten the name. "Why do you want to get there?" he wondered. I told him, and he gave an exclamation. "Good God! Of course—but how extraordinary! Jean de Réchamp's here now, in Paris, too lame for the front, and driving a motor." We stared at each other, and he went on: "He must take my place—he must go with you. I don't know how it can be done, but done it shall be."

Done it was, and the next morning I found Jean de Réchamp at the wheel of my car. He looked another fellow from the wreck I had left in the Flemish hospital; all made over, and burning with activity, but older, and with lines about his eyes. He had had news from his people in the interval, and had learnt that they were still at Réchamp, and well. What is more surprising was that Mlle. Malo was with them—had never left. Alain had been got away to England, where he remained; but none of the others had budged. They had fitted up an ambulance in the château, and Mlle. Malo and the little sister were nursing the wounded. There were not many details in the letter, and they had been a long time on their way; but their tone was so reassuring that Jean could give himself up to unclouded anticipation. You may fancy if he was grateful for the chance I was giving him; for, of course, he could not have seen his people in any other way.

Our permits, as you know, did not as a rule let us into the firing line: we only take supplies to second-line ambulances and carry back the wounded in need of delicate operations. So I wasn't in the least sure whether we should be able to go to Réchamp—though I had made up my mind to get there, anyhow.

We were about a fortnight on the way, coming and going in Champagne and the Argonne, and that gave us time to get to know each other. It was bitter cold, and after our long runs over the lonely frozen hills we used to crawl into the café of the inn if there was one—and talk and talk. We put up in fairly rough places, generally in a farmhouse or cottage packed with soldiers; for the villages have all remained empty since the autumn, except when troops are quartered in them. Usually, to get warm, we had to go up after supper to the room we shared and get under the blankets with our clothes on. Once some jolly sisters of charity took us in at their hospice, and we slept two nights in an ice-cold white-washed cell—but what tales we heard around their kitchen fire! The sisters had stayed alone to face the Germans, had seen the town burn, and had made the Teutons turn the hose on the singed roof of their hospice and beat the fire back from it. It is a pity those sisters of charity can't marry…

Réchamp told me a lot in those days. I don't believe he was talkative before the War, but his long weeks in hospital, starving for news, had unstrung him. And then he was mad with excitement at getting back to his own place. In the interval he'd heard how other people, caught in their country houses, had fared—you know the stories we all refused to believe at first, and that we now prefer not to think about…Well, he'd been thinking about those stories pretty readily for some months; and he kept repeating: "My people say they're all right, but they give no details."

"You see," he explained, "there never were such helpless beings. Even if there had been time to leave they couldn't have done it. My mother had been having one of her worst attacks of rheumatism—she was in bed, helpless, when I left. And my grandmother, who is a demon of activity in the house, won't stir out of it. We haven't been able to coax her into the garden for years. She says it is draughty, and you know how we all feel about draughts! As for my father, he hasn't had to decide anything since the Comte de Chambord refused to adopt the Tricolor. My father decided that he was right, and since then there has been nothing particular for him to take a stand about. But I know how he behaved just as well as if I had been there—he kept saying: 'One must act—one must act,' and sitting in his chair and doing nothing. Oh, I'm not disrespectful: they were *like* that in his generation! Besides—it is better to laugh at things, isn't it?" And suddenly his face would darken…

On the whole, however, his spirits were good till we began to traverse the line of ruined towns between Sainte Menehould and Bar-le-Duc. "This is the way the devils came," he kept saying to me; and I saw he was hard at work picturing the work they must have done in his own neighborhood.

"But since your sister writes that your people are safe!"

"They may have made her write that to reassure me. They'd heard I was badly wounded. And, mind you, there's never been a line from my mother."

One day, when we had passed through a particularly devastated little place, and had got, from the curé some more than usually abominable details of things done there, Réchamp broke out to me over the kitchen fire of our night's lodging. "When I hear things like that I don't believe anybody who tells me my people are all right!"

"But—you know well enough," I insisted, "that the Germans are not all alike—that it all depends on the particular officer…"

"Yes, yes, I know," he assented, with a visible effort at impartiality. "Only, you see—as one gets nearer…" He went on to say that, when he had been sent from the ambulance at the front to a hospital at Moulins, he had been for a day or two in a ward next to some wounded German soldiers—bad cases, they were and had heard them talking. They didn't know he knew German, and he had heard things…There was one name always coming back in their talk—von

Scharlach, Oberst von Scharlach. One of them, a young fellow, said: "I wish now I'd cut my hand off rather than do what he told us that night…Every time the fever comes I see it all again. I wish I'd been struck dead first." They all said "Scharlach" with a kind of terror in their voices, as if he might hear them even there and come down on them horribly. Réchamp had asked where their regiment came from, and had been told, from the Vosges. That had set his brain working, and whenever he saw a ruined village, or heard a tale of savagery, the Scharlach nerve began to quiver. At such times it was no use reminding him that the Germans had had at least three hundred thousand men in the east in August. He simply did not listen…

III

The day before we started for Réchamp his spirits flew up again, and that night he became confidential. "You've been such a friend to me that there are certain things—seeing what is ahead of us that I should like to explain." And, noticing my surprise, he went on: "I mean about my people. The state of mind in my *milieu* must be so remote from anything you are used to in your happy country…But perhaps I can make you understand…"

I saw that what he wanted was to talk to me of the girl he was engaged to. Mlle. Malo, left an orphan at ten, had been the ward of a neighbor of the Réchamps, a chap with an old name and a starred château, who had lost almost everything else at baccarat before he was forty, and had repented, had the gout, and studied agriculture for the rest of his life. The girl's father was a rather brilliant painter, who died young, and her mother, who followed him in a year or two, was a Pole. You may fancy that, with such antecedents, the girl was just the mixture to shake down quietly into French country life with a gouty and repentant guardian. The Marquis de Corvenaire—that was his name—brought her down to his place, got an old maid sister to come and stay, and really, as far as one knows, brought his ward up rather decently. Now and then she used to be driven over to play with the young Réchamps, and Jean remembered her as an ugly little girl in a plaid frock, who used to invent wonderful games and get tired of playing them just when the other children were beginning to learn how. But her domineering ways and searching questions did not meet with his mother's approval, and her visits were not encouraged. When she was seventeen her guardian died and left her a little money. The maiden sister had gone dotty. There was nobody to look after Yvonne, and she went to Paris to an aunt; broke loose from the aunt when she came of age, set up her studio, traveled, painted, played the violin, knew lots of people, and never laid eyes on Jean de Réchamp till about a year before the War, when her guardian's place was sold and she had to go down there to see about her interest in the property.

The old Réchamps heard she was coming but didn't ask her to stay. Jean drove over to the shut-up château, however, and found Mlle. Malo lunching on a corner of the kitchen table. She exclaimed: "My little Jean!" flew to him with a kiss for each cheek, and made him sit down and share her omelet...The ugly little girl had shed her chrysalis, and you may fancy if he went back once or twice!

Mlle. Malo was staying at the château all alone, with the farmer's wife to come in and cook her dinner: not a soul in the house at night but herself and her brindled sheep-dog. She had to be there a week, and Jean finally suggested to his people to ask her to Réchamp. But at Réchamp they hesitated, coughed, looked away, said the spare rooms were all upside down, and the *valet de chamber* laid up with the mumps and the cook short-handed—till finally the irrepressible grandmother broke out: "A young girl who chooses to live alone—probably prefers to live alone!"

There was a deadly silence, and Jean didn't raise the question again; but I can imagine his blue eyes getting obstinate.

Soon after Mlle. Malo's return to Paris, he followed her and began to frequent the Passy studio. The life there was unlike anything he had ever seen—or conceived as possible, short of the prairies. He had sampled the usual varieties of French womenkind, and explored most of the social layers, but he had missed the newest, that of the artistic-emancipated. I don't know much about that side myself, but from his descriptions I should think they were a good deal like intelligent Americans, except that they didn't seem to keep art and life in such watertight compartments. But his great discovery was the new girl. Apparently he had never known any before but the traditional type, which predominates in the provinces, and still persists, he tells me, in the last fastnesses of the Faubourg St. Germain. The girl who comes and goes as she pleases, reads what she likes, has opinions about what she reads, who talks, looks, and behaves with the independence of a married woman—and yet has kept the Diana freshness— think how she must have shaken up such a man's inherited view of things! Mlle. Malo did far more than make Réchamp fall in love with her: she turned his world topsy-turvy and prevented his ever again squeezing himself into his little old pigeon-hole of prejudices.

Before long they confessed their love—just like any young couple of Anglo-Saxons—and Jean went down to Réchamp to ask permission to marry her. Neither you nor I can quite enter into the state of mind of a young man of twenty-seven who has knocked about all over the globe, and been in and out of the usual sentimental coils—and who has to ask his parents' leave to get married! Don't let us try: it is no use. We should only end by picturing him an incredible ninny. But there is not a man in France who would not feel it his duty to take that step, as Jean de Réchamp did. All we can do is to accept the premise and pass on.

Well—Jean went down and asked his father and his mother and his old grandmother if they would permit him to marry Mlle. Malo; and they all with one voice said they wouldn't. There was an uproar, in fact; and the old grandmother contributed the most piercing note to the concert. Marry Mlle. Malo! A young girl who lived alone! Traveled! Spent her time with foreigners, with musicians and painters! *A young girl!* Of course, if she had been a married woman—that is, a widow—much as they would have preferred a young girl for Jean, or even, if widow it had to be, a widow of another type—still it was conceivable that, out of affection for him, they might have resigned themselves to his choice. But a young girl—bring such a young girl to Réchamp! Ask them to receive her under the same roof with their little Simone, their innocent Alain...

He had a bad hour of it; but he held his own, keeping silent while they screamed, and stiffening as they began to wobble from exhaustion. Finally he took his mother apart and tried to reason with her. His arguments were not much use, but his resolution impressed her, and he saw it. As for his father, nobody was afraid of M. de Réchamp when he said: "Never while I live and there is a roof on Réchamp!" They all knew he had collapsed inside. But the grandmother was terrible. She was terrible because she was so old, and was clever at taking advantage of it. She could bring on a valvular heart attack by just sitting and holding her breath, as Jean and his mother had long since found out; and she always treated them to one when things weren't going as she liked. Madame de Réchamp promised Jean that she would intercede with her mother-in-law; but she hadn't much faith in the result, and when she came out of the old lady's room she whispered:

"She's just sitting there holding her breath."

The next day Jean himself advanced to the attack. His grandmother was the most intelligent member of the family, and she knew he knew it, and liked him for having found it out; so when he had her alone she listened to him without resorting to any valvular tricks. "Of course," he explained, "you're much too clever not to understand that the times have changed, and manners with them, and that what a woman was criticized for doing yesterday she is ridiculed for not doing today. Nearly all the old social thou-shalt-nots have gone: intelligent people nowadays don't give a fig for them, and that simple fact has abolished them. They only existed as long as there was someone left for them to scare." His grandmother listened with a sparkle of admiration in her ancient eyes. "And, of course," Jean pursued, "that can't be the real reason for your opposing my marriage with a young girl you've always known, who has been received here—"

"Ah, that's it—we've always known her!" the old lady snapped him up.

"And what of that? I don't see—"

"Of course you don't. You are here so little: you don't hear things..."

"What things?"

"Things in the air...that blow about...You were doing your military service at the time..."

"At what time?"

She leant forward and laid a warning hand on his arm. "Why did Corvenaire leave her all that money—*why*?"

"But why not—why shouldn't he?" Jean stammered, indignant.

Then she unpacked her bag—a heap of vague insinuations, baseless conjectures, village tattle, all, at the last analysis, based, as he succeeded in proving, and making her own, on a word launched at random by a discharged maidservant who had retailed her grievances to the curé's housekeeper. "Oh, she does what she likes with M. le Marquis, the young miss! *She* knows how…" On that single phrase the whole neighborhood had raised a slander built of adamant.

Well, it will give you an idea of what a determined fellow Réchamp is when I tell you he pulled it down—or thought he had. He kept his temper, hunted up the servant's record, proved her to be a liar and dishonest, cast grave doubts on the discretion of the cure's housekeeper, and poured such a flood of ridicule over the whole clumsy fable, and those who had believed in it, that for sheer shamefacedness at having based her objection on such grounds, his grandmother gave way, and brought his parents toppling down with her.

All this happened a few weeks before the War, and soon afterwards Mlle. Malo came down to Réchamp. Jean had insisted on her coming; he wanted her presence there, as his betrothed, to be known to the neighborhood. As for her, she seemed delighted to come. I could see from Réchamp's tone, when he reached this part of his story, that he rather thought I should have expected its heroine to have shown a becoming reluctance—to have stood on her dignity. He was distinctly relieved when he found that I expected no such thing.

"She is simplicity itself—it is her great quality. Vain complications don't exist for her, because she doesn't see them…That is what my people can't be made to understand…"

I gathered from the last phrase that the visit hadn't been a complete success, and this explained his having let out, when he first told me of his fears for his family, that he was sure Mlle. Malo would not have remained at Réchamp it she could help it. Oh no, decidedly, the visit was not a success…

"You see," he explained, with a half-embarrassed smile, "it was partly her fault. Other girls as clever, but less—how shall I say?—less proud, would have adapted themselves, arranged things, avoided startling allusions. She talked to my family as naturally as she did to me. You can imagine, for instance, the effect of her saying: 'One night, after a supper at Montmartre, I was walking home with two or three pals.' It was her way of affirming her convictions, and I adored her for it—but I wished she wouldn't!"

And he depicted, to my joy, the neighbors rumbling over to call in heraldic barouches (the mothers alone, with embarrassed excuses for not bringing their daughters), and the agony of not knowing, till they were in the room, whether Yvonne would receive them with lowered lids and folded hands, sitting by in a *pose de fiancée* while the elders talked; or if she would take the opportunity to air her views on the separation of Church and State, or the necessity of making divorce easier. "It's not," he explained, "that she really takes much interest in such questions: she is much more absorbed in her music and painting. But anything her eye lights on sets her mind dancing—as she said to me once: 'It's your mother's friends' bonnets that make me stand up for divorce!'" He broke off abruptly to add: "Good God, how far off all that nonsense seems!"

IV

The next day we started for Réchamp, not sure if we could get there, but bound to, anyhow! It was the coldest day we had had, the sky still, the earth iron, and a snow-wind howling down on us from the north. The Vosges are splendid in winter. In summer they are just plump, pudding hills; when the wind strips them they turn into mountains. And we seemed to have the whole country to ourselves—the black firs, the blue shadows, the beechwoods cracking and groaning like rigging, the bursts of snowy sunlight from cold clouds. Not a soul in sight except the sentinels guarding the railways, muffled to the eyes, or peering out of their huts of pine-boughs at the cross roads. Every now and then we passed a long string of 75s, or a train of supply wagons or army ambulances, and at intervals a cavalry patrol cantered by, his cloak bellied out by the gale; but of ordinary people about the common jobs of life, not a sign.

The sense of loneliness and remoteness that the absence of the civilian population produces everywhere in eastern France is increased by the fact that all the names and distances have been scratched out and the signposts at the cross roads thrown down. It was done, of course, to throw the enemy off the track in September: and the signs have never been put back. The result is that one is for ever losing one's way, for the soldiers quartered in the district know only the names of their particular villages, and those on the march can tell you nothing about the places they are passing through. We had got badly off our road several times during the trip, but on the last day's run Réchamp was in his own country, and knew every yard of the way—or thought he did. We had turned off the main road and were running along between rather featureless fields and woods, crossed by a good many wood roads with nothing to distinguish them; but he continues to push ahead, saying: "We don't turn till we get to a manor house on a stream, with a big paper mill across the road." He went on to tell me that the millowners lived in the manor and were old friends of his people: good old local stock who had lived there for generations and had done a lot for the neighborhood.

"It's queer I don't see their village steeple from this rise. The village is just beyond the house. How the devil could I have missed the turn?" We ran on a little farther, and suddenly he stopped the motor with a jerk. We were at a cross road, with a stream running under the bank on our right. The place looked like an abandoned stoneyard. I never saw a completer ruin. To the left, a gate gaped on emptiness; to the right, a mill-wheel hung in the stream. Everything else was as flat as your dinner-table.

"Was this what you were trying to see from that rise?" I asked; and I saw a tear or two running down his face.

"They were the kindest people: their only son got himself shot the first month in Champagne—"

He had jumped out of the car and was standing staring at the level waste. "The house was there—there was a splendid lime tree in the court. I used to sit under it and have a glass of *vin gris de Lorraine* with the old people…Over there, where that cinder heap is, all their children are buried." He walked across to the graveyard under a blackened wall—a bit of the apse of the vanished church—and sat down on a gravestone. "If the devils have done this *here*—so close to us," he burst out, and covered his face.

An old woman walked toward us down the road. Réchamp jumped up and ran to meet her. "Why, Marie-Jeanne, what are you doing in these ruins?" The old woman looked at him with unastonished eyes. She seemed incapable of any surprise. "They left my house standing. I am glad to see monsieur," she simply said. We followed her to the one house left in the waste of stones. It was a two-roomed cottage, propped against a cow-stable, but fairly decent, with a curtain in the window and a cat on the sill. Réchamp caught me by the arm and pointed to the door panel. "Oberst von Scharlach" was scrawled on it. He turned as white as your table-cloth and hung on to me for a minute; then he spoke to the old woman. "The officers were quartered here: that was the reason they spared your house?"

She nodded. "Yes; I was lucky. But the gentlemen must come in and have a mouthful."

Réchamp's finger was on the name. "And this one—this was their Commanding Officer?"

"I suppose so. Is it somebody's name?" She had evidently never speculated on the meaning of the scrawl that had saved her.

"You remember him—their Captain? Was his name Scharlach?" Réchamp persisted.

Under its rich weathering the old woman's face grew as pale as his. "Yes, that was his name—I heard it often enough."

"Describe him then. What was he like? Tall and fair? They're all that—but what else? What in particular?"

She hesitated, and then said: "This one wasn't fair. He was dark and had a scar that drew up the left corner of his mouth."

Réchamp turned to me. "It's the same. I heard the men describe him at Moulins."

We followed the old woman into the house, and while she gave us some bread and wine she told us about the wrecking of the village and the factory. It was one of the most abominable stories I have heard yet. Put together the worst of the typical horrors and you will have a fair idea of it. Murder, outrage, torture: Scharlach's program seemed to be fairly comprehensive. She ended off by saying: "His orderly showed me a silver-mounted flute he always traveled with, and a beautiful paint-box mounted in silver, too. Before he left he sat down on my doorstep and made a painting of the ruins."

Soon after leaving this place of death we got to the second lines, and our troubles began. We had to do a lot of talking to get through the lines, but what Réchamp had just seen had made him eloquent. Luckily, too, the ambulance doctor, a charming fellow, was short of tetanus serum, and I had some left; and while I went over with him to the pine-branch hut, where he hid his wounded, I explained Réchamp's case and implored him to get us through. Finally, it was settled that we should leave the ambulance therefore in the lines the ban against motors is absolute—and drive the remaining twelve miles. A sergeant fished out of a farmhouse a toothless old woman with a furry horse harnessed to a two-wheeled trap, and we started off by roundabout wood-tracks. The horse was in no hurry, nor the old lady either; for there were bits of road that were pretty steadily curry-combed by shell, and it was to everybody's interest not to cross them before twilight. Jean de Réchamp's excitement seemed to have dropped: he sat beside me dumb as a fish, staring straight ahead of him. I didn't feel talkative either, for a word the doctor had let drop had left me thinking. "That poor old crony mind the shells? Not she!" he had said when our crazy chariot drove up. "She doesn't know them from snowflakes any more. Nothing matters to her now, except trying to outwit a German. They're all like that where Scharlach's been—you've heard of him? She had only one boy—half-witted: he cocked a broom-handle at them, and they burnt him. Oh, she'll take you to Réchamp safe enough."

"Where Scharlach's been"—so he had been as close as this to Réchamp! I was wondering if Jean knew it, and if that had sealed his lips and given him that flinty profile. The old horse's woolly flanks jogged on under the bare branches and the old woman's bent back jogged in time with it. She never once spoke or looked around at us. "It isn't the noise we make that'll give us away," I said at last; and just then the old woman turned her head and pointed silently with the osier-twig she used as a whip. Just ahead of us lay a heap of ruins: the wreck, apparently, of a great château and its dependencies. "Lermont!" Réchamp exclaimed, turning white. He made a move to jump out and then dropped back into the seat. "What's the use?" he muttered. He leant forward and touched the old woman's shoulder.

"I hadn't heard of this—when did it happen?"

"In September."

"They did it?"

"Yes. Our wounded were there. It's like this everywhere in our country."

I saw Jean stiffening himself for the next question. "At Réchamp, too?"

She relapsed into indifference. "I haven't been as far as Réchamp."

"But you must have seen people who'd been there—you must have heard."

"I've heard the masters were still there—so there must be something standing. Maybe, though," she reflected, "they are in the cellars."

We continued to jog on through the dusk.

V

"There is the stable," Réchamp burst out.

Through the dimness I could not tell which way to look; but I suppose in the thickest midnight he would have known where he was. He jumped from the trap and took the old horse by the bridle. I made out that he was guiding us into a long village street edged by houses in which every light was extinguished. The snow on the ground sent up a pale reflection, and I began to see the gabled outline of the houses and the stable at the head of the street. The place seemed as calm and unchanged as if the sound of war had never reached it.

In the open space at the end of the village Réchamp checked the horse.

"The elm—there is the old elm in front of the church!" he shouted, in a voice like a boy's. He reached back and caught me by both hands. "It was true, then—nothing's touched!" The old woman asked: "Is this Réchamp?" and he went back to the horse's head and turned the trap toward a tall gate between park walls. The gate was barred and padlocked, and not a gleam showed through the shutters of the porter's lodge; but Réchamp, after listening a minute or two, gave a low call twice repeated, and presently the lodge door opened, and an old man peered out. Well—I leave you to brush in the rest. Old family servant, tears and hugs, and so on. I know you affect to scorn the cinema, and this was it, tremolo and all. Hang it! This War's going to teach us not to be afraid of the obvious.

We piled into the trap and drove down a long avenue to the house. Black as the grave, of course; but in another minute the door opened and there, in the hall, was another servant, screening a light—and then more doors opened on another cinema scene: fine old drawing-room with family portraits, shaded lamp, domestic group about the fire. They evidently thought it was the servant coming to announce dinner; not a head turned at our approach. I could see them all over Jean's shoulder: a grey-haired lady knitting with stiff fingers, an old gentleman with a high nose and a weak chin sitting in a big carved armchair and looking more like a portrait than the portraits; a pretty girl at his feet, with a dog's head in her lap, and another girl who had a Red Cross on her sleeve, at the table with a book. She had been reading aloud in a rich veiled voice, and broke off her last phrase to say: "Dinner…" Then she looked up and saw Jean. Her dark face remained perfectly calm, but she lifted her hand in a just perceptible gesture of warning, and instantly understanding he drew back and pushed the servant forward in his place.

"Madame la Comtesse—it is someone outside asking for Madame."

The dark girl jumped up and ran out into the hall. I remember wondering: "Is it because she wants to have him to herself first or because she's afraid of their being startled?"

I wished myself out of the way, but she took no notice of me, and going straight to Jean flung her arms about him. I was behind him and could see her hands about his neck, and her brown fingers tightly locked. There wasn't much doubt about those two…

The next minute she caught sight of me, and I was being rapidly scanned by a pair of the finest eyes I ever saw—I don't apply the term to their setting, though that was fine, too, but to the look itself, a look at once warm and resolute, all-promising and all-penetrating. I really can't do with fewer adjectives…

Réchamp explained me, and she was full of thanks and welcome; not excessive, but—well, I don't know—eloquent! She gave every intonation all it could carry, and without the least emphasis: that is the wonder.

She went back to "prepare" the parents, as they say in melodramas; and in a minute or two we followed. What struck me at first was that these insignificant and inadequate people had command of the grand gesture—had *la ligne.* The mother had laid aside her knitting—*not* dropped it—and stood waiting with open arms. But even in clasping her son she seemed to include me in her welcome. I don't know how to describe it; but they never let me feel I was in the way. I suppose that is part of what you call distinction; knowing instinctively how to deal with unusual moments.

All the while, I was looking about me at the fine, secure, old room, in which nothing seemed altered or disturbed, the portraits smiling from the walls, the servants beaming in the doorway and wondering how such things could have survived in the trail of death and havoc we had been following.

The same thought had evidently struck Jean, for he dropped his sister's hand and turned to gaze about him, too.

"Then nothing's touched—*nothing*? I don't understand," he stammered.

Monsieur de Réchamp raised himself majestically from his chair, crossed the room, and lifted Yvonne Malo's hand to his lips. "Nothing is touched—thanks to this hand and this brain."

Madame de Réchamp was shining on her son through tears.

"Ah, yes—we owe it all to Yvonne."

"All, all I Grandmamma will tell you!" Simone chimed in; and Yvonne, brushing aside their praise with a half-impatient laugh, said to her betrothed: "But your grandmother! You must go up to her at once."

A wonderful specimen, that grandmother: I was taken to see her after dinner. She sat by the fire in a bare paneled bedroom, bolt upright in an armchair, a knitting-table at her elbow with a shaded lamp on it. She was even more withered and ancient than she looked in her photograph, and I judge she'd never been pretty; but she somehow made me feel as though I'd got through with prettiness. I don't know exactly what she reminded me of: a dried bouquet or something rich and clovy that had turned brittle through long keeping in a sandalwood box. I suppose her sandalwood box had been Good Society. Well, I had a rare evening with her. Jean and his parents were called down to see the curé, who had hurried over to the château when he heard of the young man's arrival; and the old lady asked me to stay on and chat with her. She related their experiences with uncommon detachment, seeming chiefly to resent the indignity of having been made to descend into the cellar—"to avoid French shells, if you'll believe it: the Germans had the decency not to bombard us," she observed impartially. I was so struck with the absence of rancor in her tone that finally, out of sheer curiosity, I made an allusion to the horror of having the enemy under one's roof. "Oh, I might almost say I didn't see them," she returned. "I never go downstairs any longer; and they didn't do me the honor of coming beyond my door. A glance sufficed them—*une vieille femme comme moi!*" she added with a phosphorescent gleam of coquetry.

"But they searched the château, surely?"

"Oh, a mere form; they were *très bien—très bien*," she almost snapped at me. "There was a first moment, of course, when we feared it might be hard to get Monsieur de Réchamp away with my young grandson; but Mlle. Malo managed that very cleverly. They slipped off while the officers were dining." She looked at me with the smile of some arch old lady in a Louis XV pastel. "My grandson Jean's *fiancée* is a very clever young woman: in my time no young girl would have been so sure of herself, so cool and quick. After all, there is something to be said for the new way of bringing up girls. My poor daughter-in-law, at Yvonne's age, was a bleating babe: she is so still, at times. The convent doesn't develop character. I am glad Yvonne was not brought up in a convent." And this champion of tradition smiled on me more intensely.

Little by little I got from her the story of the German approach: the distracted fugitives pouring in from the villages north of Réchamp, the sound of the distant cannonading, and suddenly, the next afternoon, after a reassuring lull, the sight of a single spiked helmet at the end of the drive. In a few minutes a dozen followed: mostly officers; then all at once the place hummed with them. There were supply wagons and motors in the court, bundles of hay, stacks of rifles, artillerymen unharnessing and rubbing down their horses. The crowd was hot and thirsty, and in a moment the old lady, to her amazement, saw wine and cider being handed about by the Réchamp servants. "Or, say, at least I was told," she added, correcting herself, "for it's not my habit to look out the window. I simply sat here and waited." Her seat, as she spoke, might have been a curule chair.

Downstairs, it seemed, Mlle. Malo had instantly taken her measures. *She* didn't sit and wait. Surprised in the garden with Simone, she had made the girl walk quietly back to the house and receive the officers with her on the doorstep. The officer in command—Captain, or whatever he was—had arrived in a bad temper, cursing and swearing, and growling out menaces about spies.

The day was intensely hot, and possibly he had had too much wine. At any rate, Mlle. Malo had known how to "put him in his place"; and when he and the other officers entered they found the dining-table set out with refreshing drinks and cigars, melons, strawberries, and iced coffee!

The effect had been miraculous. "The Captain—what was his name? Yes, Charlot, Charlot—Captain Charlot had been specially complimentary on the subject of the whipped cream and the cigars. Then he asked to see the other members of the family, and Mlle. Malo told him there were only two—two old women. He made a face at that, and said all the same he should like to meet them; and she answered: 'One is your hostess, the Comtesse de Réchamp, who is ill in bed'—for my poor daughter-in-law was lying in bed paralyzed with rheumatism—'and the other her mother-in-law, a very old lady who never leaves her room.'"

"But aren't there any men in the family?" he had then asked; and she had said: "Oh yes—two. The Comte de Réchamp and his son."

"And where are they?"

"In England. Monsieur de Réchamp went a month ago to take his son on a trip."

The officer said: "I was told they were here today"; and Mlle. Malo replied: "You had better have the house searched and satisfy yourself."

He laughed and said: "The idea *had* occurred to me." She laughed, also, and sitting down at the piano struck a few chords. Captain Charlot, who had his foot on the threshold, turned back—Simone had described the scene to her grandmother afterwards.

"Some of the brutes, it seems, are musical," the old lady explained; "and this was one of them. While he was listening, some soldiers appeared in the courtyard carrying another who seemed to be wounded. It turned out afterwards that he'd been climbing a garden wall after fruit, and cut himself on the broken glass on the top; but the blood was enough—they raised the usual dreadful cry of an ambush, and a Lieutenant clattered into the room where Mlle. Malo sat playing Stravinsky." The old lady paused for her effect, and I was conscious of giving her all she wanted.

"Well—?"

"Will you believe it? It seems she looked at her watch-bracelet and said: 'Do you generally dress for dinner? *I* do—but we've still time for a little Moussorgsky—or whatever wild names they call themselves—if you will make those people outside hold their tongues.' Our Captain looked at her again, laughed, gave an order that sent the Lieutenant right about, and sat down beside her at the piano. Imagine my stupor, dear sir: the drawing-room is directly under this room, and in a moment I heard two voices coming up to me. Well, I won't conceal from you that his was the finest. But then I always adored a baritone." She folded her shrunken hands among their laces. "After that, the Germans were *très bien*—*très bien*. They stayed two days, and there was nothing to complain of. Indeed, when the second detachment came, a week later, they never even entered the gates. Orders had been left that they should be quartered elsewhere. Of course, we were lucky in happening on a man of the world like Captain Charlot."

"Yes, very lucky. It's odd, though, his having a French name."

"Very odd. It probably accounts for his breeding," she answered placidly; and left me marveling at the happy remoteness of her age.

VI

The next morning early, Jean de Réchamp came to my room. I was struck at once by the change in him: he had lost his first glow, and seemed nervous and hesitating. I knew what he had come for; to ask me to postpone our departure for another twenty-four hours. By rights, we should have been off that morning; but there had been a sharp brush a few kilometres away, and a couple of poor devils had been brought to the château whom it would have been death to carry further that day and criminal not to hurry to a base hospital the next morning. "We have simply got to stay till tomorrow: you're in luck," I said, laughing.

He laughed back, but with a frown that made me feel I had been a brute to speak in that way of a respite due to such a cause.

"The men will pull through, you know—trust Mlle. Malo for that!" I said.

His frown did not lift. He went to the window and drummed on the pane.

"Do you see that breach in the wall, down there behind the trees? It's the only scratch the place has got. And think of Lermont! It's incredible—simply incredible!"

"But it's like that everywhere, isn't it? Everything depends on the officer in command."

"Yes; that's it, I suppose. I haven't had time to get a consecutive account of what happened: they are all too excited. Mlle. Malo is the only person who can tell me how things went," he swung about on me. "Look here, it sounds absurd, what I'm asking; but try to get me an hour alone with her, will you?"

I stared at the request, and he went on, still half-laughing: "You see, they all hang on me; my father and mother, Simone, the curé, the servants. The whole village is coming up presently: they want to stuff their eyes full of me. It's natural enough, after living here all these long months cut off from everything. But the result is I haven't said two words to her yet."

"Well, you shall," I declared; and with an easier smile he turned to hurry down to the mass of thanksgiving which the curé was to celebrate in the private chapel. "My parents wanted it," he explained; "and after that the whole village will be upon us. But after—"

"Later I will effect a diversion; I swear I will," I assured him.

By daylight, decidedly, Mlle. Malo was less handsome than in the evening. It was my first thought as she came toward me, that afternoon, under the limes. Jean was still indoors, with his people, receiving the village; I rather wondered she had not stayed there with him. Theoretically, her place was at his side; but I knew she was a young woman who did not live by rule, and she had already struck me as having a distaste for superfluous expenditure of feeling.

Yes, she was less effective by day. She looked older, for one thing; her face was pinched, and a little sallow, and for the first time I noticed that her cheekbones were too high. Her eyes, too, had lost their velvet depth: fine eyes still, but not unfathomable. But the smile with which she greeted me was charming: it ran over her tired face like a lamplighter kindling flames as he runs. "I was looking for you," she said. "Shall we have a little talk? The reception is sure to last another hour, every one of the villagers is going to tell just what happened to him or her when the Germans came."

"And you've run away from the ceremony?"

"I'm a trifle tired of hearing the same adventures retold," she said, still smiling.

"But I thought there *were* no adventures—that that was the wonder of it?"

She shrugged. "It makes their stories a little dull, at any rate. We've not a hero or a martyr to show." She had strolled further from the house as we talked, steering me in the direction of a bare horse-chestnut walk that led towards the park.

"Of course, Jean's got to listen to it all, poor boy; but I needn't," she explained.

I didn't know exactly what to answer, and we walked on a little way in silence; then she said: "If you'd carried him off this morning he would have escaped all this fuss." After a pause, she added slowly: "On the whole, it might have been as well."

"To carry him off?"

"Well, yes." She stopped and looked at me. "I wish you would."

"Would? Now?"

"Yes, now; as soon as you can. He's really not strong yet—he's drawn and nervous." ("So are you," I thought, parenthetically.)

"And the excitement is greater than you can perhaps imagine—"

I gave her back a look. "Why, I think I *can* imagine."

She colored up through her sallow skin, and then laughed away her blush. "Oh, I don't mean the excitement of seeing *me*! But his parents, his grandmother, the curé, all the old associations—"

I considered for a moment; then I said: "As a matter of fact, you're about the only person he *hasn't* seen." She checked a quick answer on her lips, and for a moment or two we faced each other silently. A sudden sense of intimacy, of complicity almost, came over me. What was it the girl's silence was crying out to me?

"If I take him away now he won't have seen you at all," I continued.

She stood under the bare trees, keeping her eyes on me. "Then take him away now!" she reiterated; and as she spoke I saw her face change, decompose into deadly apprehension and as quickly regain its usual calm. From where she stood she faced the courtyard, and glancing in the same direction I saw the throng of villagers coming out of the château. "Take him away—take him away at once!" she passionately commanded; and the next minute Jean de Réchamp detached himself from the group and began to limp down the walk in our direction.

What was I to do? I cannot exaggerate the sense of urgency Mlle. Malo's appeal gave me, or my faith in her sincerity. No one who had seen her meeting with Réchamp the night before could have doubted her feeling for him: if she wanted him away it was not because she did not delight in his presence. Even now, as he approached, I saw her face veiled by a fine mist of emotion: it was like watching a fruit ripen under a midsummer sun. But she turned sharply from the house and began to walk on.

"Can't you give me a hint of your reason?" I suggested, as I followed.

"My reason? I have given it!" I suppose I looked incredulous, for she added in a lower voice: "I don't want him to hear—yet—about all the horrors."

"The horrors? I thought there had been none here."

"All around us—" Her voice became a whisper. "Our friends...our neighbors...everyone..."

"He can hardly avoid hearing of that, can he? And, besides, since you are all safe and happy...Look here," I broke off, "he is coming after us. Don't we look as if we were running away?"

She turned around, suddenly paler; and in a stride or two Réchamp was at our side. He was pale, too; and before I could find a pretext for slipping away he had begun to speak. But I saw at once that he didn't know or care if I was there.

"What was the name of the officer in command who was quartered here?" he asked, looking straight at the girl.

She raised her eyebrows slightly. "Do you mean to say that after listening for three hours to every inhabitant of Réchamp you haven't found that out?"

"They all call him something different. My grandmother says he had a French name: she calls him Charlot."

"Your grandmother was never taught German: his name was Oberst van Scharlach." She didn't remember my presence either: the two were still looking straight in each other's eyes.

Réchamp had grown white to the lips; he was rigid with the effort to control himself.

"Why didn't you tell me it was Scharlach who was here?" he brought out at last, in a low voice.

She turned her eyes in my direction. "I was just explaining to Mr. Greer—"

"To Mr. Greer?" He looked at me, too, half-angrily.

"I know the stories that are about," she continued quietly; "and I was saying to your friend that, since we had been so happy as to be spared, it seemed useless to dwell on what had happened elsewhere."

"Damn what happened elsewhere! I don't know yet what happened here."

I put a hand on his arm. Mlle. Malo was looking hard at me, but I wouldn't let her see I knew it. "I'm going to leave you to hear the whole story now," I said to Réchamp.

"But there isn't any story for him to hear!" she broke in. She pointed at the serene front of the château, looking out across its gardens to the unscarred fields. "We are safe; the place is untouched. Why brood on other horrors—horrors we were powerless to help?"

Réchamp held his ground doggedly. "But the man's name is a curse and an abomination. Wherever he went he spread ruin."

"So they say. Mayn't there be a mistake? Legends grow up so quickly in these dreadful times. Here"—she looked about her again at the peaceful scene—"here he behaved as you see. For heaven's sake be content with that!"

"Content?" He passed his hand across his forehead. "I'm blind with joy...or should be, if only..."

She looked at me entreatingly, almost desperately, and I took hold of Réchamp's arm with a warning pressure. "My dear fellow, don't you see that Mlle. Malo? *La joie fait peur*—that's the trouble with both of you!"

He lowered his head. "Yes, I suppose it is." He took her hand and kissed it. "I beg your pardon. Greer's right: we're both on edge."

"Yes: I will leave you for a little while, if you and Mr. Greer will excuse me." She included us both in a quiet look that seemed to me extremely noble, and walked slowly away toward the château. Réchamp stood gazing after her for a moment; then he dropped down on one of the benches at the edge of the path. He covered his face with his hands. "Scharlach—Scharlach," I heard him repeat.

We stood there side by side for ten minutes or more without speaking. Finally I said: "Look here, Réchamp—she's right and you're wrong. I shall be sorry I brought you here if you don't see it before it's too late."

His face was still hidden; but presently he dropped his hands and answered me. "I do see. She's saved everything for me—my people and my house, and the ground we're standing on. And I worship it because she walks on it!"

"And so do your people: the War's done that for you, any how," I reminded him.

VII

The morning after we were off before dawn. Our time allowance was up, and it was thought advisable, on account of our wounded, to slip across the exposed bit of road in the dark.

Mlle. Malo was downstairs when we started, pale in her white dress, but calm and active. We had borrowed a farmer's cart in which our two men could be laid out on a mattress, and she had stocked our trap with food and remedies. Nothing seemed to have been forgotten. While I was settling the men Réchamp turned back into the hall to bid her good-bye; anyhow, when she followed him out a moment later he looked quieter and less strained.

He had taken leave of his parents and his sister upstairs, and Yvonne Malo stood alone in the dark doorway watching us as we drove away.

There was not much talk between us during our slow drive back to the lines. We had to go at a snail's pace, for the roads were rough; and there was time for meditation. I knew well enough what my companion was thinking about, and my own thoughts ran on the same lines. Though the story of the German occupation of Réchamp had been retold to us a dozen times, the main facts did not vary. There were little discrepancies of detail, and gaps in the narrative here and there; but all the household, from the astute ancestress to the last bewildered pantry-boy, were at one in saying that Mlle. Malo's coolness and courage had saved the château and the village. The officer in command had arrived full of threats and insolence: Mlle. Malo had placated and disarmed him, turned his suspicions to ridicule, entertained him and his comrades at dinner, and contrived during that time—or, rather, while they were making music afterwards (which they did for half the night, it seemed)—that Monsieur de Réchamp and Alain should slip out of the cellar in which they had been hidden, gain the end of the gardens through an old hidden passage, and get off in the darkness. Meanwhile,

Simone had been safe upstairs with her mother and grandmother, and none of the officers lodged in the château had—after a first hasty inspection—set foot in any part of the house but the wing assigned to them. On the third morning they had left, and Scharlach, before going, had put in Mlle. Malo's hands a letter requesting whatever officer should follow him to show every consideration to the family of the Comte de Réchamp, and if possible—owing to the grave illness of the Countess—avoid taking up quarters in the château, a request which had been scrupulously observed.

Such were the amazing but undisputed facts over which Réchamp and I, in our different ways, were now pondering. He hardly spoke, and when he did it was only to make some casual references to the road or to our wounded soldiers; but all the while I sat at his side I kept hearing the echo of the question he was asking himself, and hoping to God he wouldn't put it to me...

It was nearly noon when we finally reached the lines, and the men had to have a rest before we could start again; but a couple of hours later we landed them safely at the base hospital. From there we had intended to go back to Paris; but as we were starting there came an unexpected summons to another point of the front, where there had been a successful night attack, and a lot of Germans taken in a blown-up trench. The place was fifty miles away, and off my beat, but the number of wounded on both sides was exceptionally heavy, and all the available ambulances had already started. An urgent call had come for more, and there was nothing for it but to go; so we went.

We found things in a bad mess at the second line shanty hospital where they were dumping the wounded as fast as they could bring them in. At first we were told that none were fit to be carried further that night; and after we had done what we could we went off to hunt up a shakedown in the village. But a few minutes later an orderly overtook us with a message from the surgeon. There was a German with an abdominal wound who was in a bad way, but might be saved by an operation if he could be got back to the base before midnight. Would we take him at once and then come back for the others?

There is only one answer to such requests, and a few minutes later we were back at the hospital, and the wounded man was being carried out on a stretcher. In the shaky lantern gleam I caught a glimpse of a livid face and a torn uniform, and saw that he was an officer, and nearly done for. Réchamp had climbed to the box and seemed not to be noticing what was going on at the back of the motor. I understood that he loathed the job and wanted not to see the face of the man we were carrying; so when we had got him settled I jumped into the ambulance beside him and called out to Réchamp that we were ready. A second later an infirmier ran up with a little packet and pushed it into my hand. "His papers," he explained. I pocketed them and pulled the door shut, and we were off.

The man lay motionless upon his back, conscious, but desperately weak. Once I turned my pocket-lamp on him, and saw that he was young—about thirty—with damp dark hair and a thin face. He had received a flesh wound above the eyes, and his forehead was bandaged, but the rest of the face was uncovered. As the light fell on him he lifted his eyelids and looked at me: his look was inscrutable.

For half an hour or so I sat there in the dark, the sense of that face pressing close on me. It was a damnable face—meanly handsome, basely proud. In my one glimpse of it I had seen that the man was suffering atrociously, but as we slid along during the night he made no sound. At length the motor stopped with a violent jerk that drew a single moan from him. I turned the light on him, but he lay perfectly still, lips and lids shut, making no sign; and I jumped out and ran round to the front to see what had happened.

The motor had stopped for lack of gasoline and was stock still in the deep mud. Réchamp muttered something about a leak in his tank. As he bent over it, the lantern flame struck up into his face, which was set and businesslike. It struck me vaguely that he showed no particular surprise.

"What is to be done?" I asked.

"I think I can tinker it up; but we've got to have more essence to go on with."

I stared at him in despair; it was a good hour's walk back to the lines, and we weren't so sure of getting any gasoline when we got there! But there was no help for it; and as Réchamp was dead lame, no alternative but for me to go.

I opened the ambulance door, gave another look at the motionless man inside, and took out a remedy which I handed over to Réchamp with a word of explanation. "You know how to give a hypo? Keep a close eye on him and pop this in if you see a change—not otherwise."

He nodded. "Do you suppose he'll die?" he asked below his breath.

"No, I don't. If we get him to the hospital before morning I think he'll pull through."

"Oh, all right." He unhooked one of the motor lanterns and handed it over to me. "I'll do my best," he said as I turned away.

Getting back to the lines through that pitch-black forest and finding somebody to bring the gasoline back for me was about the worst job I ever tackled. I couldn't imagine why it wasn't daylight when we finally got to the place where I'd left the motor. It seemed to me as if I'd been gone twelve hours when I finally caught sight of the grey bulk of the car through the thinning darkness.

Réchamp came forward to meet us, and took hold of my arm as I was opening the door of the car. "The man's dead," he said.

I had lifted up my pocket-lamp, and its light fell on his face, which was perfectly composed, and seemed less gaunt and drawn than at any time since we had started for Réchamp.

"Dead? Why—how? What happened? Did you give him the hypodermic?" I stammered, taken aback.

"No time to. He died in a minute."

"How do you know he's dead? Were you with him?"

"Of course, I was with him," Réchamp retorted, with a sudden harshness that made me realize I had grown harsh myself. But I had been almost sure the man wasn't anywhere near death when I left him. I opened the door of the ambulance and slipped in with my lantern. He didn't appear to have moved, but he was dead sure enough—had been for two or three hours, by the feel of him. It must have happened not long after I left…Well, I'm not a doctor, anyhow…

I don't know that Réchamp and I exchanged a word during the rest of that run. But it was my fault and not his if we didn't. By the mere rub of his sleeve against mine as we sat outside on the motor I knew he was conscious of no bar between us: he had somehow got back, in the night's interval, to a state of wholesome stolidity, while I, on the contrary, was tingling all over with exposed nerves.

I was glad enough when we got back to the base at last, and the grim load we carried was lifted out and taken into the hospital. Réchamp waited in the courtyard beside his car, lighting a cigarette in the cold early sunlight; but I followed the bearers and the surgeon into the whitewashed room where the dead man had to be undressed. I had a burning spot at the pit of my stomach while his clothes were ripped off him and the bandages undone; I couldn't take my eyes from the surgeon's face. But the surgeon, with a big batch of wounded on his hands, was probably thinking more of the living than the dead; and, besides, we were near the front, and the body before him was an enemy's.

He finished his examination and scribbled something in a notebook. "Death must have taken place nearly five hours ago," he merely remarked. It was the conclusion I had come to myself.

"And how about the papers?" the surgeon continued. "You have them, I suppose? This way, please."

We left the half-stripped body on the blood-stained oil-cloth, and he led me into an office where a functionary sat behind a littered desk.

"The papers? Thank you. You haven't examined them? Let's see, then."

I handed over the leather note-case I had thrust into my pocket the evening before, and saw for the first time its silver-edged corners and the coronet in one of them. The official took out the papers and spread them on the desk between us. I watched him absently while he did so.

Suddenly he uttered an exclamation. "Ah—that's a haul!" he said, and pushed a bit of paper towards me. On it was engraved the name—Oberst Graf Benno von Scharlach…

"A good riddance," said the surgeon over my shoulder…I went back to the courtyard and saw Réchamp still smoking his cigarette in the cold sunlight. I don't suppose I had been in the hospital ten minutes; but I felt as old as Methuselah.

My friend greeted me with a smile. "Ready for breakfast?" he said good-humoredly; and a little chill ran down my spine…But I said: "Oh, all right—come along…" For, after all, I *knew* there wasn't a paper of any sort on that man when he was lifted into my ambulance the night before: the French officials attend to their business too carefully for me not to have been sure of that. And there wasn't the least shred of evidence to prove that he hadn't died of his wounds during the unlucky delay in the forest; or that Réchamp had known his tank was leaky when we started out from the lines.

"I could do with a *café complet*, couldn't you?" Réchamp suggested looking straight at me with his good blue eyes; and arm-in-arm we started off for the nearest hotel.

Them Others

Stacy Aumonier

I

It is always disturbing to me when things fall into pattern form, when, in fact, incidents of real life dovetail with each other in such a manner as to suggest the shape of a story. A story is a nice neat little thing with what is called a "working-up" and a climax, and life is a clumsy, ungraspable thing, very incomplete in its periods, and with a poor sense of climax. In fact, death—which is a very uncertain quantity—is the only definite note it strikes, and even death has an uncomfortable way of setting other things in motion. If, therefore, in telling you about my friend Mrs. Ward, I am driven to the usual shifts of the story-teller, you must believe me that it is because this narrative concerns visions: Mrs. Ward's visions, my visions, and your visions. Consequently I am dependent upon my own poor powers of transcription to mold these visions into some sort of shape, and am driven into the position of a storyteller against my will.

The first vision, then, concerns the back view of the Sheldrake Road, which, as you know, butts on to the railway embankment near Dalston Junction Station. If you are of an adventurous turn of mind you shall accompany me, and we will creep up on to the embankment together and look down into these back yards. (We shall be liable to a fine of £2, according to a bye-law of the Railway Company, for doing so, but the experience will justify us.)

There are twenty-two of these small buff-brick houses huddled together in this road, and there is surely no more certain way of judging not only the character of the individual inhabitants but of their mode of life than by a survey of these somewhat pathetic yards. Is it not, for instance, easy to determine the timid, well-ordered mind of little Miss Porson, the dressmaker at number nine, by its garden of neat mud paths, with its thin patch of meagre grass, and the small bed of skimpy geraniums? Cannot one read the tragedy of those dreadful Alleson people at number four? The garden is a wilderness of filth and broken bottles, where even the weeds seem chary of establishing themselves. In fact, if we listen carefully—and the trains are not making too much noise—we can hear the shrill crescendo of Mrs. Alleson's voice cursing at her husband in the kitchen, the half-empty gin bottle between them.

The methodical pushfulness and practicability of young Mr. and Mrs. Andrew MacFarlane is evident at number fourteen. They have actually grown a patch of potatoes, and some scarlet-runners, and there is a chicken-run near the house.

Those irresponsible people, the O'Neals, have grown a bed of hollyhocks, but for the rest the garden is untidy and unkempt. One could almost swear they were connected in some obscure way with the theatrical profession.

Mrs. Abbot's garden is a sort of playground. It has asphalt paths, always swarming with small and not too clean children, and there are five lines of washing suspended above the mud. Every day seems to be Mrs. Abbot's washing day. Perhaps she "does" for others. Sam Abbot is certainly a lazy, insolent old rascal, and such always seem destined to be richly fertile. Mrs. Abbot is a pleasant "body," though.

The Greens are the swells of the road. George Green is in the grocery line, and both his sons are earning good money, and one daughter has piano lessons. The narrow strip of yard is actually divided into two sections, a flower-garden and a kitchen-garden.

And they are the only people who have flower-boxes in the front. Number eight is a curious place. Old Mr. Bilge lives there. He spends most of his time in the garden, but nothing ever seems to come up. He stands about in his shirt-sleeves, and with a circular paper hat on his head, like a printer. They say he was formerly a corn merchant, but has lost all his money. He keeps the garden very neat and tidy, but nothing seems to grow. He stands there staring at the beds, as though he found their barrenness quite unaccountable.

Number eleven is unoccupied, and number twelve is Mrs. Ward's.

We come now to an important vision, and I want you to come down with me from the embankment and to view Mrs. Ward's garden from inside, and also Mrs. Ward as I saw her on that evening when I had occasion to pay my first visit.

It had been raining, but the sun had come out. We wandered round the paths together, and I can see her old face now, lined and seamed with years of anxious toil and struggle; her long bony arms, slightly withered, but moving restlessly in the direction of snails and slugs.

"Oh dear! Oh dear!" she was saying. "What with the dogs, and the cats, and the snails, and the trains, it's wonderful anything comes up at all!"

Mrs. Ward's garden has a character of its own, and I cannot account for it. There is nothing very special growing—a few pansies and a narrow border of London Pride, several clumps of unrecognisable things that haven't flowered, the grass patch in only fair order, and at the bottom of the garden an unfinished rabbit hutch. But there is about Mrs. Ward's garden an atmosphere. There is something about it that reflects in her placid eye the calm, somewhat contemplative way she has of looking right through things, as though they didn't concern her too closely. As though, in fact, she were too occupied with her own inner visions.

"No," she says in answer to my query. "We don't mind the trains at all. In fact, me and my Tom we often come out here and sit after supper. And Tom smokes his pipe. We like to hear the trains go by."

She gazes abstractedly at the embankment.

"I like to hear things…going on and that. It's Dalston Junction a little further on. The trains go from there to all parts, right out into the country they do…ever so far…My Ernie went from Dalston."

She adds the last in a changed tone of voice. And now perhaps we come to the most important vision of all—Mrs. Ward's vision of "my Ernie."

I ought perhaps to mention that I had never met "my Ernie."

I can only see him through Mrs. Ward's eyes. At the time when I met her, he had been away at the War for nearly a year. I need hardly say that "my Ernie" was a paragon of sons. He was brilliant, handsome, and incredibly clever. Everything that "my Ernie" said was treasured. Every opinion that he expressed stood. If "my Ernie" liked anyone, that person was always a welcome guest. If "my Ernie" disliked anyone they were not to be tolerated, however plausible they might appear.

I had seen Ernie's photograph, and I must confess that he appeared a rather weak, extremely ordinary looking young man, but then I would rather trust to Mrs. Ward's visions than the art of any photographer.

Tom Ward was a mild, ineffectual-looking old man, with something of Mrs. Ward's placidity but with nothing of her strong individual poise. He had some job in a gas works. There was also a daughter named Lily, a brilliant person who served in a tea-shop, and sometimes went to theatres with young men. To both husband and daughter Mrs. Ward adopted an affectionate, mothering, almost pitying attitude. But with "my Ernie," it was quite a different thing. I can see her stooping figure, and her silver-white hair gleaming in the sun as we come to the unfinished rabbit-hutch, and the curious wistful tones of her voice as she touches it and says:

"When my Ernie comes home…"

The War to her was some unimaginable but disconcerting affair centred round Ernie. People seemed to have got into some desperate trouble, and Ernie was the only one capable of getting them out of it. I could not at that time gauge how much Mrs. Ward realized the dangers the boy was experiencing. She always spoke with conviction that he would return safely. Nearly every other sentence contained some reference to things that were to happen "when my Ernie comes home." What doubts and fears she had were only recognisable by the subtlest shades in her voice.

When we looked over the wall into the deserted garden next door, she said:

"Oh dear! I'm afraid they'll never let that place. It's been empty since the Stellings went away. Oh, years ago, before this old war."

II

It was on the occasion of my second visit that Mrs. Ward told me more about the Stellings. It appeared that they were a German family, of all things! There was a Mr. Stelling, and a Mrs. Frow Stelling, and two boys.

Mr. Stelling was a watchmaker, and he came from a place called Bremen. It was a very sad story Mrs. Ward told me. They had only been over here for ten months when Mr. Stelling died, and Mrs. Frow Stelling and the boys went back to Germany.

During the time of the Stellings' sojourn in the Sheldrake Road it appeared that the Wards had seen quite a good deal of them, and though it would be an exaggeration to say that they ever became great friends, they certainly got through that period without any unpleasantness, and even developed a certain degree of intimacy.

"Allowing for their being foreigners," Mrs. Ward explained, "they were quite pleasant people."

On one or two occasions they invited each other to supper, and I wish my visions were sufficiently clear to envisage those two families indulging this social habit.

According to Mrs. Ward, Mr. Stelling was a kind little man with a round fat face. He spoke English fluently, but Mrs. Ward objected to his table manners.

"When my Tom eats," she said, "you don't hear a sound—I look after that! But that Mr. Stelling...Oh dear!"

The trouble with Mrs. Stelling was that she could only speak a few words of English, but Mrs. Ward said "she was a pleasant enough little body," and she established herself quite definitely in Mrs. Ward's affections for the reason that she was so obviously and so passionately devoted to her two sons.

"Oh, my word, though, they do have funny ways—these foreigners," she continued. "The things they used to eat! Most peculiar! I've known them eat stewed prunes with hot meat!"

Mrs. Ward repeated, "Stewed prunes with hot meat!" several times, and shook her head, as though this exotic mixture was a thing to be sternly discouraged. But she acknowledged that Mrs. Frow Stelling was in some ways a very good cook; in fact, her cakes were really wonderful, "the sort of thing you can't ever buy in a shop."

About the boys there seemed to be a little divergence of opinion. They were both also fat-faced, and their heads were "almost shaved like convicts." The elder one wore spectacles and was rather noisy, but:

"My Ernie liked the younger one. Oh yes, my Ernie said that young Hans was quite a nice boy. It was funny the way they spoke, funny and difficult to understand."

It was very patent that between the elder boy and Ernie, who were of about the same age, there was an element of rivalry which was perhaps more accentuated in the attitude of the mothers than in the boys themselves. Mrs. Ward could find little virtue in this elder boy. Most of her criticism of the family was levelled against him. The rest she found only a little peculiar. She said she had never heard such a funny Christian name as Frow. Florrie she had heard of, and even Flora, but not *Frow*. I suggested that perhaps Frow might be some sort of title, but she shook her head and said that that was what she was always known as in the Sheldrake Road, "Mrs. Frow Stelling."

In spite of Mrs. Ward's lack of opportunity for greater intimacy on account of the language problem, her own fine imaginative qualities helped her a great deal. And in one particular she seemed curiously vivid. She gathered an account from one of them—I'm not sure whether it was Mr. or Mrs. Frow Stelling or one of the boys—of a place they described near their home in Bremen. There was a narrow street of high buildings by a canal, and a little bridge that led over into a gentleman's park. At a point where the canal turned sharply eastwards there was a clump of linden-trees, where one could go in the summer-time, and under their shade one might sit and drink light beer, and listen to a band that played in the early part of the evening.

Mrs. Ward was curiously clear about that. She said she often thought about Mr. Stelling sitting there after his day's work. It must have been very pleasant for him, and he seemed to miss this luxury in Dalston more than anything. Once Ernie, in a friendly mood, had taken him into the four-ale bar of "The Unicorn" at the corner of the Sheldrake Road, but Mr. Stelling did not seem happy. Ernie acknowledged afterwards that it had been an unfortunate evening. The bar had been rather crowded, and there was a man and two women who had all been drinking too much. In any case, Mr. Stelling had been obviously restless there, and he had said afterwards:

"It is not that one wishes to drink only…"

And he had shaken his fat little head, and had never been known to visit "The Unicorn" again.

Mr. Stelling died quite suddenly of some heart trouble, and Mrs. Ward could not get it out of her head that his last illness was brought about by his disappointment and grief in not being able to go and sit quietly under the linden-trees after his day's work and listen to a band.

"You know, my dear," she said, "when you get accustomed to a thing it's *bad* for you to leave it off."

When poor Mr. Stelling died, Mrs. Frow Stelling was heartbroken, and I have reason to believe that Mrs. Ward went in and wept with her, and in their dumb way they forged the chains of some desperate understanding. When Mrs. Frow Stelling went back to Germany they promised to write to each other. But they never did, and for a very good reason. As Mrs. Ward said, she was "no scholard," and as for Mrs. Frow Stelling, her English was such a doubtful quantity, she probably never got beyond addressing the envelope.

"That was three years ago," said Mrs. Ward. "Them boys must be eighteen and nineteen now."

III

If I had intruded too greatly into the intimacy of Mrs. Ward's life, one of my excuses must be, not that I am "a scholard," but that I am in any case able to read a simple English letter. I was, in fact, on several occasions "requisitioned." When Lily was not at home, someone had to read Ernie's letters out loud. The arrival of Ernie's letters was always an inspiring experience. I should perhaps be in the garden with Mrs. Ward when Tom would come hurrying out to the back, and call out:

"Mother! a letter from Ernie!"

And then there would be such excitement and commotion. The first thing was always to hunt for Mrs. Ward's spectacles. They were never where she had put them. Tom would keep on turning the letter over in his hands, and examining the postmark, and he would reiterate:

"Well, what did you do with them, mother?"

At length they would be found in some unlikely place, and she would take the letter tremblingly to the light. I never knew quite how much Mrs. Ward could read. She could certainly read a certain amount. I saw her old eyes sparkling and her tongue moving jerkily between her parted lips, as though she were formulating the words she read, and she would keep on repeating:

"T'ch! T'ch! Oh dear, oh dear, the *things* he says!"

And Tom impatiently by the door would say:

"Well, what *does* he say?"

She never attempted to read the letter out loud, but at last she would wipe her spectacles and say: "Oh, you read it, sir. The *things* he says!"

They were indeed very good letters of Ernie's, written apparently in the highest spirits. There was never a grumble, not a word. One might gather that he was away with a lot of young bloods on some sporting expedition, in which football, rags, singsongs, and strange feeds played a conspicuous part. I read a good many of Ernie's letters, and I do not remember that he ever made a single reference to the horrors of war, or said anything about his own personal discomforts. The boy must have had something of his mother in him in spite of the photograph.

And between the kitchen and the yard Mrs. Ward would spend her day placidly content, for Ernie never failed to write. There was sometimes a lapse of a few days, but the letter seldom failed to come every fortnight.

It would be difficult to know what Mrs. Ward's actual conception of the War was. She never read the newspapers, for the reason, as she explained, that "there was nothing in them these days except about this old war." She occasionally dived into *Reynolds' Newspaper* on Sundays to see if there were any interesting law cases or any news of a romantic character. There was nothing romantic in the war news. It was all preposterous. She did indeed read the papers for the first few weeks, but this was for the reason that she had some vague idea that they might contain some account of Ernie's doings. But as they did not, she dismissed them with contempt.

But I found her one night in a peculiarly preoccupied mood.

She was out in the garden, and she kept staring abstractedly over the fence into the unoccupied ground next door. It appeared that it had dawned upon her that the War was to do with "these Germans," that in fact we were fighting the Germans, and then she thought of the Stellings. Those boys would now be about eighteen and nineteen. They would be fighting too. They would be fighting against Ernie. This seemed very peculiar.

"Of course," she said, "I never took to that elder boy—a greedy, rough sort of a boy he was. But I'm sure my Ernie wouldn't hurt young Hans."

She meditated for a moment as though she were contemplating what particular action Ernie would take in the matter. She knew he didn't like the elder boy, but she doubted whether he would want to do anything very violent to him.

"They went out to a music-hall one night together," she explained, as though a friendship cemented in this luxurious fashion could hardly be broken by an unreasonable display of passion.

IV

It was a few weeks later that the terror suddenly crept into Mrs. Ward's life. Ernie's letters ceased abruptly. The fortnight passed, then three weeks, four weeks, five weeks, and not a word. I don't think that Mrs. Ward's character at any time stood out so vividly as during those weeks of stress. It is true she appeared a little feebler, and she trembled in her movements, whilst her eyes seemed abstracted as though all the power in them were concentrated in her ears, alert for the bell or the knock. She started visibly at odd moments, and her imagination was always carrying her tempestuously to the front door, only to answer—a milkman or a casual hawker. But she never expressed her fear in words. When Tom came home—he seemed to have aged rapidly—he would come bustling into the garden, and cry out tremblingly:

"There ain't been no letter today, mother?"

And she would say quite placidly:

"No, not today, Tom. It'll come tomorrow, I expect."

And she would rally him and talk of little things, and get busy with his supper. And in the garden I would try and talk to her about her clumps of pansies, and the latest yarn about the neighbors, and I tried to get between her and the rabbit-hutch with its dumb appeal of incompletion. And I would notice her staring curiously over into the empty garden next door, as though she were being assailed by some disturbing apprehensions. Ernie would not hurt that eldest boy...but suppose...if things were reversed...there was something inexplicable and terrible lurking in this passive silence.

During this period the old man was suddenly taken very ill. He came home one night with a high temperature and developed pneumonia. He was laid up for many weeks, and she kept back the telegram that came while he was almost unconscious, and she tended him night and day, nursing her own anguish with a calm face.

For the telegram told her that her Ernie was "missing and believed wounded."

I do not know at what period she told the father this news, but it was certainly not till he was convalescent. And the old man seemed to sink into a kind of apathy. He sat feebly in front of the kitchen fire, coughing and making no effort to control his grief.

Outside the great trains went rushing by, night and day. Things were "going on," but they were all meaningless, cruel.

We made inquiries at the War Office, but they could not amplify the laconic telegram.

And then the winter came on, and the gardens were bleak in the Sheldrake Road. And Lily ran away and married a young tobacconist, who was earning twenty-five shillings a week. And old Tom was dismissed from the gasworks. His work was not proving satisfactory. And he sat about at home and moped. And in the meantime the price of foodstuffs was going up, and coals were a luxury. And so in the early morning Mrs. Ward would go off and work for Mrs. Abbot at the wash-tub, and she would earn eight or twelve shillings a week.

It is difficult to know how they managed during those days, but one could see that Mrs. Ward was buoyed up by some poignant hope. She would not give way. Eventually old Tom did get some work to do at a stationer's. The work was comparatively light, and the pay equally so, so Mrs. Ward still continued to work for Mrs. Abbot.

My next vision of Mrs. Ward concerns a certain winter evening. I could not see inside the kitchen, but the old man could be heard complaining. His querulous voice was rambling on, and Mrs. Ward was standing by the door leading into the garden. She had returned from her day's work and was scraping a pan out into a bin near the door. A train shrieked by, and the wind was blowing a fine rain against the house. Suddenly she stood up and looked at the sky; then she pushed back her hair from her brow and frowned at the dark house next door. Then she turned and said:

"Oh, I don't know, Tom; if we've got to do it, we *must* do it. If them others can stand it, we can stand it. Whatever them others do, we can do."

And then my visions jump rather wildly. And the War becomes to me epitomized in two women. One in this dim doorway in our obscure suburb of Dalston, scraping out a pan, and the other perhaps in some dark high house near a canal on the outskirts of Bremen. Them others! These two women silently enduring. And the trains rushing by, and all the dark, mysterious forces of the night operating on them equivocally.

Poor Mrs. Frow Stelling! Perhaps those boys of hers are "missing, believed killed." Perhaps they are killed for certain. She is as much outside "the things going on" as Mrs. Ward. Perhaps she is equally as patient, as brave.

And Mrs. Ward enters the kitchen, and her eyes are blazing with a strange light as she says:

"We'll hear tomorrow, Tom. And if we don't hear tomorrow, we'll hear the next day. And if we don't hear the next day, we'll hear the day after. And if we don't…if we don't never hear…again…if them others can stand it, we can stand it, I say."

And then her voice breaks, and she cries a little, for endurance has its limitations, and—the work is hard at Mrs. Abbot's.

And the months go by, and she stoops a little more as she walks, and—someone has thrown a cloth over the rabbit-hutch with its unfinished roof. And Mrs. Ward is curiously introspective. It is useless to tell her of the things of the active world. She listens politely but she does not hear. She is full of reminiscences of Ernie's and Lily's childhood. She recounts again and again the story of how Ernie when he was a little boy ordered five tons of coal from a coal merchant to be sent to a girls' school in Dalston High Road.

She describes the coal carts arriving in the morning, and the consternation of the head-mistress.

"Oh dear, oh dear," she says; "the things he did!"

She does not talk much of the Stellings, but one day she says meditatively:

"Mrs. Frow Stelling thought a lot of that boy Hans. So she did of the other, as far as that goes. It's only natural like, I suppose."

V

As time went on Tom Ward lost all hope. He said he was convinced that the boy was killed. Having arrived at this conclusion he seemed to become more composed. He gradually began to accustom himself to the new point of view. But with Mrs. Ward the exact opposite was the case.

She was convinced that the boy was alive, but she suffered terribly.

There came a time—it was in early April—when one felt that the strain could not last. She seemed to lose all interest in the passing world and lived entirely within herself. Even the arrival of Lily's baby did not rouse her. She looked at the child queerly, as though she doubted whether any useful or happy purpose was served by its appearance.

It was a boy.

In spite of her averred optimism she lost her tremulous sense of apprehension when the bell went or the front door was tapped.

She let the milkman—and even the postman—wait.

When she spoke it was invariably of things that happened years ago.

Sometimes she talked about the Stellings, and one Sunday she made a strange pilgrimage out to Finchley and visited Mr. Stelling's grave. I don't know what she did there, but she returned looking very exhausted and unwell. As a matter of fact she was unwell for some days after this visit, and she suffered violent twinges of rheumatism in her legs.

I now come to my most unforgettable vision of Mrs. Ward.

It was a day at the end of April, and warm for the time of the year. I was standing in the garden with her and it was nearly dark. A goods train had been shunting, and making a great deal of noise in front of the house, and at last had disappeared. I had not been able to help noticing that Mrs. Ward's garden was curiously neglected for her for the time of year. The grass was growing on the paths, and the snails had left their silver trail over all the fences. I was telling her a rumor I had heard about the railway porter and his wife at number twenty-three, and she seemed fairly interested, for she had known John Hemsley, the porter, fifteen years ago, when Ernie was a baby. There were two old broken Windsor chairs in the garden, and on one was a zinc basin in which were some potatoes. She was peeling them, as Lily and her husband were coming to supper. By the kitchen door was a small sink. When she had finished the potatoes, she stood up and began to pour the water down the sink, taking care not to let the skins go too. I was noticing her old bent back, and her long bony hands gripping the sides of the basin, when suddenly a figure came limping round the bend of the house from the side passage, and two arms were thrown around her waist, and a voice said:

"Mind them skins don't go down the sink, mother. They'll stop it up!"

VI

As I explained to Ernie afterwards, it was an extremely foolish thing to do. If his mother had had anything wrong with her heart, it might have been very serious. There have been many cases of people dying from the shock of such an experience.

As it was, she merely dropped the basin and stood there trembling like a leaf, and Ernie laughed loud and uproariously. It must have been three or four minutes before she could regain her speech, and then all she could manage to say was:

"Ernie!…My Ernie!"

And the boy laughed and ragged his mother, and pulled her into the house, and Tom appeared and stared at his son, and said feebly:

"Well, I never!"

I don't know how it was that I found myself intruding upon the sanctity of the inner life of the Ward family that evening. I had never had a meal there before, but I felt I was holding a sort of watching brief over the soul and body of Mrs. Ward. I had had a little medical training in my early youth, and this may have been one of the reasons which prompted me to stay.

When Lily and her husband appeared we sat down to a meal of mashed potatoes and onions stewed in milk, with bread and cheese, and very excellent it was.

Lily and her husband took the whole thing in a boisterous, high comedy manner that fitted in with the mood of Ernie. Old Tom sat there staring at his son, and repeating at intervals:

"Well, I never!"

And Mrs. Ward hovered round the boy's plate. Her eyes divided their time between his plate and his face, and she hardly spoke all the evening.

Ernie's story was remarkable enough. He told it disconnectedly and rather incoherently. There were moments when he rambled in a rather peculiar way, and sometimes he stammered, and seemed unable to frame a sentence. Lily's husband went out to fetch some beer to celebrate the joyful occasion, and Ernie drank his in little sips, and spluttered. The boy must have suffered considerably, and he had a wound in the abdomen, and another in the right forearm which for a time had paralyzed him.

As far as I could gather, his story was this:

He and a platoon of men had been ambushed and had had to surrender. When being sent back to a base, three of them tried to escape from the train, which had been held up at night. He did not know what had happened to the other two men, but it was on this occasion that he received his abdominal wound at the hands of a guard.

He had then been sent to some infirmary, where he was fairly well treated; but as soon as his wound had healed a little, he had been suddenly sent to some fortress prison, presumably as a punishment. He hadn't the faintest idea how long he had been confined there. He said it seemed like fifteen years. It was probably nine months. He had solitary confinement in a cell, which was like a small lavatory. He had fifteen minutes' exercise every day in a yard with some other prisoners, who were Russians, he thought. He spoke to no one. He used to sing and recite in his cell, and there were times when he was quite convinced that he was "off his chump." He said he had lost "all sense of everything" when he was suddenly transferred to another prison. Here the conditions were somewhat better and he was made to work. He said he wrote six or seven letters home from there, but received no reply. The letters certainly never reached Dalston. The food was execrable—but a big improvement on the dungeon. He was only there a few weeks when he and some thirty prisoners were sent suddenly to work on the land at a kind of settlement. He said that the life there would have been tolerable if it hadn't been for the fact that the Commandant was an absolute brute. The food was worse than in the prison, and they were punished severely for the most trivial offenses.

It was here, however, that he met a sailor named Martin, a Royal Naval Reservist, an elderly, thick-set man with a black beard and only one eye. Ernie said that this Martin "was an artist. He wangled everything. He had a genius for getting what he wanted. He would get a beef-steak out of a stone." In fact, it was obvious that the whole of Ernie's narrative was colored by his vision of Martin. He said he'd never met such a chap in his life. He admired him enormously, and he was also a little afraid of him.

By some miraculous means peculiar to sailors, Martin acquired a compass. Ernie hardly knew what a compass was, but the sailor explained to him that it was all that was necessary to take you straight to England. Ernie said he "had had enough of escaping. It didn't agree with his health," but so strong was his faith and belief in Martin that he ultimately agreed to try with him.

He said Martin's method of escape was the coolest thing he'd ever seen. He planned it all beforehand. It was the fag-end of the day, and the whistle had gone, and the prisoners were trooping back across a potato field. Martin and Ernie were very slow. They lingered apparently to discuss some matter connected with the soil. There were two sentries in sight, one near them and the other perhaps a hundred yards away. The potato field was on a slope; at the bottom of the field were two lines of barbed wire entanglements. The other prisoners passed out of sight, and the sentry near them called out something, probably telling them to hurry up. They started to go up the field when suddenly Martin staggered and clutched his throat. Then he fell over backwards and commenced to have an epileptic fit. Ernie said it was the realest thing he'd ever seen. The sentry ran up, at the same time whistling to his comrade. Ernie released Martin's collar-band and tried to help him. Both the sentries approached, and Ernie stood back. He saw them bending over the prostrate man, when suddenly a most extraordinary thing happened. Both their heads were brought together with fearful violence. One fell completely senseless, but the other staggered forward and groped for his rifle.

When Ernie told this part of the story he kept dabbing his forehead with his handkerchief.

"I never seen such a man as Martin, I don't think," he said. "Lord! he had a fist like a leg of mutton. He laid 'em out neatly on the grass, took off their coats and most of their other clothes, and flung 'em over the barbed wire, and then swarmed over like a cat. I had more difficulty, but he got me across too, somehow. Then we carted the clothes away to the next line.

"We got up into a wood that night, and Martin draws out his compass and he says: 'We've got a hundred and seven miles to do in night shifts, cully. And if we make a slip we're shot as safe as a knife.' It sounded the maddest scheme in the world, but somehow I felt that Martin would get through it. The only thing that saved me was that—that I didn't have to think. I simply left everything to him. If I'd started thinking I should have gone mad. I had it fixed in my mind, 'Either he does it or he doesn't do it. I can't help it.' I really don't remember much about that journey. It was all a dream like. We did all our travelin' at night by compass, and hid by day. Neither of us had a word of German. But Gawd's truth! that man Martin was a marvel! He turned our trousers inside out, and made 'em look like ordinary labourers' trousers. He disappeared the first night and came back with some other old clothes. We lived mostly on raw potatoes we dug out of the ground with our hands, but not always. I believe Martin could have stole an egg from under a hen without her noticing it. He was the coolest card there ever was. Of course there was a lot of trouble one way and another. It wasn't always easy to find wooded country or protection of any sort. We often ran into people and they stared at us, and we shifted our course. But I think we were only addressed three or four times by men, and then Martin's methods were the simplest in the world. He just looked sort of blank for a moment, and then knocked them clean out and bolted. Of course they were after us all the time, and it was this constant tacking and shifting ground that took so long. Fancy! he had never a map, you know, nothing but the compass. We didn't know what sort of country we were coming to, nothing. We just crept through the night like cats. I believe Martin could see in the dark…He killed a dog one night with his hands…It was necessary."

VII

It was impossible to discover from Ernie how long this amazing journey lasted—the best part of two months, I believe. He was himself a little uncertain with regard to many incidents, whether they were true or whether they were hallucinations. He suffered greatly from his wound and had periods of feverishness. But one morning, he said, Martin began "prancing." He seemed to develop some curious sense that they were near the Dutch frontier.

And then, according to Ernie, "a cat wasn't in it with Martin."

He was very mysterious about the actual crossing. I gather that there had been some "clumsy" work with sentries. It was at that time that Ernie got a bullet through his arm. When he got to Holland he was very ill. It was not that the wound was a serious one, but, as he explained:

"Me blood was in a bad state. I was nearly down and out."

He was very kindly treated by some Dutch Sisters in a convent hospital. But he was delirious for a long time, and when he became more normal they wanted to communicate with his people in England, but this didn't appeal to the dramatic sense of Ernie.

"I thought I'd spring a surprise packet on you," he said, grinning.

We asked about Martin, but Ernie said he never saw him again. He went away while Ernie was delirious, and they said he had gone to Rotterdam to take ship somewhere. He thought Holland was a dull place.

During the relation of this narrative my attention was divided between watching the face of Ernie and the face of Ernie's mother.

I am quite convinced that she did not listen to the story at all.

She never took her eyes from his face, and although her tongue was following the Row of his remarks, her mind was occupied with the vision of Ernie when he was a little boy, and when he ordered five tons of coal to be sent to the girls' school.

When he had finished, she said:

"Did you meet either of them young Stellings?"

And Ernie laughed rather uproariously and said no, he didn't have the pleasure of renewing their acquaintance.

On his way home, it appeared, he had reported himself at headquarters, and his discharge was inevitable.

"So now you'll be able to finish the rabbit-hutch," said Lily's husband, and we all laughed again, with the exception of Mrs. Ward.

I found her later standing alone in the garden. It was a warm spring night. There was no moon, but the sky appeared restless with its burden of trembling stars. She had an old shawl drawn round her shoulders, and she stood there very silently with her arms crossed.

"Well, this is splendid news, Mrs. Ward," I said.

She started a little, and coughed, and pulled the shawl closer round her.

She said, "Yes, sir," very faintly.

I don't think she was very conscious of me. She still appeared immersed in the contemplation of her inner visions. Her eyes settled upon the empty house next door, and I thought I detected the trail of a tear glistening on her cheeks. I lighted my pipe. We could hear Ernie, and Lily, and Lily's husband still laughing and talking inside.

"She used to make a very good puddin'," Mrs. Ward said suddenly, at random. "Dried fruit inside, and that. My Ernie liked it very much…"

Somewhere away in the distance—probably outside "The Unicorn"—someone was playing a cornet. A train crashed by and disappeared, leaving a trail of foul smoke which obscured the sky. The smoke cleared slowly away. I struck another match to light my pipe.

It was quite true. On either side of her cheek a tear had trickled. She was trembling a little, worn out by the emotions of the evening.

There was a moment of silence, unusual for Dalston.

"It's all very…perplexin' and that," she said quietly.

And then I knew for certain that in that great hour of her happiness her mind was assailed by strange and tremulous doubts. She was thinking of "them others" a little wistfully. She was doubting whether one could rejoice—when the thing became clear and actual to one—without sending out one's thoughts into the dark garden to "them others" who were suffering too. And she had come out into this little meagre yard at Dalston, and had gazed through the mist and smoke upwards to the stars, because she wanted peace intensely, and so she sought it within herself, because she knew that real peace is a thing which concerns the heart alone.

And so I left her standing there, and I went my way, for I knew that she was wiser than I.

War Dog

John W. Thomason, Jr.

Greta was a war dog in the service of H. M. the Kaiser and King. They bred her in the kennels of a Pomeranian Junker who was reported dead at Contalmaison, on the Somme, in 1916. With the bleak autumn of that year his widow found that she could not endure alone the rambling old estate on the dark North German plain; so she closed it, and went down to Berlin, where, in the bitter war-time, there was at least company for loneliness and misery.

Greta, with other matters pertaining to the house of a landed German gentleman, came up for sale. A purchasing officer of the signal service, waiting for a train in Pommern, saw her and bought her for the Army. She was then five months old, but the signal officer had a good eye.

She went across Germany and into France, boxed up in a military train, and came to Seventh Army Headquarters, behind Laon. On a winter morning they let her out of her crate into a swept courtyard where there were soldiers and dogs, and you heard the guns along the Chemin des Dames sound sharp and angry from the south-west across the new snow; then someone thrust a mess of horse-meat stew under her nose, and she found no concern for the far-off thunder.

The gross Wachtmeister of the Seventh Army *Meldehund-Trupp*—on detail from a Uhlan regiment because of his handiness with animals—observed the lanky puppy while, all legs and appetite, she wolfed her food. Writing down her points in his book as he noted them, he decided that she had a good head and good legs, and when it caught up with her belly, her chest would be broad and deep enough.

The color, too, was right—greyish, like the good German uniform; you did not want blacks and tans in this war, where the harder you were to see the longer you lasted. And she was the seventh puppy in this draft, so her name must begin with a G—Gertrude—Garda—Gretchen—Greta. Greta would do. Here, having polished her pan, she sat back to ease her stomach, and cocked an amiable ear at the big man in the tight cavalry tunic.

"Attention, you!" he rumbled at her. "Your name is Greta. To begin with, you will learn that name—Greta—" Thereafter, the "Prussian Regulations for the Care, Training, and Handling of War Dogs, 1913: Revised, with Notes on the Recent Fighting, 1915," ordered her life.

More than any other detail of modern battle, the war dog has been swamped in sentimental nonsense. The fact is that the German armies found them useful in a certain limited field and employed them from sound tactical considerations where they were effective; for there was never any sentimentality about the German service.

Of course you saw nondescript and various mascots among the regiments, since there is a natural affinity between soldiers and dogs the world over; and in the trench sectors, where the War settled into routine, the men in the listening-posts in front of the wire used to take out small alert animals that raised a helpful row when people approached from the wrong direction. But the real war dogs, rationed and quartered and borne on the regimental strength, were the clever brutes of the German shepherd breed, selected and trained to carry messages from a regimental headquarters to its battalions on the line.

This German shepherd dog is a northern strain, as old as history, and until late years entirely utilitarian, the colleague of herders and the assistant of the Continental police. He is sturdy and faithful, he takes kindly to discipline, and he is capable of a high degree of training along open-air lines. Commonly he is called the police dog, and he has other names.

His remote ancestors crossed the Rhine with the flocks of the Cimbri and the Teutons, and medieval manuscripts show him exactly in appearance as he is now. More remotely, he is kin to the wolves that roamed the North German plain, and to this day the wolfish look is written large upon him.

In battle, they found that he could replace to a certain extent the regimental runner, that unfortunate whose duty takes him most frequently across the blazing forward zone of combat, maintaining touch between one post and another. Therefore, it was common sense to use him, because you can grow a dog in two years where a man takes twenty, and a dog may get through where a man cannot.

The war dogs, then, in the German service were the affair of the army signal officer, along with radio, telegraph, the field-telephone, carrier-pigeons, flags, and signal-lanterns, and all the diverse means whereby a field army talks between its elements. In battle, everything mechanical has a way of going out of commission: there is a heat at the point of contact which fuses things.

A Colonel in action might be able to talk over his field-telephone to Berlin, and not be able to get through to his forward battalion half a kilometre away. To be certain, therefore, he must fall back on the means of communication that Caesar used; he must send somebody with his message. The messenger may be a dog.

Buried in the war archives in Potsdam there is the final opinion in the matter: After exhaustive tests it was found that five dogs would do the regimental messenger work of sixteen soldier runners. The arithmetic is plain—five men to look after five dogs, and eleven rifles more for the firing line. So they used dogs when they could.

The army *Meldehund-Trupp*—messenger dog outfit took Greta and moulded her to pattern in half a year. There were two basic lessons: the first was obedience to orders, and the second concerned the grey-green uniform of the German soldier. A puppy idled in the courtyard of the billet with Drina and

Blitz and Eric and a dozen or so others, playing gravely after the fashion of the breed and keeping a watchful eye on the soldiers in the light grey shoulder straps of the communication troops.

When one called Greta, you went swiftly to receive instruction, paying no attention to any other name. You carried things from one soldier to another, things fastened to your collar. First it was just across the courtyard, then it would be around the corner, and, later, your man would deliberately hide, so that you had to trail and cast about to find him.

Presently the affair took you out into the fields and up and down ravines, and there must be no loitering on the way. They worked you from one place to another place, and they worked you at night. Simple things, done over and over, they came to be second nature. And through every exercise ran the other lesson, respect for the uniform.

"Because, *Liebchen*," the *Herr Wachtmeister*, with his heavy voice and remarkably gentle hands, would say, "it would be frightful if, when you get Out There, you should take up with the wrong fellows. Those Frenchmen in their dirty blue breeches, or the English *Schwein* in khaki—So!" There were practical lessons.

The *Feld-grau* fed and cherished you. It cleaned your quarters and dispensed work and play and food and caresses. With civilians a dog had no contacts— dubious, mean persons, passed aloofly on the street. And once, Greta, carrying a message to the young *Gemeiner* on the other end of her run, found him in the place he ought to have been, wearing strange blue clothes.

It was puzzling; but the hands and the face and the smell of this private were familiar, and she accepted his blandishments and made him free of the tin cylinder at her neck. She never forgot what happened to her after that, for the *Wachtmeister* had a way of impressing things.

Again, it was a fellow in an English uniform; and when, the next day, a sorry file of khaki prisoners passed on the street, Greta had to be restrained. The conclusion was inevitable: people in grey-green were all right; otherwise, they were to be avoided if possible and attacked if not. In any case, they meant trouble.

Later, they ran Greta about the firing ranges of the army small-arms schools, and loosed off rifles and machine-guns near her, and exploded things around her. The French planes also helped her education along with the occasional bombing-raids that an army headquarters must expect behind an active front.

Steady nerves and discipline and custom dissipated any gun-shyness she might have had. At the field trials of the new blood, which the *Meldehund-Trupp* held in the early summer, she got a message over a kilometre of broken ground in less than four minutes, which is classed as good in the Prussian service, and she received the compliments of exalted personages, even officers of the General Staff, turned out to observe the event.

She was a grave, upstanding dog, approaching her full growth, with a fine head and clean hard legs, and a close, greyish-tawny coat, when, in the late summer of '17, they certified her fit for field duty and drafted her to the 40th Fusilier Regiment in the 28th Infantry Division, the old Regular division that they called the Conquerors of Lorette.

The 28th Division had been fighting in Caurieres Wood before Verdun and needed replacements of every kind. They went down into Alsace and entered the line north-west of Altkirch, which was a quiet sector and a suitable place for a division to renew itself; and here Greta had her first combat experiences, sharp enough and not too crowded, as is best for recruits, both men and dogs.

The War flicked languidly across the great still valleys of the region. Greta became acquainted with shell-fire and learned to cock an ear and gauge them, proceeding with a contemptuous flick of her tail when the thing howled high or wide, and squatting like a soldier when the whine of it increased to a shattering roar and crashed down near at hand.

Incautiously quartering over a ridge, between reserve and the forward position, she drew long-range machine-gun fire and she deduced from that the wisdom of avoiding the sky-line and keeping away from the open. She watched the war-wise soldiers and patterned her conduct on theirs.

She followed her occasions up and down black ravines in the night, and under the flares of the front line she learned what dead men are like.

When the division, much restored, went up into the Champaigne around the Butte de Mesnil, Greta went competently with them and did good service with the 1st Battalion of the 40th Regiment, which was her particular assignment, in that wilderness of shell-holes and wire and old trenches where the War was always bitter.

Her division was one of those which rushed north for the counter-battle at Cambrai, and Greta saw her first tanks—disconsolate monsters, out of gasoline beyond the Nord Canal—and her first fighting Englishmen, and took the rifle-fire of a platoon of them at bay in the wreck of a wood; and there began to be stories about her in the regiment. The 28th wintered in the Ardennes and had a post of honour in the great March drive that rolled down to the gates of Amiens, and thereafter drew out and practised the arts of open warfare in the country behind Laon, through April and early May of 1918.

Near the last of the month the Seventh Army pounded across the Chemin des Dames, and four days later, in a red sunset full of crackling shrapnel, Greta lapped water from the Marne and heard her dusty soldiers, filling their canteens by the blue river, talk of a place called Paris. Then they went back a little way and rested.

Always keen to the moods of soldiers, Greta sensed the anger and disgust in the ranks when the division was alerted and moved up to the front barely a week afterward. It was not their turn, the grey-green files growled. What was the War coming to, when the 10th Division—which had always been fairly good as front-troops went—lost a town to these Yankee amateurs the beaten French were putting in to plug their holes! However, they added with sour pride, the

28th would show them—and this is the proper and healthy frame of mind for soldiers.

Greta's Fusilier Regiment took over a narrow front, with the 1st Battalion in the corner of a wood through which the right division prolonged the line, and the 2nd facing down on a battered village where shells were always falling. Going in with Regimental Headquarters, you noted that things here were quite lively. The columns did not tramp confidently along the roads, but went in hurrying groups across the fields and kept to the woods where it was possible. There was shelling always and everywhere, and many dead men and horses.

Greta's particular signalman—the stubby little private who always looked after her—was killed taking her over her route the first time. They went from the wood where Headquarters lived in holes, down a gully to the road. Then a ditch covered the way, as far as a railroad embankment.

That had to be crossed; here the enemy got the signalman and came near getting Greta. Bullets rung dust into her nose and ripped into the ground around her, and she fled straight across a wheat-field to the edge of the wood and found her own people, more concerned about her than about the poor *Gemeiner*, who lay now in plain sight on the embankment with his knees drawn up.

She was fired at in the dusk when she went back, and every time afterwards when she had to move in daylight. There were no trenches; and things happened as often and as quickly as they did in the Champaigne.

About the third day matters became very bad. All afternoon and all night the shells crashed down on the woods and along the roads. The telephones went out. Greta, catching cat-naps in her hole, as a war dog must, was awakened by the heavy boots of the reserve battalion, brought up to Headquarters before dawn, from rest billets in the rear area.

They sent her out when the sky was getting grey, and a machine-gun, very near, spat a stream of bullets around her ears when she scuttled across the railroad. She made the shelter of the wood with her tongue out, and was confused. The place had changed its very shape. Some of her best landmarks were gone, and many dead lay about in field-grey uniforms.

In the place where battalion command post should have been, there was nothing but a great shell-hole and an untidy litter of corpses. One of these was the Signal *Feldwebel*, who always took her messages. He lay now partly under a fallen branch, with dew on his yellow moustache, and Greta licked his cold jowl and permitted herself to grieve softly in her throat.

She went on with bristling shoulders and cast about through the wood to find her people, as she had been trained. She came to a narrow clearing, where a body lay in a strange khaki uniform. Stepping around it with distaste, she halted at the edge of the open, some wolfish instinct sounding an alarm.

Private Hense Jordan, of the Fifth Marines, noted with satisfaction that the night was about finished. A sickly bluish light came sifting into the woods. Shredded tree-tops and splintered branches grew sharp against a pale green sky.

The flailed and broken timber and trampled underbrush around him took form in the shadows. The dawn chill bit into his bones, and he shifted himself in the shallow hole he had scooped the night before, and drew his salvaged German blanket closer around his shoulders.

An agonizing cramp—in his thigh jerked him painfully on his feet, to ease the tortured muscle. That spasm passing, he propped his rifle in a convenient crotch and remained standing, hunched over, his hands thrust into his breeches for warmth. He yawned and shivered miserably, his teeth chattering and his bony knees knocking together. It was the time of day when battles start and raids may be expected and reveille turns you out, and the time of day a man always feels the lowest!

Of all the duty you got, these listening-posts, out in front in a place like this, were the meanest. And double watches, because the Major said there weren't enough men left in the battalion to run regular reliefs...Where, by the way, was that damn sergeant with his relief? He'd been out here since the Major-General Commandant was a corporal.

Meantime, his trained hard eyes searched restlessly in the brush for any movement; Private Hense Jordan was an old soldier, and he had no intention of dying for his country—not through carelessness, anyway. It was quiet, right here. Over on the left, toward the Veuilly Woods and Hill 142, the guns of the French division were shelling something, and you heard chaut-chauts and Hotchkiss guns. On the eastern face of this wood single rifles were going— snipers, most likely; Heine had good snipers.

Some of our machine-guns were bickering with the Maxims across the fields from Bouresches. A quiet morning. Well, after last night, Private Jordan considered, everybody ought to have his belly full—and here *Minenwerfer* shells began to break regularly in the right rear, where the ravine that bordered the southern edge of the wood led back to the town of Lucy.

"Steppin' 'em up an' down that there gully, where the chow detail has to go," considered Private Jordan sadly. "Heine's on the job, an' Gawd help them poor greaseballs, if they's any of them in there—hope some of them gets through with grub—an' oh, Lawd, let there be coffee." He couldn't remember when he had eaten, and he felt too weak to stand. He reached back and shook his canteen, although he knew it was empty, and he spat cotton from a dry mouth, and small irritations gravelled him.

It was, he decided, no life for a white man. Lying out nights. And being shelled. And fighting blind in the woods, and never getting any rations. "Gettin' us all bumped off like this, they might at least feed us." He hadn't had his shoes off for eleven days. He wished he was back on a battleship, where they piped for chow three times a day an' mornin' coffee before turn-to; and he regretted all the evil things he had said in his time about the Navy.

"Leastways, you wear marine uniform 'board ship." He crooked a torn khaki sleeve and regarded it with disgust. "First thing the Army done was take away our Lewis guns an' give us chautchauts—take away our greens an' give us khaki—" That last rankled. Every man in the marine brigade considered it a blow struck at their morale by the envious Army when they were informed that in France they would receive no more of the forester green winter field uniforms of the marine corps, but would go garbed in olive-drab.

"Same as any odd lot of doughboys—yeh!" What if it was very like the German uniform? "Time a Boche gets near enough to tell the difference, he's in danger, I'll tell the cock-eyed worl'!" Only a few officers in the brigade clung to the old greens of the corps. The Major was one.

Private Jordan considered him briefly, the memory of his last court-martial sour on his mind. A hard son of a dog, but he was up here last night with his little stick, when they reorganized after the attack, looking things over. "Well, if I was a Major, they wouldn't get me in no army O.D., neither. Wouldn't have a chance. Recruitin' Office, Kansas City, Mizzouri: that would be my billet."

There was, in the brush ahead, something that moved. Private Jordan's rifle was by his knee, and his hands were in his pockets, which was bad; but he was too old a stager to duck and grab. He froze motionless, every sense alert. The weakness flowed out of him, and his eyes narrowed to slits. Which way, and what—

It was a dog, a dust-grey, tall fellow with pointed ears, and when it lifted its wolfish head, pale color on its throat. It materialized from around a bush a dozen yards away and stood, a forefoot lifted, considering the next move. Private Hense Jordan remembered the order, reiterated when they came up to this fight: "Kill all dogs. We don't use them, and the French don't. The Germans use them for messengers. Kill them, wherever seen and search the remains— they're usually carrying something."

Private Jordan also reflected that the Boche was very close to him, on ahead through the woods, and he did not want to shoot or otherwise demonstrate from his position if he could help it. But he'd have to get that dog…Looked like the critter might come on out into the open, where a snap shot would have a better chance—easy does it. Strictly as an afterthought, he loved dogs. But orders were orders.

Greta settled it for him. The day before she had been right through here. There should be a section of her infantrymen and two light machine-guns just past the clearing. She trotted out, her head low, taking a confusion of scents from the trampled ground, and the marine saw that she would come within a yard of him.

Try it with the bayonet—no noise—He caught up his rifle and lunged in one motion, sudden as a snake's, but she was a split-second quicker, and recoiled.

In her schooled brain, as she faced him, the cold face of her *Feldwebel* back there, and the little *Gemeiner* on the railroad, and the mad things that zipped and droned around her in the wheat, all connected at once with this lean brown man. Here was the enemy. She flung herself at him, slashing for the thigh, as a wolf does. He shifted his bayonet and caught her on it; the point slid inside her fore-leg and back, by the angle of her leap, across her shoulder-blade.

But her weight overbalanced the man, and they went down together in a tangle which the rifle dominated. Rolling clear of her ringing jaws, Private Jordan brought one hobnailed boot down on her head and considered that it was enough. He got up, wrenched the blade clear, shot a quick glance around, and bent over the long, crumpled body, which quivered briefly and relaxed.

At her neck, hooked to the leather collar, was a thin aluminum cylinder.

"Active Boche, all right—in the messenger business…Dam' it, I had to do it! An' it's a bitch, too! Arh! But there wasn't no way out of it—guess that got her in the heart." Kneeling, much distressed, he investigated the battered head and felt along her chest.

A sergeant and a private of marines came noiselessly up behind him. They spoke in husky whispers. "Got one, Hense? Seen anything else? If the mutt's got anything on 'im, rush it on back to the skipper. An' report to your platoon—moved it to the right this mornin'—Corporal Kent's in charge; they got some slum up. Here's the lay-out, guy," and the sergeant turned to instruct the relief.

Meantime Private Jordan had noted that the dog's chest still bled, and the flow was bright and not sluggish. "Say," he said, without looking up, "she ain't dead! I never killed her. She—"

"Well, kill it an' get back from here," snapped the sergeant in disgust. "This any place to be sobbin' over our dumb friends, you—" And Private Jordan slung his rifle, picked her up, and dodged into the brush to the rear, where he set her down and clumsily applied his first-aid bandage to stop the flow of blood.

Her skull didn't seem to be smashed, and although she was still entirely limp, he thought her heart went a little. Then he walked swiftly down through the position, along a very thin line of men in holes, who regarded him without curiosity and gulped cold slum and lukewarm coffee.

"Battalion?—down that there trail, fella." For he wasn't going to the company commander, a man not sympathetic to dogs or to irregularities.

"If the skipper says how come I went over his head, I'll tell him I thought orders was to take Boche dope right to the Major. Major used to have a dog," he planned uneasily; and passed through two platoons of the 2nd Engineers, unkempt and competent and constituting the battalion reserve; and found battalion headquarters group disposed in the ravine.

The Major sat on a rock and drank coffee from a canteen cup. He was unshaven, and his eyes were red-rimmed from loss of sleep, and the shine had departed from his field boots; but he wore his stained forester-green uniform with an air, and his helmet, the chin-strap looped up over the brim, was slanted at a cocky angle. He conversed casually with his Adjutant, and did not look around when Private Jordan, strangely burdened, slid down the bank of the ravine and was halted by the important sergeant-major.

"Private Jordan wants permission to speak to the battalion commander—got a Boche dog here, carryin' messages."

The Adjutant, a young man in a soldier's blouse and Quartermaster breeches everywhere too large for him, turned to hear, with a cold, bad-tempered eye.

"Sir, I'm on listenin'-post on the left, back there, an' just now, this here dog—I think she's a Boche messenger-houn', sir, like it says in orders—she tries to get by me, an'—" Then Greta came alive. Her lax body, sagging in the man's arms, quickened. She slashed Private Jordan's wrist wickedly, threw herself down and away from him, rolled over on her wrecked shoulder, and came in frantic haste to her three good feet, every tooth showing and her back hair all on end.

The Adjutant swore and plucked out his pistol, and the battalion gas non-com clubbed his rifle, and Private Jordan, clutching at his wrist, rocked on his feet and pleaded foolishly: "Aw, don' kill her—don' kill her. She's a bitch, too." The Major walked toward her.

Sick and dizzy, with an unaccountable weakness dragging at her, and surrounded by khaki, Greta whirled on this new enemy, to do what she could. The fire went out of her eye. For the man had on a green uniform and had also the stiff, high look of her own officers. It was all very confusing, but with her people here it would be all right. He held out his hand, and stooped to her, and spoke softly. Greta lunged painfully to him, tried to lick his hand, and collapsed against his boots.

The Major detached the aluminium cylinder, and thrust it at his Adjutant. "See if it's anything, Le Grand. And my compliments to the surgeon—want him here. Now, old lady, did they do you wrong? Damnation! Bayonet—and you've bashed her eye out, you—"

"Sir"—Private Jordan, much distressed, pulled away from the file who was working at his wrist—"I done my best not to kill her. Sir, I never hurt a dawg in my life—I—"

"Oh, all right. All right. Surgeon, give me a hand here—maybe we can patch her up. Dam' fine animal, I think. Yes, what is it?"

The Adjutant, with the aid of a Navy hospital corps man who had studied in Vienna, had a translation. "It's addressed in code and signed in code, sir, but I think it's from Headquarters to battalion. Says KTK Battalion will approach position under cover from the right, pass through you, and attack to recover lost position. Says you will support attack after it has passed through. Says half hour SMW—must mean heavy *Minenwerfer*—preparation, starting at five-fifteen—a.m., sir. And the time sent is four-thirty-five—don't get that, for it's just after four now—and it says acknowledge with two yellow smokes."

Said the Major, his head on one side: "Their time's an hour ahead of ours. Sergeant-major, you inventoried those captured pyrotechnics, you said. Ought to be yellow smoke rockets among 'em. Go forward a little way and send up two. Pick a place in the clear, so they'll get above the knees." The sergeant-major saluted and set off at a trot. "Where's that engineer officer? Mr. Shank, have your platoons stand by to reinforce the left company in half an hour. Go up there now and look it over; you'll put them in as the company commander directs. Tell him about it; they'll come that way. Work in through the woods and hit the left, I think. Le Grand, get Headquarters. I want some artillery."

A runner said: "Hi! Ol' sergeant-major sure made knots there go them yellow smokes!" And very soon afterward the *Minenwerfer* shells began to crash into the woods. In the 40th Fusilier Regiment they never understood why their counter-attack failed so disastrously. The Lieutenant-Colonel had a very bad time explaining it.

And Greta lives now in Quantico, when she's at home. Her Major has a regiment there. She carries her years well, although she is one-eyed and has a heavy limp. She is an aloof, unfriendly dog to every other person but her Colonel; yet it is noted that in the fall and winter, when the marines go in forester-green, her temper becomes more genial, and she allows familiarities on the part of the rank and file.

Réchoussat's Christmas
(from *Civilization*)

Georges Duhamel

Réchoussat repeated in a shrill, strained voice: "I tell you, they're not coming after all."

Corporal Têtard turned a deaf ear to this. He was sorting out his stock on a table: lints, oil, rubber gloves reminiscent of the fencer, probes enclosed in a tube like vanilla cornets, a basin of enamelled sheet-iron resembling a big bean, and a bulging vase with a wide gaping mouth, looking like nothing at all.

Réchoussat affected an air of indifference. "They needn't come if they don't wish to. Anyway, I don't care."

Corporal Têtard shrugged his shoulders. "But I tell you they will come," he said.

The wounded man obstinately shook his head. "Not here, old boy, nobody'll come here. All those who visit downstairs never come up here. I'm only telling you. I don't really care, you know."

"You may be sure they will come."

"Really, I don't know why I have been placed here alone in the room."

"Probably because you must have quiet."

"Whether they come or not, it's all one to me."

Réchoussat frowned to show his pride, then he added, sighing:

"You can begin now with your bag of tricks."

As a matter of fact Corporal Têtard was ready. He had lighted a candle-end and in one movement drew back the sheets.

Réchoussat's body was revealed, extraordinarily thin, but Têtard scarcely noticed it, and Réchoussat had for three months now been fairly accustomed to his misery. He knew quite well that to have a piece of shell in the back is a serious matter, and that, when a man's legs and abdomen are paralyzed, he is not going to recover quickly.

"Feeling better?" asked Têtard in the course of his operation.

"Yes," he replied. "Now it's six o'clock and they haven't come. Good thing! I don't mind."

The corporal did not reply; with a weary expression he rubbed together his rubber gloves. Riveted to the wick, the candle-flame leaped and struggled, like a wretched prisoner yearning to escape and fly up alone in the blackness of the room, and beyond, higher, higher, in the winter sky, in regions where the sounds of the war of men are no longer heard. Both the patient and the orderly watched the flame in silence, with wide-open vague eyes. Every second a gun, far away, snapped at the panes, and each time the flame of the candle started nervously.

"It takes a long time! You're not cold?" asked Têtard.

"The lower part of my body does not know what cold means."

"But it will, one day."

"Of course it will. It's dead now, but it must become alive again. I am only twenty-five; it's an age when the flesh has plenty of vigour."

The corporal felt awkward, shaking his head. Réchoussat seemed to him worn out; he had large sores in the places where the body rested on the bed. He had been isolated in order that his more fortunate comrades should be spared the sight of his slow, dragging death.

A long moment went by. The silence was so oppressive that for a moment they felt their small talk quite inadequate. Then, as if he was continuing a mental discussion, Réchoussat suddenly remarked:

"And, you know, I'm so easily satisfied. If they came for two minutes only."

"Hush!" said Têtard. "Hush!"

He leaned, listening, towards the door. Obscure sounds came from the passage.

"Ah, here they are!" said the orderly.

Réchoussat craned his neck. "Bah! No, I tell you."

Suddenly a wonderful light, rich in reflections of gold and crimson—a strange fairy light-filled the passage. The wall in front stood out; ordinarily as pale as December woods, now it suddenly exhibited the splendour of an Eastern palace or of a princess' gown. In all this light there was the sound of happy voices and of laughter. No one could be heard singing, yet the light itself seemed to be singing a magnificent song. Réchoussat, who could not move, stretched his neck the more vigorously, and raised his hands a little above the sheets, as if he wanted to feel this beautiful sound and light.

"You see, you see!" said Têtard. "I told you they would come."

Then there was a big blaze. Something stopped before the door; it was a tree—a real fir-tree from the forests, planted in a green box. There were so many Chinese lanterns and pink candles hanging from its branches that it looked like an enormous torch. But there was something grander to come; the wise and learned kings now entered. There was Sorri, a Senegalese gunner, Moussa, and Cazin. Wrapped in cloaks from Adrianople, they wore long white beards made of cotton wool.

They walked right into Réchoussat's room. Sorri carried a little packet tied with ribbon. Moussa waved aloft two cigars, and Cazin a bottle of champagne. The three of them bowed punctiliously, as they had been told, and Réchoussat found himself suddenly with a box of chocolates in his right hand, two cigars in his left, and a glass of foaming wine on his little table.

"Ah, boys! No, no; you're joking, boys."

Moussa and Cazin laughed. Sorri showed his teeth.

"Ah, boys!" repeated Réchoussat, "I don't smoke, but I'm going to keep the cigars as a souvenir. Pass me the wine."

Sorri took the goblet and offered it as if it were a sacred cup. Réchoussat drank it gently and said:

"It's some wine! Good stuff!"

There were more than a score of faces at the door, and they all smiled at the gentle naive Réchoussat.

Afterwards, a veritable sunset! The wonderful tree receded, jolting into the passage. The venerable kings disappeared, with their flowing cloaks and their sham beards. Réchoussat still held the goblet and gazed at the candle as if all the lights existed there. He laughed, slowly repeating, "It's some wine!" Then he continued to laugh and never said a word.

Quite gently the darkness entered the room again and lodged itself everywhere, like an intimate animal disturbed in its habits.

With the darkness something very sad insinuated itself everywhere, which was the odor of Réchoussat's illness. A murmuring silence rested on every object like dust. The face of the patient ceased to reflect the splendour of the Christmas tree; his head sunk down, he looked at the bed, at his thin, ulcerated legs, the glass vessel full of unclean liquid, the probe, all these incomprehensible things, and he said, stammering with astonishment:

"But…but…what is the matter then? What is the matter?"

Armistice
(from *Waiting for Daylight*)

H. M. Tomlinson

The tumult of that year, desperate and stupefying, lessened. We had leisure to breathe again. The Germans were expended. Ludendorff had gambled with his last reserves, and he had lost. The threatening colossus suggested by his name dissolved in vapour. His armies, wasted in spendthrift recklessness, stood dangerously upon an enlarged front. Behind them was a nation which had stoutly endured starvation within frontiers locked fast by the war fleets of its enemies while hope maintained it. Hope had gone. It saw starkly a reality which no device of words could hide. The victories of its heroes had brought it to this; and the Americans, who could never cross the seas, were in fact in France, ready to begin a new war. Poch and Haig struck back rapidly alternating blows at the disheartened German front. Germany collapsed.

The guns would cease fire on this November day, so we were told. It was true, maybe. We had been told many things. Now They who ruled everything, even what we should read and know, even the number of potatoes we should eat—They who had taken so much from us, for our good, that only ashes were left, They said the guns would cease to fire. We hoped so. But it was late.

It was a quiet winter morning. The perspective of the long trial was too deep. Nothing could be seen in it now, nothing but the wan sky over the Thames. We waited, lethargic, hardly believing. It was near the hour. London was still. Then a rocket burst over the river.

The end! That was the end of it!

A window was flung open. Someone was cheering across the street. Sirens began to hoot on the river. The whistles of locomotives kept up their whistling. There was shouting and singing below.

I looked out. The city was erupting. An Australian soldier sat on the roof of a cab with a nurse on his lap. People were flooding from every door; clouds of papers and official forms fell over the cheering crowds from the windows of offices; the street already was a congested, tumultuous torrent of released people.

When I turned to the room my own office was deserted. It was oddly quiet. The staff had dropped everything and had gone. Discipline had departed to sing and dance elsewhere. One had better join it, perhaps?

But as I made for the door, there, only just visible in the shadow of a recess, was an old bowler hat on a peg. It was ancient with dust. It was ridiculously out of fashion. I stood and looked at it. That was Charley Bolt's old hat. He left it there, to go to war, four years ago. It seemed very much by itself. I got out a pipe; took a chair; I might just as well keep it company, on such a day.

Honours Easy
(from *Fiery Particles*)

C. E. Montague

I

When Colin March, a younger son of a famous diplomatist, played in a British Embassy garden abroad his foreign nurse gave him a tortoise. "A useful beast," she explained. "It devours cockroaches; they are its passion."

Colin wanted to see this beneficent passion at work. So he captured one of the Embassy's many cockroaches and put it down in front of the tortoise's nose, like an early Christian presented to a lion. The tortoise eyed the offered feast and mused deeply. The cockroach did not muse. It was a cockroach of action. Without any apparent need for reflection it bolted for cover, like a flash of blackness, right into the tortoise's shell, and hid itself in that profound thinker's armpit.

The cadet of a dynasty of ambassadors was charmed with the cockroach's wit. He filed the whole affair in a pigeon-hole of his cute little mind. As he grew up he would often chuckle to think of it. Piquant parallels would occur to him. For a fox to go to earth under the kennels, for landsmen to go out to sea to escape from a press-gang, for cannon-fodder to hide at the back of the cannon this was the wit of life put into a kind of practical epigram, salt and impudent. He adored it.

When Colin was twenty the War came. "*C'est beau, ça,*" he said, when he saw what was done on the spot by most of the young men he knew. He was a connoisseur. He could tell a fine gesture. "It makes fools," he said, "of us scoffers. It is as if God had broken loose out of the churches. Little new peers, like my dear cousin Grax, are becoming patrician. The rich are fairly jumping through the needle's eye, flocks of 'em—sheep at a gap."

Colin was not to be carried off his own feet by any rush to take arms. He made no holy excuses about the omission: his sense of humor saved him from that. The only kind of humbug that it would allow him to practice was humbug conscious and gleeful not Pecksniff's humbug; only Sganarelle's. It was a vital interest to him, he demurely said, not to be dead. And how could a ruling class rule from the tomb? Might not one honestly praise Father Damien without rushing off to nurse lepers? Besides, his elder brother was badly wounded already; life, he pointed out, might at any moment become vastly more worth living than ever.

And yet the War, and the way that his caste thought about it, were not to be easily talked out of his path. Like lions, they straddled across it; like tortoises, they impended over our quick-witted cockroach. Perhaps he remembered. He seemed to. For one day he spoke to his father, his father spoke to the proper person, and Colin was given a temporary commission for "special employment" in France. From war he thus found refuge in the Army. The cockroach was safe in the tortoise's armpit.

There were many strange "special employments" in France. One special employee wrote tracts upon the duty of desertion for airmen to drop on the enemy's lines. Another kept a country house for visiting magnates to stay at. Another met dying officers' wives at the boat, and whisked them away in fleet cars to the death-bed. All these had something to do. And there were others, who may have done little harm. Colin was one of them: "G.H.Q., Fifth Echelon," was his army address. By day he sat in a tin hut, properly warmed. His casement opened on the Channel's foam. A sergeant-major brought him forms to sign, and said: "The place, sir, for the name is 'ere." He had a telephone soon—a great help in crying off dinner engagements whenever a more amusing one came. He made the right faces when anyone called. He was always game for a round of golf with the Brigadier at Le Touquet. For these duties his qualifications were excellent French and Italian. He may not have borne any physical part in the great westward retreat. But how could he? What good would it do to wade into the sea?

II

For three months Colin had led a life of rude health, brightened by spirited tiffs with other saviours of the country. Ruder disputes going on elsewhere formed a dim, distinguished background for these engaging figures: battles and sieges, the Marne and the Aisne, the fall of Antwerp, the first Battle of Ypres. Colin was highly aware of the value of all this forest distance of tapestried gloom against which his own foreground figure was planted. He knew what was what. All this was romance, like the whining of winds that have blown over deserts of snow when they sniff at night round the house where a person, who knows what is what, lies in bed, with the firelight leaping or musing.

Then came the Deluge. Or, rather, one of the Deluges. Colin would say: "Poor old G.H.Q. was made to be inundated and reinundated, like Holland, on proper occasions. Or it's like England, with Picts and Brythons and Angles and Normans all rushing it in their turns. All of us here are ex-conquerors, layer on layer of us. First to charge in were the War Office braves, the old hands, the mighty hunters of good jobs before the Lord. I came as a sutler with them. I'm the *jeune premier arriviste*. Then, after three months of the War, the notes of a distant recessional march strike our ears, a thunderous tramping is heard in the east, and there burst in upon us the pick of the old Regulars from the front—oh, not all of them, only those who had found that it was not the right sort of war, and that they had the right sort of friends. Approaching, they took a short run, and fairly butted and rammed their way into shelter, with all their mothers and uncles pushing them hard from behind—fell right in on top of us here with their cavalry spurs and their Guards knickerbockers and buttons and swashing and martial outsides. They were like the saints taking the Kingdom of Heaven by storm. We tried to be nice to them; sat as close as we could to make room; cut our work in two and gave them half, like St. Martin; talked to them kindly and wittily. They only stared. Then I knew them—the poor old Army Class worthies at school. Look at Claude, *par exemple*—his eyes! 'There is no speculation in those eyes.'"

Claude Barbason's brain, it may be, was not all air and fire. And Colin was yoked to him now. They bit wooden penholders in the same hut, and perfected a dislike of each other that they had roughed out in peace-time in London.

"Ever see," Colin would pleasantly ask you, "such a good German as Claude? *Tout ce qu'il a de Boche absolument!*" Claude's face indeed, with its pink and white gravity, heavy blue eyes and straw hair, did call up visions of some German officer prisoners. No doubt, he had, through his ancestors, sojourned in England a good thirteen hundred years. Still, you could fancy him, that long ago, full of home thoughts of West Saxony, marching Londonward from the sea, mopping the sweat from pink cheeks and shaking the yellow hair away from China-blue eyes, to see, for the first time, from the Kentish chalk downs, the Thames shining below through the trees.

Claude would take his own part, without positive sparkle, in this commerce in compliments. Colin to him was "the mountebank," with his "bounding cleverness" and his "beastly quotations." Colin, he said, dirtied everything that he touched; he seemed to like rolling himself and everyone else in the mud; he called the scarlet staff tabs—which they were both seeking—the Red Badge of Funk; he said the Job Lot Mess, where they and other odds-and-ends ate, ought to hang out a sign on a board "*Au Ravitaillement des Embusqués*"; he called Fifth Echelon "Chelsea" and "Greenwich"—because, as he idiotically said, it gave a secure and honoured old age to so many young men; he was always dragging in rotten gobbets of verse, with foul under-meanings: "Soldier, rest, thy warfare o'er"; "Keep thou still when clans are arming"; "His tin hat now shall be a hive for bees"—oh, there was no end to his loathsomeness!

"Speak for yourself," Claude often wanted to say. Let the fellow befoul his own nest, and not decent people's. What could an amateur soldier like that know about what a real soldier must feel? Yet Claude's scorching retorts did not get themselves uttered—only something dry and austere, like "I suppose we all get our orders and have to obey them," or, "Well, if you don't mind, I'll get on with my work. There's a war on," said with a reproving stiffness. Then Claude would bite his penholder pretty severely.

III

I fancy it was in the gloom following one of these indecisive engagements with

Colin that Claude's eyes were suddenly opened, like Adam's and Eve's, and he saw that, for the high purpose of conflict with Colin, he, Claude, was little better than naked. If, now, he had a ribbon or two on his bosom, all the darts of Colin's flashy, trashy wit would be deflected; Claude would be armour-plated, like capital ships; like generals, he would be able to score without saying a word, just by sitting behind the front of his tunic and letting it tell.

Somebody said in his hearing that night that the King of Alania—we'll call it Alania—was soon to visit our front. Claude listened. After dinner he cast a long, passionate look at a framed thing that hung on the ante-room wall. It looked from afar like a colored plate of the full solar spectrum, but it was labeled, "The Ribbons of all the World. Orders of Honour." Yes, an Alanian ribbon was there—a blue one, a beauty! Fie, thought Claude, upon this quiet life in a hut, yoked with an unbeliever. Swiftly he wrote to three uncles of his—wrote as he had not written since the days when he first perceived that the trenches were no place for him.

The uncles were loyal; Claude, if a babe in some ways, was no Babe in the Wood. And they were soldiers, and well placed for doing good deeds to a nephew. One of the three was in actual charge of the plans for giving this Alanian King a good time, *vice* somebody else who was ill.

The King duly came. He was reverentially motored about from meal to meal, well in the rear of our front. And who but Claude sat in state beside the chauffeur, except when he—Claude, not the chauffeur—leapt down to open the door! In this great office Claude bore himself meekly through three dusty midsummer days. On the third evening the King and his British guides, nurses, and gillies of every degree stood somewhat self-consciously grouped at Amiens on one of that city's desolate lengths of low railway platform. The guest was going away. Abruptly the fountain of honour was turned full on, and it played in the twilight.

Nervous and kind, wishful to do the right thing by Britain, but not to keep one of France's trains waiting, the King dealt out stars of Alania with shy expedition to all the British officers who had done anything for him. An A.D.C. stood beside him and fed the blue-ribboned trinkets into the gracious hand. Claude went in last. But even when he was bestarred three stars were visibly left over. The King held one of them, ready to shed. The A.D.C. was still holding an unmistakable brace. Somebody must have miscounted. Or else, as Claude came to believe later, the devil was in it. The fountain of honour looked like slopping over the edge of its basin.

A little way off, in the gathering dusk, three British officers, not attached to the King's party, were standing—perhaps awaiting the train, perhaps not. The Alanian A.D.C. cast a look towards them. Then he looked at the King and drew the King's eyes towards the trio. The King nodded. "There iss," he said sweetly, "no British officer who iss not worthy." The red-eyed train for Paris was now clanking out of the tunnel into the station. "Quick, please!" said the King, in Alanian.

The three unpremeditated vessels of the royal grace were informed. And the angel of this annunciation was Claude. To his unaffected distaste he found, on approach, that one of the three was Colin. Still, Claude's not to reason why, at any rate until later. He delivered royalty's summons. In three minutes the three remainder stars had settled into their new, fortuitous homes, the King had peace in the quickening train, and Claude had briefly let himself go on the question of unearned increment, and was hearing a little from Colin about the divine super-equity of the ruling that he who had borne the burden and heat of three full days' work in the vineyard should not receive more than he who had wrought for one hour only.

"An hour!" objected the literal Claude. "Why, you only paraded for pay!"

"Absolutely," said Colin. But he was too modest. That dramatic scene at the station had really taken some skill and pains to bring off. Drama, they say, is the art of preparation.

Claude simmered and fumed. "Anyhow," Colin said like an angel, "it has all ended happily."

"Not that I wanted," Colin explained to me later, "this acrid Alanian blueblob. Red is the only wear, to my mind, on this obscene khaki. Still, one has to take life as it comes. So I went to the station. I even took other trouble. Why should I have to, though? Why should Claude have to eat dust all over the Pas de Calais before he can stick what he likes on his coat? Let's have Free Trade in all ribbons. Then they'd give real distinction. A man would write himself down just what he is by the things he'd put on. All the born base wallahs would put up three rows on the spot, if they'd not got them now. The Samurai at the front would take care to wear nothing—they'd be like the patriciate we're getting in England at last, the fellows who won't take the peerages. I should wear dozens, but I'd be an artist about it. I'd paint like a Rubens and wear my own picture. I'd start from that deep Russian red with the bottomless lustre—the Cross of St. George, or what is it?—and fight it out in that key all the summer. Oh, I see red; I can hear it—whole chords of red, peals of it. Isn't any Grand Duke ever coming this way?"

IV

None came. But some bird of the air must soon have carried to Colin the news that a mission of British officers, heroes of Mons and the Marne, was about to visit the Russian front. For Colin wrote, swiftly and well, to the proper person in London. He had heard that for this mission ten hard-bitten fighters were needed; they had to have manners, know French, and be able to carry their wine. Colin answered the call of his country the moment he got it to come to him. It was, he saw, no case for delay. Empires perish. Before such another call came, the Russians might have a republic, and no decorations about, like the poor Yanks, and then—too late, the saddest words in life, too late. Plenty of time, later on, for Colin to prosecute his conquests in France. He took his stand now with the nine other courteous and capacious linguists.

In holy Russia the primitive virtue of hospitality was so ardently practiced that Colin came back crying out for a separate peace. Only a cure at Marienbad, he declared, could patch up his old body for heaven. No mere London season, he vowed, had ever made such demands upon the digestive force of the celebrants as this Muscovite joy-ride. Still, that profoundly lustrous red ribbon was his.

He brought back, besides, a lot of good stories. One was about a Japanese Colonel, another guest of the Tsar's. In a Russian trench this child of the sunrise had strayed from the side of his guides and fallen in with four Russian privates. They were good lads from the country, simple but careful. They were not sure whether the War was still the old one with Japan or another. Anyhow, they considered it safer to kill a loose Jap. The faithful souls did it, and Colin declared that the consequent Russian apologies to Japan were a classic for young attachés to study, apart from their primary worth as light fiction. Richer still in comedy was the Japanese government's plight. For, by way of good manners, it had to pretend to believe that the murder was not got up by the Tsar. And, to keep up this pose, a Russian staff Captain, the guide who had not succeeded in keeping the Japanese Colonel alive, had to be given a Japanese Order.

"That gaud," said Colin to the Job Lot Mess, "was a treasure, a sovereign prince of enamels. We ought to make more of the Japs. We ought to shift the whole war farther East. We might hold all the gorgeous East in fee. Churchill is right."

V

Claude did not hear this address upon strategy. Claude, too, had gone East, though less far. When left alone in the hut he had thought deeply about A.D.C.s. Peace, perfect peace, was their lot in this war. They toiled not, neither did they fight; yet honour found them; beauty fell, as it were, from the air, and was caught upon their tunics. Claude, as the New World says, figured upon it. Then he acted. Nature may not have made him expressly for action; rather, perhaps, for the contemplation of himself in some becoming light. But Colin's own devout self was not surer than Claude of the efficacy of prayer, directed to the right quarter. Had not he, too, seen the Red Sea cut in two for his safety, and passed across dry? And now the right quarter was clear. It was that bachelor uncle of Claude's who had lately got the command of a corps. "Claude is descended," Colin explained, "from a long line of bachelor uncles. All Barbasons are. That's why they're so rich."

On the second day of the Battle of Loos, Claude rallied round this beneficent uncle. The new A.D.C. took the place of a wild young peer who had gone mad and swindled and lied his way back to the head of an equally wild Irish platoon, then diminishing in the lost battle. The uncle told Claude about this eccentric: "Damn little fool! I'd just been thinking of putting him up for an M.C. I hope *you'll* know when you're well off." Claude did. Like Issachar, he "saw that rest was good." And the corps headquarters were pleasant. There would he see no enemy but winter and rough weather; and these are not lethal in well-built châteaux. "Fritz has got a new gun," I was once told by an infantry private in that corps, "as will carry thirty-eight miles." "Goowan," another put in, "that ain't nothing. He's got a gun would hit our corps H.Q." The corps, as a whole, felt sure its commander was safe.

To this essential of safety a nephew's love added several subsidiary blessings. Claude labored, as in God's sight, to get the General's coffee milk really boiled and not just heated—a test of capacity which the General knew to be crucial. "If a man," as he said, "can't get a little thing like that right, he'll never win battles." Neither did Claude disdain to make sure that the General's boots were done just as he liked them. Of myrrh and frankincense less material Claude offered unstintingly all that his talents allowed. He was not as many A.D.C.s are. Some of the most contumacious of men are those who do little personal things for the great. Valets to emperors, ushers to Solons, batmen to heroes—too often nothing is great to such men, and nobody either. Nearly all the most mutinous blasphemy that was talked during the War was talked in the A.D.C. rooms of the mighty. But Claude revered his chief. To him his uncle was one in whom the soul of "the real army" lived on, pestered, indeed, but still nobly unswamped by the rag, tag, and bobtail of Kitcheners and Territorials. Claude could feel for the corps commander. Had he not too, for long months, endured the manners of Colin, the New Army man, in the wilderness?

To those who knew what most people did not, the uncle was known as "The Derby Winner," or, more succinctly, "The Crook." He had come out to France in command of a division. The first time it went into action his genius miscarried and lost a mile of ground and half his men. It was only then that the General showed his full speed. Some said he had leapt into a waiting aeroplane the moment the battle was lost. Anyway, he was in London incredibly soon, and seeing the proper person about a mark of distinction so signal that, when the bad news came in, it would look silly to turn round and give him a post on the shelf. Still, the news came in the end; some of these things will get out, whatever you do. Clearly The Crook was not born to command divisions. So he was given a corps to command, and the corps was now in the line, in a pretty hot corner, expiating this stroke of humor in high places. The Crook, however, cannot have been a wholly bad man. He must have had some natural affection. Claude had not served him a month when the uncle sent up his name for a Military Cross. "You'll get it too," he told him. "Whenever these lists of recommendations look a bit long to the people upstairs they start lopping off names from the tail-end and work up. So I've wedged yours in near the middle, well up."

Claude knocked off work for the day, he was so moved. He went to lie on his bed, to get at more leisure the feel of the full warmth of Fortune's benediction upon him. All things were well.

Through the tall window, across the bejewelled dewy grass of the park, he could see a white road and troops on it: a New Army battalion—he could tell that; they had no smartness—arching up to the front, to go into the line, the undersized men bending under their packs, to ease the cut of their straps on the shoulder, and chorusing one of their contumacious songs of mock funk:

> Oh my! I don't want to die;
> I want to go home.

Then the road was vacant and white for a time, till a wailing of bagpipes arose, and a kilted battalion, dwarfed to the size of a company, hove into sight, marching the opposite way—four little companies like platoons, and few officers anywhere; the pipes skirling some fearful lament, almost animal, like a moaning or keening of primitive women over their dead; the men with a stiff, savage gait of sombre defiance—scorn of the enemy they had smashed, of the staff that had thrown Scottish valour away, of the non-Scottish troops that had failed on a flank, of the non-Scottish commander-in-chief that had loosed the fool battle.

Claude was no great hand at reading that sort of print. Still, he did make out something. War was the great game; he saw that more clearly than ever; he saw, too, how great beyond all other wars was this war, how much more important a business to shine in.

And, gosh! what a facer this M.C. would be for the Mountebank!

VI

It was "at the front," of all places, that this blow fell upon Colin; not quite at the place where the smell of rotting meat hung all that autumn, but still pretty near it—at a brigade headquarters. It counted all right for his purpose.

After his travels in Russia, Colin had felt it was time he became a full G.S.O., a staff officer proper. Base was the slave who remained for ever merely "attached to" the staff. But so many Colins had felt this before, and had carried their point so completely, that scandal was feared. To avert it, a ruling had gone forth that all G.S.O.s appointed thenceforth must have had some trench service. Poor Colin, to compass his end, had to take kit for a whole fortnight's stay in a new brigade commander's charmless dug-out, and listen in candle-lit frost to the banalities talked by the Brigadier, brigade Major, staff Captain, and some odds-and-ends of medicine, signals, and the Church. Each of these, he found, had some two things to say about life, and three jokes, so that the conversation of each was a sort of recurring decimal of five places. Each of them watched, with bitter foreknowledge, the countless revolutions of the others' antique decimals. One day, however, Colin heard a new thing.

A Major, an acting battalion commander, had come in to tea. He knew the Brigadier well, and, like a good soldier, he was blaspheming the great for the sweat that they will often give you for nothing. "Hardly a fortnight ago, sir," he said to his host, "just before you came to us, a corps order came round to say some foreign devils—the Japs, I believe—had sent a wad of their 'Crosses for

Valour'—sort of V.C.s—one for the absolute ace—any rank—in each British corps. Every C.O. was to pick out the hottest man-eater he got for the corps to select the tip-topper. I took days at the job, worried my officers, ricked my own brain with being judgmatic. I sent in a beauty at last—a sergeant. He'd got cut off in a post with five men and had held up the Boches for two days till we got him away. He'd had a broken arm all the time—a great fellow! All the other C.O.s in the corps ran their prize tigers, too, for all they were worth. No good. It was all a waste of time. The Cross never got past the corps. An A.D.C. got it, a fellow just up from the base—Barton, Brabazon, Brasner; some name like that."

"The ribbon was—what color, sir?" Colin asked.

"Mouldy bluish, I heard," said the Major, "like Stilton."

"I think the name," Colin said, "must be Barbason."

"That's right," said the Major, suddenly interested in Colin. "You know him?"

"I thought everyone did," said Colin, the man from the centre of things, almost severely. Ignorance seems, at times, as if it must almost be affectation.

"We're pretty provincial out in these parts," said the Brigadier softly. Colin laughed, and looked at the Brigadier with new respect. Colin could take with good humor any rebuke that had wit.

"What has this beggar done?" the Major vindictively asked him.

"He doesn't exactly *do* things," said Colin. "He *wears* them. Like me. Only he goes in for blue. He has just got an M.C. That's three different blues on his coat—a whole Blue Ribbon Army. No arrangement in blue, like a Whistler, but more chaste and nattya glove fit of the blues. He's Little Boy Blue, and he blows his own horn." Where other people get cross, Colin becomes a few degrees more copiously vivacious.

The two seniors looked at each other. The dull plum ribbon of the Victoria Cross was the only one on the Brigadier's tunic. The Major had fought well in three battles, and he had not even one. The Brigadier pointed to where a bar of ruddy Oriental radiance, that no Western loom could have made, glowed on Colin's breast, next to the lustrous Russian crimson. "That's pretty," the Brigadier said.

"It should be," said Colin; "it's old, and Chinese. I won it by running away."

"Now, now—" The Brigadier, as a Colonel, had often had to curb the plunging modesty of subalterns.

"No idle boast, sir," said Colin. "Some Chinese Moltke came to G.H.Q. I was told to 'take the old euchre-player away out of this—anywhere up to the front and get him shot over.' So we set off in a car for the front. The Far East didn't like the idea. Nor did the West. But pride ruled our will. We got down four miles from the front and walked on up a road that felt naked and cocked up right into the air. Then the trouble came. There was a sort of *émeute* going on in the air. A flock of white puff-balls was straying about the blue sky, always advancing by having a new puff break out on ahead of it. Then something venomous fell into the road, six feet away, and hissed in a puddle—a thing like a bolt, or a nut, from the blue."

The Brigadier put in a note: "A chip from one of our own Archie shells."

"No doubt, sir," said Colin. "I did not examine. I fell back. So did my lovely charge. Let nobody say a Chinese cannot run. The man who could beat me that day to the car must have been an Achilles. As we sped home my companion gave thanks, and made promises: first to God, then to me for my lead. He was a faithful fellow! *Ecce signum!*" Colin touched the beautiful new ribbon on his bosom.

An orderly came in for his kit. His trench service was over. When he had gone the two elder officers stared at each other. Simple souls abounded on our front and near it. Else how could we have won?

VII

Honours, as old-fashioned whist players say, were now easy three all. But March had the pull in one way. For he was first to be back at the base, the honoriferous seaboard, washed by such tides as a man may take at the flood and be led on to fortune. "Always stick to the base in a war," a fatherly Regular on the Q. side once advised him; "don't be led away by love of excitement. Most of the good things go to the base at the end of a war, and most of the big chances come to it now." But Colin needed no man's help to see a church by daylight.

Colin's prestige at the seats of the mighty was rising. The Chinese hero had lauded, in august ears, Colin's daring and skill as a guide to the front. But the next call on his gifts was to be for a virtue more distinctively Christian. Appendicitis had suddenly smitten another illustrious guest of our army, a Spanish-American Marshal, a neutral, and therefore more to be cherished than an ally. While he lay sick unto death in an inn at Bruay, the British officer who had led him about in the time of his health, and who hated the sight of natural deaths, was telephoning all day to beg that some bedside mannerist might be sent up to carry on smoothing the pillow, *vice* himself. "The Dago only wants," he said, "a sort of Angel in the House."

Colin was offered this errand of mercy. He pondered. A long time ago he had tried for some days to learn Spanish; he might find he could talk it a little now if he tried. And that Russian story showed how from the pure and unpolluted flesh of deceased foreign officers violet and other beautiful colors may spring. Possibly red. Red, he hoped. He looked carefully into the same colored plate on the ante-room wall at which Claude had once tenderly gazed. Yes, both the Aureate Harvest (with Swords) and the Bleeding Heart (with Swords, too) had red ribbons. The sick must be visited. Colin accepted.

He was back at the sea in eight days, better thought of than ever. His choice of official wreaths to put on the coffin, his turning of phrases on those little cards that are tied to the wreaths, were felt to have aided the cause. Spanish-America, too, must have felt he had done the thing well. For in due time the Aureate Harvest came in as the other kindly fruits of the earth do for the use of her Colins.

"A somewhat ghoulish business," said Claude, when this just award was gazetted. Claude, at the time, was just back from the corps. The uncle's drafts upon Britain's man-power had grown so exacting that he was transferred to a more august job, where any diminutions he made in the population of these islands would be less violently observable. Colin said he was changed from a fatal accident into an obscure mortal disease. Anyhow, he had no use for Claude any longer; nor had Claude for him. Restored to the coast, Claude was working out a new way of fighting the Germans, a quite new engine of war. It was to have a great vogue, this new weapon. It could be used almost anywhere except in a regiment. It was called "the reorganization of the establishment" of the department or unit of which the reorganising person had charge.

Even in those early days the G.H.Q. heaven was one that had many mansions. They were of all sizes, and growing like melons—so fast that in some of them little time could be found for any work except settling where everybody should sit. Officers in command of departments, sub-departments, and sections, and sections and sub-sections of sub-departments would draft and re-draft plans for the further sub-division of each into two or more parts, according to the earliest and best biological precedents, each of the new parts to be as important as the existing hole, each, therefore, to be commanded by an officer of as high rank as the existing commander of the whole, with the natural corollary that the existing commander should get a step of promotion in order to have proper authority over these branch subordinates, all of whose labours he would have to superintend if the draft should be approved. Claude, now a Captain, was senior officer at the Sink, as his and Colin's little department was called by its irreverent neighbors. At first the Sink had been Colin; then Colin and Claude; six officers, doers of miscellaneous odd jobs, now reposed within it; there were a score of attendant orderlies, clerks, and chauffeurs. Why not cut it in two and house the two portions apart, with Claude to coordinate the exertions of both, as a G.S.O. 2 and a Major? Claude fell to work on a draft, fortified with a kind of genealogical tree to establish the lawful descent of disciplinary power over each of his expected twins, all the way down from the commander-in-chief. While he was writing the draft and drawing the tree he sometimes felt more apt to the sword than to the pen. But he stuck to the pen gamely.

VIII

Something, I think, must have made Colin suspicious. Perhaps he saw Claude writing with an abnormal fluency. Or, of course, he may just have had a pricking in his thumbs. Anyhow, like the intelligent dog whom God has taught to scent in good time his master's intention to drown him, Colin took himself off before Claude's draft was approved by the proper person. My next letter from Colin was from a ducal, delectable house in Mayfair:

"You see, they have combed me out of the trenches. Is it that I am seconded, or what is the term used by you militarists? *Tout court*, England hath need of me here. I work in this weatherproof house, the new Ministry of Liaison. No, I am not the Minister—only his eyes and ears, or a portion of these, and of his understanding. A *raison d'être* for the Ministry is being prepared. Meanwhile it offers asylum to young men of quality fleeing from Military Tribunals. Rods of the houses of signatories to Magna Charta rush in daily and cling to the horns of the altar. It is a dock-leaf planted by merciful nature where the nettles grow."

It seems that some gifted Scottish statesman, out of a job at the time, had been going up and down with a dirk, as it were, in his stocking, till all the statesmen in office wanted to find him something nice to play with, lest he should stick the knife into one of their wames. To save life in this way the Ministry of Liaison was founded, and this man of mettle was placed at its head. The Ministry was "to coordinate the functions of various administrative departments."

Colin wrote to me later:

"My reverence for this foundation grows. In this kicked ant-heap of a Europe it must be about the last abode of peace on earth and of goodwill towards men, all men.

> Nae German lays his scaith to us,
> We ne'er did ony harm.

"To us the harried Anglo-German flies, and we make him a confidential clerk or an interpreter. Here he spends happy days of Government time in writing letters to London newspapers, mostly to 'show up the Hun in our midst.' Like medieval monasteries, we cherish through a dark and bloody age the endangered graces of life. Here, in the best types of chair, sleep the brave; here knit or crochet the fair, or, within seemly limits, carry on with the brave.

> Liaison our name;
> And I will not deny,
> In respect to the same,
> What that name might imply.

"A free, gallant life. To take me to the club, to lunch, my country has a car like Tennyson's full tide that 'moving, seems asleep.' Not a speck in the sky, except passing thoughts of what Claude may be up to. Are we not members one of another, and, if aught befall him, shall I not feel?"

Under that peaceful surface considerable forces were stirring. For nearly three years our Napoleons, Alexanders, and Caesars had been collecting merited marks of distinction. The skill of collectors had almost outgrown the supply of colligible matter. The most skilful were wearing about every ribbon there was; they had gained the whole world, and unless the world were enlarged they might as well bid an early farewell to the neighing steed and shrill trump and go home. To keep their ardour from going the way of the former warmth of the moon, as well as for other good reasons, the O.B.E was invented.

The new species of laurel was sent, very justly, in bulk to the Ministry of Liaison, to show how well the sender had done in creating a Ministry so worthy of reward. But Colin, through some unfortunate slip, was not on the list of those whom the King, on first thoughts, delighted to honour. He wrote to me:

> "They must have put me down third reserve only. The stones that these builders reject! Still, I was jammed in, head of a corner, later. Three high-stomached civilians, who work with us here, rejected the bauble, with a slight wave of the hand. I commend, I can even envy them. A civilian is free; he may guard his own honour. But to us soldiers, you know, an order's an order; mine not to make reply. In I went, third wicket down. With canine loyalty I wagged an unoffended tail, and accepted my one-third of the crumbs that had fallen from the table of the proud."

You see, Colin, to my mind, had no real humbug about him, as I understand humbug. He had not the lie in his soul. He did not tell lies to himself, nor really very many to anyone else. Humbug was Claude's special subject, not his. Colin's special subject was reds, and for that plummy red of the O.B.E. ribbon there was a place ready in his heart, or about a couple of inches above it.

The danger of being saddled with some undesirable job, as a vicegerent of Claude's, had now had time to blow over, and Colin began to hear the great wars and the tented or hutted field call him again. One month of tactful importunacy in the right place and he was gone, now in the full rosy red of a G.S.O., with the red and blue brassard of G.H.Q. too—with every guarantee, in fact, of life, liberty, and the pursuit of happiness. To begin with, he travelled from London in the uncrowded staff train, after his luncheon, instead of rising at six in the morning to catch the common, crammed leave train, like the ruck of regimental officers. These, on their way back to be killed, were carried off early to cool their heels for half a day at Folkestone till the staff train should arrive at the pier and its occupants have time to dig themselves on all the best sites on the boat. "A kindly precaution," said Colin that night in the new mess at Bligny, to which he found himself carried away by the car that awaited him on the quay at Boulogne—"one of the many kindly precautions we take to set the moribund free from too much love of living."

Colin found Claude commanding at Bligny. Such a find might not seem elating. But it inspired Colin at dinner that night with a fine mischievous brightness. Taking a quick look at Claude now and then, to see how the stimulant worked, Colin rattled on about that slouching file of *condamnés*, the infantry and artillery subalterns coming back from their leave, trailing up the steep gangway at Folkestone on to the deck, with all their lumpish kits on their backs, and their eternal pipes and mud-sick uniforms, and looking awkwardly round them, shy among all the seated staff people, for some solid object to sit on.

Claude rose to the fly; his face lit up a little when Colin played on his sense of the "New Army bounders" social deficiencies. Yes, he had noticed those fellows—anyone would—when he last went on leave. "Appalling crowd of navvies!" He felt himself, for the moment, in quite warm agreement with Colin—with what he took to be Colin. Colin described to me later this tender reunion. "You should have heard him!" said Colin. "Claude is simply so much natural born prey for irony. He is like one of the little guinea-pigs that they give to the snakes at the Zoo. A plain shirker like me is almost decent beside him. I only deny Christ right out—I frankly skulk by the fire while He's getting crucified. Claude would sneer at the cut of the clothes that Christ wore on the Cross. We're the two thieves, but Claude is the one that sniggered. 'Bill Sikeses in Sam Brownes'—that's what the little rodent calls the fellows that he and I have deserted. 'Really rather awful,' he says—'these new officers. Quite five-sixths of them the sort of people you'd expect to touch their caps to you in civil life.' Imagine the lice on one of our Tommies finding fault with the Tommy's pedigree! Then he remembered that he was an acting Major, and also the only Regular there, so he quenched his familiar smile, like the ass in the play, with an austere regard of control."

I had never seen Colin angry before. Any common vexation only made him more gaily ironical. He may be cutting jokes in heaven yet when Claude lies howling.

IX

So far our two heroes had had to work, if only an hour, for all they got. The next thing to come in was, as Colin vulgarly said, a bit of a war bonus.

For months our gallant London Press had felt a painful dearth of "hero stunts" and "sob stories." Lord Jellicoe had meanly preferred the continued existence of his fleet to the proper provision of good matter for "scare heads." Heroic editors began to shake their heads over Sir Douglas Haig's want of "snap," "go," and "punch" in maintaining the daily ration of thrills for bald men in armchairs at home. Pending the proper measures for "gingering up" these commanders there might be some market still for a little emotionalising about the old stunt of "the heroes of Mons." Just to fill up the gap, why not a "whirlwind campaign" for giving a special medal or star to the few living men who had stemmed the German rush upon Paris in 1914?

It was rather a daring piece of stop-gappery. Legends of Mons were wilting already under the first rays of the higher criticism. Irreverent people at home were comparing the casualties of 1914 with the rates at which a gifted old Regular staff had since extinguished so many New Army battalions. It had leaked out that in that infant war of 1914 there had been no bombardments that would not now seem like seasons of relative rest and release from the true, high-pressure hells of the later dispensation. Heartless rationalists had begun to reflect that perhaps it was not really so much more meritorious to join the Army in times of deep peace, to get off the streets or to escape harder and grimier work, than it was to join it when joining meant embracing, almost at once, the fairest chance of an early death that had ever smiled on British recruits; that to the old Regular officers, in especial, the war had not brought the surrender of worldly good things, of beloved work or the plans and hopes of their lives, but a suddenly opened prospect of these happinesses—more pay, quicker promotion, a paradise of professional opportunity, and, after the one great toss-up with death in 1914, safety and ease in the odour of certified glory for most of those who had not lost the toss.

Still, it was a cheap "stunt." It needed no telegraphing; it could be "done in the office." And there was no risk of actions for libel and of "exemplary damages," as in "stunts" of detraction against great Generals and Admirals and Ministers and leaders of industry who failed in their several ways to act up to the needs of stunt presses. So the stunt Press took courage, and ranted and gushed, boomed and bleated and shrilled. And, the War Office having no courage to take, the Mons Star was invented when nearly all the men who might have deserved it were dead. Thus do the Colins and Claudes of this world build better than they know. They fight with their back to the walls of good bedrooms against every foe that would take a job from them, and at the close of the long day, or earlier, some unsought meed is added unto them, besides all that they seek.

Alike in gaining this guerdon, our two pretty men were not alike in the emotions raised by its possession. Colin crowed with frank joy at the scandal. Scandals, he said, were too few in these colorless times. Scandal was only a reverberation of adventure, the fuming of timid mobs when taller spirits hustled and pushed their way through. Wherever a high plume had stirred in the world, and big throws had been made and the costly unreason of romance had been properly prized, scandal had smoked up to heaven like dust from winning chariot wheels. This wisdom of life he imparted to Claude, adjuring him also not to misuse the new ribbon. Blue at one end and red at the other, and all shaded, watered, transitional and connective—why, it was clearly sent by Heaven for purposes of liaison, to hitch on the garden of gentians, forget-me-nots, heliotrope and cornflower that had first bloomed on Claude's tunic to any later sallies he might meditate in red, green, even black. Only let Claude beware of minding the foolish orders issued by pokerfed Generals, men blind to the arts, as to the order in which ribbons should be arranged on the martial bosom. Imagine Velasquez or Tintoret laying his colors on in obedience to General

Routine Orders! "No; blue to blue, red to red, each after its kind arrange we them."

Claude hated all such talk. Raffish gammon, only fit for a radical hairdresser! If the King thought it good enough to honour a man, what loyal soldier would jeer or belittle? Claude had the Old Army's fine sense of relative values well lodged in his soul. Gazetted awards were no mere measures of worth: they were worth itself, crystallised, capitalised. "Perhaps it isn't easy," he said to Colin, with solemn concessiveness, "for other people to understand what these things mean to a soldier."

Somehow Colin did not seem so confounded by this as he ought to be. Instead, he only looked at Claude as if Claude were a curious exhibit in a museum, and this wounded afresh Claude's soldierly consciousness of his own irreproachable normality. Claude felt at these times an intense and burning wish that Colin were not the son of a peer. The craving was almost physically painful, like retching. If Colin were scrubby by birth, somehow the world would seem more coherent.

But all this was an interlude. Back now to the grim realities of the War.

X

War hath her triumphs of company—floating no less deserving renown than peace's. Claude had drafted and drawn to some purpose. With help from on high the Sink had become thrice itself, not merely twice, and one of these three Sinks alone was more capacious than the great original. Unhappily, Claude had not secured command of the whole trinity. Some more majestic bird of prey, a G.H.Q. Colonel, had dropped like a stone out of the upper sky, somewhere close to the sun, and stuck his claws firmly into Claude's kill. But, subject always to this depredator, Claude received the fattest of the three distinct commands which owed him their being.

At Bligny he could not quite say what most of his six officers did. He felt surer about the chauffeurs. One of the officers he suspected of plans for salvaging solder from old bully-beef tins—a low job. He fancied another to be the minute early embryo of a demobilisation unit. A third was in unmistakable travail, writing a novel. A fourth seemed to have something to do with some of the Army's visitors from abroad. A fifth moved obscurely about in a dim borderland between letters and war; rumor said that he "smuggled the dope" into papers at Amsterdam and Madrid—"a Wolff in sheep's clothing, you know," Colin told me. The sixth was said to be sure that if only the War went on long enough we should end it decisively at last by feeding all the outer world's "movies" with the right stuff, and to this happy issue it was hoped that he was making some larger contribution than anyone saw.

Anyhow, they all kept moving. Cars were there for all, and petrol failed not. How was Claude to check the things they did or left undone? He walked, unpolluted by such inquisitive cares, among the mysteries of his command.

The place itself had amenity. It was a white, classical pre-Revolution château in a hollow between two chalk downs and beside a trout stream. G.H.Q., with its possibly critical eyes, was safely far off. No one at G.H.Q. cared about Bligny. It was a mere trousers-button, a thing to be put out of mind until it should, hang it, come off. Claude "ran his own show," and as it and everything in it were things without precedent there was no binding routine; he might fashion the show after his own image. And, in the course of nature, some honour accrued to every head of a show in the course of a year, and where would Colin be then?

Colin, also, asked himself that. No specific job had been given him yet. He had only been dumped on Bligny because there was no valid reason for dumping him anywhere else. There he lay down to sleep of a night and rose up of a morning to ring for a car and roll off to visit some proper person and bring to his mind the parable of the Importunate Woman. This time he had quite a long run in the rôle of that excellent female, and, like her, he got there at last. He prayed himself into a job—not, he felt, one that was quite what it should be. Still, it was not at Bligny; it was at G.HQ. proper, near the heart of the rose. And so Colin rolled off for good, as it seemed.

He left Claude sitting rather moodily in his "office"—the absent Comtesse de Bligny's boudoir. Claude always sat there for several hours a day. It was the bridge of his ship, and a captain looks best on the bridge. He was moody, because in these last weeks he had found that, however little a Captain may do on his bridge, he may still make some sort of a mess. Two or three times he had almost had to act in some way or other, to take an absolute plunge, adopting one course and rejecting another. That was the trouble; alternatives were like horses: he couldn't guess which was a winner. So Claude had tried hard each time to take either both courses or none, and now some captious god in the G.H.Q. heaven was not taking this so well as he might. Rumors of grand muddles at Bligny began to circulate in Olympus. "Silly little devil!" Colin was soon to hear a dangerous Brigadier-General say of Claude. "Of two evils, choose both—that's his idea."

In giving the Bligny billet to Claude the proper person concerned had not entertained extravagant hopes. Barbason, he had said at the time, wasn't a flyer; still, he was clearly fed-up with the job he had had before. And the new Bligny show was too much of a pearl to cast before any New Army swine. So the proper person had hoped as hard as he could about Claude, and then had looked the other way as hard as he could, hoping no harm would come. But Claude made a truly wonderful mess of it all. What made things worse was the way that opportunities for making messes were growing. The show itself grew, as everything grew in that tropical army. More and more officers came after Colin had gone. The work of some of these had all sorts of civilian connections. Visitors came, British and foreign, some of them famous, some subterraneanly powerful, some open-eyed and quick-witted. They went away, all over the earth, telling funny stories of croppers that Claude had come in his kingdom. Colin heard some of them. Faint but disturbing echoes of horrid laughter found their way round, even to Claude. He grew angry, first, at all this vulgar demand for the unsoldierly cleverness that fools called efficiency. But he grew anxious, too, for G.H.Q. had been weak before now in the face of the howlings of beasts; men had been thrown to the wolves. To be safe, he supposed he must get in some brainy bounder as an assistant at Bligny.

With mingled pride and embarrassment, Claude found, on reflection, how few brainy bounders he knew. Colin was much the brainiest of the few—a beast, but a clever beast. And Colin, he fancied, was only marking time just at present. Claude gallantly fought down his natural aversion, went to see Colin, and found him sparkling with health and good-humor after three hours' squash rackets. Claude set forth his proposition frankly. The trout fishing at Bligny was not surpassing, but it was good. There was some work, it was true, but no coolie work of routine to be done on the nail, as at G.H.Q. proper, and no office hours. No Generals came blowing in to inspect. All the great people from London, who ran things, came through the place sooner or later. Colin would meet them at Bligny. A clever devil like him would put it all over them, so as to do himself no end of good.

There was certainly something in that, Colin thought. He thought a good deal. The tall ship of his warlike career had lately been lying becalmed, and Heaven knew how much longer these doldrums might last. He knew that Claude had been slipping up, with good comic effect. He might slip up more, and then—yes, there were good troubled waters at Bligny; there might be a little good fishing, besides that for the trout. He temporised and prepared.

While, for some weeks, he continued to do so, things went no better at Bligny. G.H.Q. rocked with mirth at Claude's misadventures. Pedantic precisians began to ask how this entertainment helped to beat Germany. Comic paragraphs crept into London and Paris newspapers. Somebody asked a sarcastic question in Parliament. Then at last it was felt that Claude had to go. But some of the great and wise were sorry for Claude. They felt he had his points. Nosing civilians had hounded him out of his job. The like might happen to anyone. So the wise and the great said he should stay for a month more, and meanwhile be given a little something to make him feel better. Claude's D.S.O. was the most piquant thing in the next list of rewards for special gallantry and devotion. A month after this piece of justice appeared in the *Gazette*, Claude got his orders to hand over the Bligny command—yea, to hand it over to the forethoughtful Colin.

"You know why I'm unstuck," Claude said to his officers when the blow fell. "Because March is a New Army man. Some ticks in the Press have been blowing hot air about the 'Regular Army trade union,' saying it corners all the good jobs—that sort of bilge. So some New Army man has got to be jumped into something—any old job—just to have him ready to show. All very well if there weren't a war on. But how're we to win if they're always taking the heart out of the backbone of the Army?" Claude, you see, was no great commander of metaphors, either. "I know one thing," he continued: "I'm not taking any hand in this ramp."

To keep this vow not to touch pitch, Claude, strictly speaking, did not "hand over" to Colin at all. He never explained to Colin the work of the place, the lie of the land, the things that had to be seen to. A stand had to be made against all this handing over to the unworthy, so Claude felt, and went out for the day in his car. He did this every day of the week during which he was to hand over, Colin and he being both in the house. He breakfasted early so as not to see Colin. Towards the end of one of these last breakfasts some tactless officer let fall a hint that a few tips about the routine of the show might help the new commander to vanquish the Germans.

"No! let him rip," said Claude, with an air of stern virtue. "If he slips up, all the better—show that wars are not won by sham soldiers."

Colin came in at the moment, and Claude left it at that, and finished his coffee inflexibly. Already his car stood at the door; another long day's service to the petrol trade had dawned. He gone, Colin frankly commended his love of the road and of his kinsfolk. "It's time he hopped round," Colin said to the rest of the table, "and talked to those uncles." No "reserve" or "discretion" for Colin. War, he said, was quite enough of a morgue, anyhow, without that.

XI

For the next two months Colin was kept pretty busy. The chase engaged him by day. He rode a great many partridges down on the swelling chalk hills, where the air and turf were divine. A sterner task was teaching an Irish retriever how to course hares. At night, any time he could spare from French billiards and bridge, he employed in making up war arrears of light reading. Unto his officers he did as he would that his superiors should do unto him. "*Continuez, mes enfants,*" he would benignantly say to them, whatsoever they did. After a Claude, he said, the land ought to have rest for some years. As to the men, he quoted distinguished authorities on the subject of "trusting the lads." He owned that he desired his command to have the charms of an ancient and untended garden, diverse and engaging with wayward, self-sowing flowers, unmarred by the desolating militarist symmetries and uniformities of geometric "carpet" flower-beds. In short, even as Claude had trusted, Colin "ripped."

He ripped so visibly and audibly that, long before the next harvest of decorations had time to come in, he was, even in G.H.Q.s clement eyes, "ripe for booting," as Claude elatedly said. And booted he was, in his turn. But to boot Colin was like booting a large polygonal stone. It might hurt. Not for nothing had Colin practised all his social charms at Bligny for the last two months. Many visitors—editors, politicians, miscellaneous powers of light or of darkness—had gone back to England enslaved by Colin's little ways. One enamoured magnate had said before going away: "If any old fool in the Army tries to get in your way, let me know." Colin had formed a Pretorian Guard, upside down—a little band of lusty civilians ready to hustle an army.

At Colin's cry for help his trusty bravoes fell to work like firemen. They pulled long wires, spread sinister rumors, warned proper persons, and made incipient booming sounds through certain megaphones of the Press which were known to be capable of giving forth, when in full blast, the most horrific bellowings. Nervous superior officers sought to appease Colin with a long leave at home. He only used it to prime his redoubtable backers with nastier facts and more vitriolic suggestions.

You see, he was in quite a strong position: he had no regiment to be bundled back to; his unit was "General List"; so he might win, but he could not be smashed—he was dormy. He took up high ground—that the "Old Army Gang" had pushed him out by jade's tricks; that, if he had to go back to civil life now with a black mark to his name, some of those wanglers must howl for it. Then he would moderate slightly this rhadamanthine tone, and would temper justice with mercy: if they had the sense to rub out the black mark, he would not be vindictive. But he must have something done to prove to the world that he had done his duty and not been turned down in disgrace.

"Oh, give him his blasted M.C. and be done with it," somebody said at last, looking up from an office table at somebody else.

"Afraid we can't, sir," said somebody else. "This new rule, you know, sir— about keeping M.C.s for things done in action."

"Oh, damn! D.S.O., then."

"Very good, sir."

So Colin left with a new red and blue stain on his coat, and none at all on his character as a soldier. He bore no grudge against his persecutors. He was too deeply amused. What tickled him most was that he was the very last, he believed, of all the old-world D.S.O.s, the men to whom the gaud came, like the Garter, with "no damned merit about it." A rule came into force, almost immediately after, that D.S.O.s were not to be given any longer for telephoning or clerking, or any other mode of escape from the Germans; they were all to be for the mere hack-work of fighting.

"I'm like the last Groom of the Posset," said Colin, "or Clerk of the Royal Backstairs. I'm the Last British Wolf. I ought to be stuffed, when I die, and bought for the nation, and put up on the Horse Guards Parade. It has a kind of brain, you know, the dear old Regular Army; its madness has method. For three years of war all of it gorges itself with these D.S.O.s—I mean all of it that is not busy fighting. Meanwhile it invents the M.C., and settles on that also, till every unconscientious objector in France has got one or both. Then it sees all the Vandals and Goths of the New Army approaching the sanctuaries, so up goes this rule. It hath a twofold operation, like old Falstaff's drinks—keeps out any future staff crowd, and runs up the stock for the crowd who got in on the ground-floor. Look at my own little investment. Every new D.S.O. from this day forth will only prove more and more what a terrible fellow I was in the trenches."

I found that Claude, too, gave the new regulation his blessing. We met and dined, on my way back from a leave, at the splendid new G.H.Q. Officers' Club at Montreuil. Presently the benign operation of Louis Roederer 1906 slightly unlaced and unbuttoned the fine Prussian greatcoat and boots of Claude's mind.

"I seriously think," he seriously said, "that at least a large proportion of these decorations ought to be given for purely physical acts of valour. Otherwise they may lose caste, as it were, in the sight of the public. You may say to me, 'Why not just do our duty and let the public be damned?' Still, the public is there, and it's only fair to ourselves to mind, in some slight degree, what it thinks. When I got my own D.S.O. and M.C. I knew myself, and I think my friends knew, that I had earned them. But how is the public to know, or even to guess? All you can do to help it, and make the most hard-earned distinctions worth having, is to keep them connected, in people's minds, with the more obvious sorts of good work—front-line stunts and so on, the only things, I suppose, that the man in the street can understand about soldiering."

I tried to work this clear in my mind, assisted by the illuminating radiance of the H.A.C. band, the foaming grape of Eastern France, and the beautiful W.A.A.C. waitresses dressed as comicopera gitanas—all rendered curiously intoxicant by the sound of the rain on the roof and the imminence of my return to a little wet home in the earth of the salient. "So the bread of the children," I construed, thinking aloud, "ought to be sometimes—rather often—given to dogs, because somehow its being half-eaten by dogs makes it still more nice for the children."

"I don't call those brave fellows in the trenches dogs," said Claude somewhat distantly. He had a way of talking about the trenches, to us who lived in them, that made us feel it must only be in some incomplete unreal sense that we lived there at all; whereas in a spiritually higher and more valid sense he, the authentically rugged soldier, abode there himself, so that, in the sight of Heaven, his were war's thorns and ours her roses.

"Nor I," said I, "really," somewhat discomfited. I scarcely ever touch irony without getting into some mess and showing up badly.

Claude, still severe, said: "And I wouldn't exactly call the staff children."

"Nor I," said I, feeling I must have been rude.

"Then I don't see your point," Claude austerely pursued.

"No?" said I, still believing that somewhere or other I had one, but not feeling quite sure. And how could one waste in ill-humor the last night of music and light, the shine of clean glasses and white tablecloths?

XII

I next heard of Claude from Colin, in London. A portion of me had gone the way of all flesh in the salient, and Colin came to liven me up in a desolate Belgravian palace used as a hospital. Colin never grudged the War Office's time to any work of good nature. Some men took it all for themselves.

"You've not heard about Claude?" he answered my question. "Why, Claude has entered into his kingdom. Claude has done the impossible, the unthinkable—

found a new seam, a very Bonanza, where the most piercing eyes in the Army had only seen level sand. You know how all the princes and counsellors of the earth go out to visit Douglas Haig. D. H. believes they must all be longing to get sniped and bombarded, just because he likes it himself. So, in pure kindness of heart, he puts them into a car and packs them off for long days at the front. But Claude really knoweth man's heart. He has found them a way of escape—some sort of 'safety-first' apparatus, no one quite knows what—whether it's a quiet shebeen in the wilds of the Somme, where they can lie *perdu* all day till it's time to go home, or a whole dummy battlefield, well out of harm's way, with old German helmets and rifles lying about for the visitors to absorb as war souvenirs. Some brain-wave like that." Perhaps I looked puzzled. How could a mere acting Major have so happy a thought, and no Colonel or General knock him down and take it away and use it himself?

"Oh, Claude worked the flotation all right," Colin assured me. "Claude knew his chief, Blunt, was a fool—with a temper. So he unfolded his little idea at nine on a morning when old Blunt was looking his cheapest and blackest.

"'Think it a good idea, do you?' said Blunt. 'Well, I think it a damn bad idea, so you shall work it out yourself—and don't come whining to me when you've failed.' Can't you imagine him saying it?"

Yes, I knew that dodge of drowning new-born reformers like kittens in bucketfuls of detail.

"Of course," Colin said sagely, "Blunt was right in a way. If you're a downy old serpent, you don't want any infant Hercules kicking about. And yet Blunt was a fool. Claude had got him on the ground hop, just as he'd planned. For then he was able to go right on with his plan of the funk-hole. He did, and now this contraption of his is the envy of all G.H.Q. They say the proud and the great of this world are tumbling over each other to get in at the door. I hear that unless you're of royal blood, or a premier, Claude becomes quite short and dry with you. Once he had two live Kings and two Queens in the place, all at once—all the Court cards in one hand—the sort of thing people write to the *Field* about. When he comes home from the wars he'll sell his visitors' book and buy land and live on his rents. When the august go away they always give him an order apiece before stepping into the car. His Legion of Honour is said to be lost in the crush. It's thought the ribbons will soon go all round his back, like a gym belt, in a broad band. I fear it can't last, though."

"Why?" said I. "Are there not enough Kings in the world?"

"When a rather small hen," said Colin, "finds a large hunch of bread in the run, is a welter-weight cock to look on unmoved? Is Blunt, because he has been a fool once, to be a fool always? Believe me, he suffers remorse for his harshness to Claude. He will say: 'I have sinned.' He will undo the past. He will reorganise the establishment. Claude will be in the outer darkness, and Blunt will feed all the auriferous geese out of his own lily hand."

XIII

Then Colin talked about himself. He always had frankness, almost to the point of disease. He was, he said, eaten by care, because he had never yet failed to overtrump little Claude, and now little Claude had played such a whacking big trump. Colin said he had known an old woman once, in the country, who died of lying awake at night fearing the patchwork quilt of the old woman next door was getting on faster than hers. Colin avowed he was hag-ridden too, with the thought of that textile mosaic on Claude's bosom expanding swiftly and inexorably. Things, he said, must be thought out, lest he should die.

With Colin, to think was to talk; his thought worked best along a kind of paper-chase track of vivid words laid for the pursuing intellect by the forerunning tongue. So there he sat, by my bed, and made more picturesquely clear, to himself as well as to me, the thing that had struck him most in all his war travels across Northern France between the coast and our front—how, as he went east, the ribbons on passing men's breasts seemed always to die down and wither, just as the corn and the roses did, by the road, till on the wastes of thistle and poppies where the shell-fire began you would seldom see a decorated man. He thought, aloud, of that Brigade H.Q. where he had slept for a resonant fortnight his nearest point of approach to the firing line. That thrice-wounded Major there had not had a ribbon at all. None of the officers and men who had come in to that place from the actual front had had any. Color had only begun to break forth again where, on Colin's way back to the sea, he had passed a Divisional H.Q. five miles farther west—"first streaks of auroral rose breaking out," Colin said, "only—not in the east. No stars in the east; precious little dayspring to visit it—

> In front the sun climbs slow, how slowly,
> But westward, look, the land is bright!

"And then it was only at corps headquarters, twenty miles farther away from the fight, that the real thing came, all the flora of valour well out, the 'high midsummer pomp,' and so forth, fully on. The Army H.Q. again, when I got there, seemed like the tropics. I've worked it out that on the average the number of ribbons a British officer gets in this war varies in direct proportion to the square of his distance from the front. It's a 'law,' like the laws about heat and the conservation of energy."

I knew he hadn't worked it out before; he was only doing it now, led on by his own talk, that wildly intuitive advance-guard of his marching mind. And then, from ascertained facts, unquestionable laws, he went on visibly to speculate. Why should the working of any such law of nature as this—a law of the nature of man—be interrupted by any mere physical accident such as a sea? Was it not of the very nature of things that the London clays should be to the payable sands of Boulogne and the rich quartz rock of Montreuil as these soils were to the utter deserts of Ypres and La Bassee? All civilisation, the great world movement, had always been westward. Was not human experience now confirming this scientific hypothesis?—rain ribbons as it might in maritime France, it poured in Whitehall. That was the centre of things; there all the fountains of honour played most freshly and amply, unexhausted as yet with watering the thirsty fields of France.

Colin left me in rather a hurry at last. He had seen a great light. Things had come clear. He had to be off and withdraw his application for fresh employment in France. Not there, but on British soil, must Claude be outshone.

The job that Colin, under this new inspiration, sought from the proper person, and presently got, was, I fancy, that of a kind of occasional A.D.C. to be lent to august foreigners passing through town on their way to visit our front. Princes and Premiers, Marshals and Admirals, Colin saw them safe through the great wicked city. Claude might draw on them later, but Colin tapped the stream nearer its source. He had his reward. When I caught sight of him next the thin red lines across his tunic had been—well, reinforced.

This narrative has to end without any climax. If it were fiction it might, no doubt, culminate in some one superlative masterpiece of acquisition by one or other of its heroes. But life does not work in that way: we constantly have to put up with the ineffectiveness of truth. The two seemed to pass out of my sight like two racing yachts on a day of light airs. First one of them would catch a little local breeze and skim away with a lead, and then would run into some patch of dead air while the other would pick up a puff and be carried ahead, to be then becalmed in his turn. I heard they looked most beautiful, with three full rows of ribbons apiece, like commanders-in-chief, and that people turned round to look at them in the street, marvelling that men so young should have had time for so much valour.

Introduction to the Trenches
(from *Death of a Hero*)

Richard Aldington

Winterbourne had an easy initiation into trench warfare. The cold was so intense that the troops on both sides were chiefly occupied in having pneumonia and trying to keep warm. He found himself in a quiet sector, which had been fought over by the French in 1914 and had been the scene of a fierce and prolonged battle in 1915, after the British took over the sector. During 1916, when the main fighting shifted to the Somme, the sector had settled down to ordinary trench warfare. Trench raids had not then been much developed, but constant local attacks were made on battalion or brigade fronts. A little later the sector atoned for this calm.

To Winterbourne, as to so many others, the time element was of extreme importance during the war years. The hour goddesses who had danced along so gaily before, and have fled from us since with such mocking swiftness, then paced by in a slow, monotonous file as if intolerably burdened. People at a distance thought of the fighting as heroic and exciting, in terms of cheering bayonet charges or little knots of determined men holding out to the last Lewis gun. That is rather like counting life by its champagne suppers and forgetting all the rest. The qualities needed were determination and endurance, inhuman endurance. It would be much more practical to fight modern wars with mechanical robots than with men. But then, men are cheaper, although in a long war the initial outlay on the robots might be compensated by the fact that the quality of men deteriorates while they cost more in upkeep. But that is a question for the War Departments. From the point of view of efficiency in war, the trouble is that men have feelings; to attain the perfect soldier we must eliminate feelings. To the human robots of the last war, time seemed indefinitely and most unpleasantly prolonged. The dimension then measured as a "day in its apparent duration approached what we now call a month." And the long series of violent stalemates on the Western front made any decision seem impossible. In 1916 it looked as if no line could be broken, because so long as enough new troops were hurried to threatened points the attacker was bound to be held up; and the supplies of new troops seemed endless. It became a matter of which side could wear down the other's manpower and moral endurance. So there also was the interminable. The only alternatives seemed an indefinite prolongation of misery, or death, or mutilation, or collapse of some sort. Even a wound was a doubtful blessing, a mere holiday, for wounded men had to be returned again and again to the line.

For the first six or eight "weeks," Winterbourne, like all his companions, was occupied in fighting the cold. The Pioneer company to which he was attached were digging a sap out into No Man's Land and making trench-mortar emplacements just behind the front line. They worked on these most of the night and slept during the day. But the ground was frozen so hard that progress was tediously slow.

The company were billeted in the ruins of a village behind the reserve trenches, over a mile from the front line. The landscape was flat, almost treeless except for a few shell-blasted stumps, and covered with snow frozen hard. Every building in sight had been smashed, in many cases almost level with the ground. It was a mining country, with great queer hills of slag and strange pit-head machinery in steel, reduced by shell-fire to huge masses of twisted rusting metal. They were in a salient, with the half-destroyed, evacuated town of M— in the elbow-crook on the extreme right. The village churchyard was filled with graves of French soldiers; there were graves inside any of the houses which had no cellars, and graves flourished over the bare landscape. In all directions were crosses, little wooden crosses, in ones and twos and threes, emerging blackly from the frozen snow. Some were already askew; one just outside the ruined village had been snapped short by a shellburst. The dead men's caps, mouldering and falling to pieces, were hooked on to the tops of the crosses—the grey German round cap, the French blue and red kepi, the English khaki. There were also two large British cemeteries in sight—rectangular plantations of wooden crosses. It was like living in the graveyard of the world—dead trees, dead houses, dead mines, dead villages, and dead men. Only the long steel guns and the transport wagons seemed alive. There were no civilians, but one of the mines was still worked about a mile and a half further from the line.

Behind Winterbourne's billet were hidden two large howitzers. They fired with a reverberating crash which shook the ruined houses, and the diminishing scream of the departing shells was strangely melancholy in the frost-silent air. The Germans rarely returned the fire—they were saving their ammunition. Occasionally a shell screamed over and crashed sharply among the ruins; the huge detonation spouted up black earth or rattling bricks and tiles. Fragments of the burst shell-case hummed through the air. But it was the cold that mattered. In his efforts to defend himself against it, Winterbourne, like the other men, was strangely and wonderfully garbed. Round his belly, next the skin, he wore a flannel belt. Over that, a thick woollen vest, grey flannel shirt, knitted cardigan jacket, long woollen underpants, and thick socks. Over that, service jacket, trousers, puttees, and boots; then a sheepskin coat, two mufflers round his neck, two pairs of woollen gloves, and over them trench gloves. In addition came an equipment-box respirator on the chest, steel helmet, rifle, and bayonet. The only clothes he took off at night were his boots. With his legs wrapped in a greatcoat, his body in a grey blanket, a ground-sheet underneath, pack for pillow, and a dixie of hot tea and rum inside him, he just got warm enough to fall asleep when very tired.

Through the broken roof of his billet Winterbourne could see the frosty glitter of the stars and the white rime. In the morning, when he awoke, he found his breath frozen on the blanket. In the line his short moustache formed icicles. The boots beside him froze hard, and it was agony to struggle into them. The bread in his haversack froze greyly; and the taste of frozen bread is horrid. Little spikes of ice formed in the cheese. The tins of jam froze and had to be thawed before they could be eaten. The bully beef froze in the tins and came out like chunks of reddish ice. Washing was a torment. They had three tubs of water between about forty of them each day. With this they shaved and washed—about ten or fifteen to a tub. Since Winterbourne was a late-comer to the battalion, he had to wait until the others had finished. The water was cold and utterly filthy. He plunged his dirty hands into it with disgust, and shut his eyes when he washed his face. This humiliation, too, he accepted.

He always remembered his first night in the line. They paraded in the ruined village street about four o'clock. The air seemed crackling with frost, and the now familiar bloody smear of red sunset was dying away in the south-west. The men were muffled up to the ears, and looked grotesquely bulky in their sheep or goat skin coats, with the hump of box respirators on their chests. Most of them had sacking covers on their steel helmets to prevent reflection, and sacks tied round their legs for warmth. The muffled officer came shivering from his billet as the men stamped their feet on the hard, frost-bound road. They drew picks and shovels from a dump, and filed silently through the ruined street behind the officer. Their bayonets were silhouetted against the cold sky. The man in front of Winterbourne turned abruptly left into a ruined house. Winterbourne followed, descended four rough steps, and found himself in a trench. A notice said:

HINTON ALLEY
To the Front Line.

To be out of the piercing cold wind in the shelter of walls of earth was an immediate relief. Overhead shone the beautiful ironic stars.

A field-gun behind them started to crash out shells. Winterbourne listened to the long-drawn wail as they sped away and finally crashed faintly in the distance. He followed the man ahead of him blindly. Word kept coming down: "Hole here; look out." "Wire overhead." "Mind your head—bridge." He passed the messages on, after tripping in the holes, catching his bayonet in the field telephone wires, and knocking his helmet on the low bridge. They passed the reserve line, then the support, with the motionless sentries on the fire-step, and the peculiar smell of burnt wood and foul air coming from the dug-outs. A minute later came the sharp message: "Stop talking; don't clink your shovels." They were now only a few hundred yards from the German front line. A few guns were firing in a desultory way. A shell crashed outside the parapet about five yards from Winterbourne's head. It was only a whizz-bang, but to his unpracticed ears it sounded like a heavy. The shells came in fours—crump, Crump, CRUMP, CRRUMP; the Boche was bracketing. Every minute or so came a sharp ping!—fixed rifles firing at a latrine or an unprotected piece of trench. The duckboards were more broken. Winterbourne stumbled over an unexploded shell, then had to clamber over a heap of earth where the side of the trench had been smashed in a few minutes earlier. The trench made another sharp turn, and he saw the bayonet and helmet of a sentry silhouetted against the sky. They were in the front line.

They turned sharp left. To their right were the fire-steps, with a sentry about every fifty yards. In between came traverses and dug-out entrances, with their rolled-up blanket gas-curtains. Winterbourne peered down them—there was a faint glow of light, a distant mutter of talk, and a heavy stench of wood and foul air. The man in front stopped and turned to Winterbourne:

"Halt! Password tonight's 'Lantern.'" Winterbourne halted, and passed the message on. They waited. He was standing almost immediately behind a sentry, and got on the fire-step beside the man to take his first look at No Man's Land.

"'Oo are you?" asked the sentry in low tones.

"Pioneers."

"Got a bit o' candle to give us, chum?"

"Awfully sorry, chum, I haven't."

"Them muckin' R.E.s gets 'em all."

"I've got a packet of chocolate, if you'd like it."

"Ah! Thanks, chum."

The sentry broke a bit of chocolate and began to munch.

"Muckin' cold up here, it is. Me feet's fair froze. Muckin' dreary, too. I can 'ear ole Fritz coughin' over there in 'is listenin' post—don't 'arf sound 'ollow. Listen."

Winterbourne listened, and heard a dull, hollow sound of coughing.

"Fritz's sentry," whispered the man. "Pore ole—Needs some liquorice."

"Move on," came the word from the man in front. Winterbourne jumped down from the fire-step and passed on the word.

"Good-night, chum," said the sentry.

"Good-night, chum."

Winterbourne was put on the party digging the sap out into No Man's Land. The officer stopped him as he was entering the sap.

"You're one of the new draft, aren't you?"

"Yes, sir."

"Wait a minute."

"Very good, sir."

The other men filed into the sap. The officer spoke in low tones:

"You can take sentry for the first hour. Come along, and don't stand up."

The young crescent moon had risen and poured down cold, faint light. Every now and then a Verey light was fired from the German or English lines, brilliantly illuminating the desolate landscape of torn, irregular wire and jagged shell-holes. They climbed over the parapet and crawled over the broken ground past the end of the sap. The officer made for a shell-hole just inside the English wire, and Winterbourne followed him.

"Lie here," whispered the officer, "and keep a sharp lookout for German patrols. Fire if you see them and give the alarm. There's a patrol of our own out on the right, so make sure before you fire. There's a couple of bombs somewhere in the shell-hole. You'll be relieved in an hour."

"Very good, sir."

The officer crawled away, and Winterbourne remained alone in No Man's Land, about twenty-five yards in front of the British line. He could hear the soft, dull thuds of picks and shovels from the men working the sap, and a very faint murmur as they talked in whispers. A Verey light hissed up from the English lines, and he strained his eyes for the possible enemy patrol. In the brief light he saw nothing but the irregular masses of German wire, the broken line of their parapet, shell-holes and debris, and the large stump of a dead tree. Just as the bright magnesium turned in its luminous parabola, a hidden machine-gun, not thirty yards from Winterbourne, went off with a loud crackle of bullets like the engine of a motor-bicycle. He started, and nearly pulled the trigger of his rifle. Then silence. A British sentry coughed with a deep hacking sound; then from the distance came the hollow coughing of a German sentry. Eerie sounds in the pallid moonlight. "Ping!" went a sniper's rifle. It was horribly cold. Winterbourne was shivering, partly from cold, partly from excitement.

Interminable minutes passed. He grew colder and colder. Occasionally a few shells from one side or the other went wailing overhead and crashed somewhere in the back areas. About four hundred yards away to his left began a series of loud, shattering detonations. He strained his eyes, and could just see the flash of the explosion and the dark column of smoke and debris. These were the German trench-mortars, the dreaded "minnies," although he did not know it.

Nothing different happened until about three-quarters of an hour had passed. Winterbourne got colder and colder, felt he had been out there at least three hours, and thought he must have been forgotten. He shivered with cold. Suddenly he thought he saw something move to his right, just outside the wire. He gazed intently, all tense and alert. Yes, a dark something was moving. It stopped, and seemed to vanish. Then near it another dark figure moved, and then a third. It was a patrol, making for the gap in the wire in front of Winterbourne. Were they Germans or British? He pointed his rifle towards them, got the bombs ready, and waited. They came nearer and nearer. Just before they got to the wire, Winterbourne challenged in a loud whisper:

"Halt, who are you?"

All three figures instantly disappeared.

"Halt, who are you?"

"Friend," came a low answer.

"Give the word or I fire."

"Lantern."

"All right."

One of the men crawled through the wire to Winterbourne, followed by the other two. They wore balaclava helmets and carried revolvers.

"Are you the patrol?" whispered Winterbourne.

"Who the muckin' 'ell d'you think we are? Father Christmas? What are you doin' out here?"

"Pioneers digging a sap about fifteen yards behind."

"Are you Pioneers?"

"Yes."

"Got a bit o' candle, chum?"

"Sorry, I haven't; we don't get them issued."

The patrol crawled off, and Winterbourne heard an alarmed challenge from the men working in the sap and the word "Lantern." A Verey light went up from the German lines just as the patrol were crawling over the parapet. A German sentry fired his rifle and a machine-gun started up. The patrol dropped hastily into the trench. The machine-gun bullets whistled cruelly past Winterbourne's head—zwiss, zwiss, zwiss. He crouched down in the hole. Zwiss, zwiss, zwiss. Then silence. He lifted his head and continued to watch. For two or three minutes there was complete silence. The men in the sap seemed to have knocked off work, and made no sound. Winterbourne listened intently. No sound. It was the most ghostly, desolate, deathly silence he had ever experienced. He had never imagined that death could be so deathly. The feeling of annihilation, of the end of existence, of a dead planet of the dead arrested in a dead time and space, penetrated his flesh along with the cold. He shuddered. So frozen, so desolate, so dead a world—everything smashed and lying inertly broken. Then "crack ping!" went a sniper's rifle, and a battery of field-guns opened with salvoes about half a mile to his right. The machine-guns began again. The noise was a relief after that ghastly dead silence.

At last the N.C.O. came crawling out from the sap with another man to relieve him. A Verey light shot up from the German line in their direction just as the two men reached him. All three crouched motionless as the accurate German machine-gun fire swept the British trench parapet. Zwiss, zwiss, zwiss, the flights of bullets went over them. Winterbourne saw a strand of wire just in front of him suddenly flip up in the air where a low bullet had struck it.

Quite near enough—not six inches above his head.

They crawled back to the sap, and Winterbourne tumbled in. He found himself face to face with the platoon officer, Lieutenant Evans. Winterbourne was shivering uncontrollably; he felt utterly chilled. His whole body was numb, his hands stiff, his legs one ache of cold from the knees down. He realized the cogency of the Adjutant's farewell hint about looking after feet, and decided to drop his indifference to goose grease and neat's-foot oil.

"Cold?" asked the officer.

"It's bitterly cold out there, sir," said Winterbourne through chattering teeth.

"Here, take a drink of this"; and Evans held out a small flask. Winterbourne took the flask in his cold-shaken hand. It chinked roughly against his teeth as he took a gulp of the terrifically potent army rum. The strong liquor half choked him, burned his throat, and made his eyes water. Almost immediately he felt the deadly chill beginning to lessen. But he still shivered.

"Good Lord, man! You're frozen," said Evans. "I thought it was colder than ever tonight. It's no weather for lying in No Man's Land. Corporal, you'll have to change that sentry every half hour—an hour's too long in this frost."

"Very good, sir."

"Have some more rum?" asked Evans.

"No, thanks, sir," replied Winterbourne; "I'm quite all right now. I can warm up with some digging."

"No; get your rifle and come with me."

Evans started off briskly down the trench to visit the other working parties. About a hundred yards from the sap he climbed out of the trench over the parades; Winterbourne scrambled after, more impeded by his chilled limbs, his rifle, and heavier equipment. Evans gave him a hand up. They walked about another hundred yards over the top, and then reached the place where several parties were digging trench-mortar emplacements. The N.C.O. saw them coming, and climbed out of one of the holes to meet them.

"Getting on all right, sergeant?"

"Ground's very hard, sir."

"I know, but—"

Zwiss, zwiss, zwiss, zwiss, came a rush of bullets, following the rapid tat-tat-tat-tat-tat-tat-tat of a machine-gun. The sergeant ducked double. Evans remained calmly standing. Seeing his unconcern, Winterbourne also remained upright.

"I know the ground's hard," said Evans, "but those emplacements are urgently needed. Headquarters were at us again today about them. I'll see how you're getting on."

The sergeant hastily scuttled into one of the deep emplacements, followed in a more leisurely way by the officer. Winterbourne remained standing on top, and listened to Evans as he urged the men to get a move on. Tat-tat-tat-tat-tat. Zwiss, zwiss, zwiss, very close this time. Winterbourne felt a slight creep in his spine; but since Evans had not moved before, he decided that the right thing was to stand still. Evans visited each of the four emplacements, and then made straight for the front line. He paused at the parados.

"We're pretty close to the Boche front line here. He's got a machine-gun post about a hundred and fifty yards over there."

Tat-tat-tat-tat-tat-tat. Zwiss, zwiss, zwiss.

"Look! Over there."

Winterbourne just caught a glimpse of the quick flashes.

"Damn!" said Evans. "I forgot to bring my prismatic compass tonight. We might have taken a bearing on them, and got the artillery to turf them out."

He jumped carelessly into the trench, and Winterbourne dutifully followed. About fifty yards further on he stopped.

"I see from your paybook that you're an artist in civil life."

"Yes, sir."

"Paint pictures and draw?"

"Yes, sir."

"Why don't you apply for a draughtsman's job at Division? They need them."

"Well, sir, I don't particularly covet a hero's grave, but I feel very strongly I ought to take my chance in the line along with the rest."

"Ah! Of course. Are you a pretty good walker?"

"I used to go on walking tours in peace time, sir."

"Well, there's an order that every officer is to have a runner. Would you like the job of platoon runner? You'd have to accompany me, and you're supposed to take my last dying orders! You'd have to learn the lie of the trenches, so as to act as guide, take my orders to N.C.O.s, know enough about what's going on to help them if I'm knocked out, and carry messages. It's perhaps a bit more dangerous than the ordinary work, and you may have to turn out at odd hours, but it'll get you off a certain amount of digging."

"I'd like it very much, sir."

"All right; I'll speak to the Major about it."

"It's very good of you, sir."

"Can you find your way back to the sap? It's about two hundred yards along this trench."

"I'm sure I can, sir."

"All right. Go back and report to the corporal, and carry on."

"Very good, sir."

"You haven't forgotten the password?"

"No, sir—'Lantern.'"

About thirty yards along the trench there was a rattle of equipment, and Winterbourne found a bayonet about two feet from his chest. It was a gas sentry outside a company H.Q. dug-out.

"Halt! Who are yer?"

"Lantern."

The sentry languidly lowered his rifle.

"Muckin' cold tonight, mate."

"Bloody cold."

"What are you—Bedfords or Essex?"

"No; Pioneers."

"Got a bit of candle to give us, mate? It's muckin' dark in them dug-outs."

"Very sorry, chum, I haven't."

Rather trying, this constant demand for candle-ends from the Pioneers, who were popularly supposed by the infantry to receive immense "issues" of candles. But without candles the dug-outs were merely black holes, even in the daytime, if they were of any depth. They were deep on this front, since the line was a captured German trench reorganised. Hence the dug-outs faced the enemy instead of being turned away from them.

"Oh, all right; good-night."

"Good-night."

Winterbourne returned to the sap, and did two more half-hour turns as sentry, and for the rest of the time picked or shovelled the hard clods of earth into sandbags. The sandbags were then carried back to the front line and piled there to raise the parapet. It was a slow business. The sap itself was camouflaged to avoid observation. Winterbourne hadn't the slightest idea what its object was. He was very weary and sleepy when they finally knocked off work about one in the morning. An eight-hour shift, exclusive of time taken in getting to and from the work. The men filed wearily along the trench, rifles slung on the left shoulder, picks and shovels carried on the right. Winterbourne stumbled along, half asleep with the cold and the fatigue of unaccustomed labour. He felt he didn't mind how dangerous it was—if it was dangerous—to be a runner, provided he got some change from the dreariness of digging and filling and carrying sandbags.

After they passed the support line, the hitherto silent men began to talk incessantly. At reserve they got permission to smoke. Each grabbed in his pockets for a fag, and lighted it as he stumbled along the uneven duck-boards. After what seemed an endless journey to Winterbourne, they reached the four steps, climbed up, and emerged into the now familiar ruined street. It was silent and rather ghostly in the very pale light of the new moon. They dumped their picks and shovels, went to the cook to draw their ration of hot tea, which was served from a large black dixie and tasted unpleasantly of stew. They filed past the officer, who gave each of them a rum ration.

Winterbourne drank some of the tea in his billet, then took off his boots, wrapped himself up, and drank the rest. Some real warmth flushed into his chilled body. He was angry with himself for being so tired, after a cushy night on a cushy front. He wondered what Elizabeth and Fanny would say if they saw his animal gratitude for tea and rum. Fanny? Elizabeth? They had receded far from him; not so far as all the other people he knew, who had receded to several light years, but very far. "Elizabeth" and "Fanny" were now memories and names at the foot of sympathetic, but rather remote letters. Drowsiness came rapidly upon him, and he fell asleep as he was thinking of the curious zwiss, zwiss made by machine-gun bullets passing overhead. He did not hear the two howitzers when they fired a dozen rounds before dawn.

Defeat

(from *Six Short Plays*)

John Galsworthy

She had been standing there on the pavement a quarter of an hour or so after her shilling's worth of concert. Women of her profession are not supposed to have redeeming points, especially when—like May Belinski, as she now preferred to dub herself they are German; but this woman certainly had music in her soul. She often gave herself these "music baths" when the Promenade Concerts were on, and had just spent half her total wealth in listening to some Mozart and a Beethoven symphony.

She was feeling almost elated, full of divine sound, and of the summer moonlight that was filling the whole dark town. Women "of a certain type" have, at all events, emotions—and what a comfort that is, even to themselves! To stand just there had become rather a habit of hers. One could seem to be waiting for somebody coming out of the concert, not yet over—which, of course, was precisely what she *was* doing. One need not for ever be stealthily glancing and perpetually moving on in that peculiar way, which, while it satisfied the police and Mrs. Grundy, must not quite deceive others as to her business in life. She had only "been at it" long enough to have acquired a nervous dread of almost everything—not long enough to have passed through that dread to callousness. Some women take so much longer than others. And even for a woman "of a certain type" her position was exceptionally nerve-racking in war-time, going as she did by a false name. Indeed, in all England there could hardly be a greater pariah than was this German woman of the night.

She idled outside a book-shop humming a little, pretending to read the titles of the books by moonlight, taking off and putting on one of her stained yellow gloves. Now and again she would move up as far as the posters outside the hall, scrutinizing them as if interested in the future, then stroll back again. In her worn and discreet dark dress, and her small hat, she had nothing about her to rouse suspicion, unless it were the trail of violet powder she left on the moonlight.

For the moonlight this evening was almost solid, seeming with its cool still vibration to replace the very air; in it the war-time precautions against light seemed fantastic, like shading candles in a room still full of daylight. What lights there were had the effect of strokes and stipples of dim color laid by a painter's brush on a background of ghostly whitish-blue. The dreamlike quality of the town was perhaps enhanced for her eyes by the veil she was wearing in day time no longer white. As the music died out of her, elation also ebbed. Somebody had passed her, speaking German, and she was overwhelmed by a rush of nostalgia. On this moonlit night by the banks of the Rhine—whence she came—the orchards would be heavy with apples; there would be murmurs and sweet scents; the old castle would stand out clear, high over the woods and the chalky-white river. There would be singing far away, and the churning of a distant steamer's screw; and perhaps on the water a log raft still drifting down in the blue light. There would be German voices talking. And suddenly tears oozed up in her eyes, and crept down through the powder on her cheeks. She raised her veil and dabbed at her face with a little, not-too-clean handkerchief, screwed up in her yellow-gloved hand. But the more she dabbed the more those treacherous tears ran. Then she became aware that a tall young man in khaki was also standing before the shop-window, not looking at the titles of the books, but eyeing her askance. His face was fresh and open, with a sort of kindly eagerness in his blue eyes. Mechanically she drooped her wet lashes, raised them obliquely, drooped them again, and uttered a little sob…

This young man, captain in a certain regiment, and discharged from hospital at six o'clock that evening, had entered Queen's Hall at half-past seven. Still rather brittle and sore from his wound, he had treated himself to a seat in the grand circle, and there had sat, very still and dreamy, the whole concert through. It had been like eating after a long fast—something of the sensation Polar explorers must experience when they return to their first full meal. For he was of the New Army, and before the war had actually believed in music, art, and all that sort of thing. With a month's leave before him, he could afford to feel that life was extraordinarily joyful, his own experiences particularly wonderful; and, coming out into the moonlight, he had taken what can only be described as a great gulp of it, for he was a young man with a sense of beauty. When one has been long in the trenches, lain out wounded in a shell-hole twenty-four hours, and spent three months in hospital, beauty has such an edge of novelty, such a sharp sweetness, that it almost gives pain. And London at night is very beautiful. He strolled slowly towards the Circus, still drawing the moonlight deep into his lungs, his cap tilted up a little on his forehead in that moment of unmilitary abandonment; and whether he stopped before the book-shop window because the girl's figure was in some sort a part of beauty, or because he saw that she was crying, he could not have made clear to anyone.

Then something—perhaps the scent of powder, perhaps the yellow glove, or the oblique flutter of the eyelids—told him that he was making what he would have called "a blooming error," unless he wished for company, which had not been in his thoughts. But her sob affected him, and he said:

"What's the matter?"

Again her eyelids fluttered sideways, and she stammered:

"Not'ing. The beautiful evening—that's why!"

That a woman of what he now clearly saw to be a "certain type" should perceive what he himself had just been perceiving, struck him forcibly, and he said:

"Cheer up."

She looked up again swiftly. "All right! But you are not lonelee like me."

For one of that sort she looked somehow honest; her tear-streaked face was rather pretty, and he murmured:

"Well, let's walk a bit and talk it over."

They turned the corner and walked east, along streets empty and beautiful, with their dulled orange-glowing lamps, and here and there the glint of some blue or violet light. He found it queer and rather exciting—for an adventure of just this kind he had never had. And he said doubtfully:

"How did you get into this? Isn't it an awfully hopeless life?"

"Ye-es, it ees—" her voice had a queer soft emphasis. "You are limping—have you been wounded? "

"Just out of hospital."

"The horrible war—all the misery is because of the war. When will it end?"

He looked at her, and said:

"I say—what nationality are you?"

"Rooshian."

"Really! I never met a Russian girl."

He was conscious that she looked at him, then very quickly down. And he said suddenly:

"Is it as bad as they make out?"

She slipped her yellow-gloved hand through his arm.

"Not when I haf anyone as nice as you; I never haf yet, though;" she smiled—and her smile was like her speech, slow, confiding. "You stopped because I was sad; others stop because I am gay. I am not fond of men at all. When you know, you are not fond of them."

"Well! You hardly know them at their best, do you? You should see them at the front. By George! they're simply splendid—officers and men, every blessed soul. There's never been anything like it just one long bit of jolly fine self-sacrifice; it's perfectly amazing."

Turning her blue-grey eyes on him, she answered:

"I expect you are not the last at that. You see in them what you haf in yourself, I think."

"Oh! not a bit—you're quite out. I assure you when we made the attack where I got wounded there wasn't a single man in my regiment who wasn't an absolute hero. The way they went in never thinking of themselves—it was simply superb!"

Her teeth came down on her lower lip, and she answered in a queer voice: "It is the same too, perhaps, with—the enemy."

"Oh, yes, I know that."

"Ah! You are not a mean man. How I hate mean men!"

"Oh! they're not mean really—they simply don't understand."

"Oh! you are a baby—a good baby, aren't you?"

He did not quite like being called a baby, and frowned; but was at once touched by the disconcertion in her powdered face. How quickly she was scared!

She said clingingly:

"But I li-ike you for it. It is so good to find a ni-ice man."

This was worse, and he said abruptly:

"About being lonely? Haven't you any Russian friends?"

"Rooshian! No! The town is so beeg! Haf you been in the concert?"

"Yes."

"I, too—I love music."

"I suppose all Russians do."

She looked up at his face again, and seemed to struggle to keep silent; then she said quietly:

"I go there always when I haf the money."

"What! Are you so on the rocks?"

"Well, I haf just one shilling now." And she laughed.

The sound of that little laugh upset him—she had a way of making him feel sorry for her every time she spoke.

They had come by now to a narrow square, east of Gower Street.

"This is where I lif," she said. "Come in!"

He had one long moment of violent hesitation, then yielded to the soft tugging of her hand, and followed. The passage-hall was dimly lighted, and they went upstairs into a front room, where the curtains were drawn, and the gas turned very low. Opposite the window were other curtains dividing off the rest of the apartment. As soon as the door was shut she put up her face and kissed him—evidently formula. What a room! Its green and beetroot coloring and the prevalence of cheap plush disagreeably affected him. Everything in it had that callous look of rooms which seem to be saying to their occupants: "You're here today and you'll be gone tomorrow." Everything except one little plant, in a common pot, of maidenhair fern, fresh and green, looking as if it had been watered within the hour; in this room it had just the same unexpected touchingness that peeped out of the girl's matter-of-fact cynicism.

Taking off her hat, she went towards the gas, but he said quickly:

"No, don't turn it up; let's have the window open and the moonlight in." He had a sudden dread of seeing anything plainly—it was stuffy, too, and, pulling the curtains apart, he threw up the window. The girl had come obediently from the hearth, and sat down opposite him, leaning her arm on the window-sill and her chin on her hand. The moonlight caught her cheek where she had just renewed the powder, and her fair crinkly hair; it caught the plush of the furniture, and his own khaki, giving them all a touch of unreality.

"What's your name?" he said.

"May. Well, I call myself that. It's no good askin' yours."

"You're a distrustful little soul, aren't you?"

"I haf reason to be, don't you think?"

"Yes, I suppose you're bound to think us all brutes?"

"Well, I haf a lot of reasons to be afraid all my time. I am dreadfully nervous now; I am not trusting anybody. I suppose you haf been killing lots of Germans?"

He laughed.

"We never know, unless it happens to be hand to hand. I haven't come in for that yet."

"But you would be very glad if you had killed some?"

"Glad? I don't think so. We're all in the same boat so far as that's concerned. We're not glad to kill each other. We do our job—that's all."

"Oh! it is frightful. I expect I haf my broders killed."

"Don't you get any news ever?"

"News! No indeed, no news of anybody in my country. I might not haf a country; all that I ever knew is gone—fader, moder, sisters, broders, all—never any more I shall see them, I suppose, now. The war it breaks and breaks—it breaks hearts." Her little teeth fastened again on her lower lip in that sort of pretty snarl. "Do you know what I was thinkin' when you came up? I was thinkin' of my native town and the river there in the moonlight. If I could see it again I would be glad. Were you ever homeseek?"

"Yes, I have been—in the trenches; but one's ashamed, with all the others."

"Ah! ye-es!" It came from her with a hiss. "Ye-es! You are all comrades there. What is it like for me here, do you think, where everybody hates and despises me, and would catch me, and put me in prison, perhaps?"

He could see her breast heaving with a quick breathing painful to listen to. He leaned forward, patting her knee, and murmuring: "So sorry."

She said in a smothered voice:

"You are the first who has been kind to me for so long! I will tell you the truth—I am not Rooshian at all—I am German."

Hearing that half-choked confession, his thought was: "Does she really think we fight against women?" And he said:

"My dear girl, who cares?"

Her eyes seemed to search right into him. She said slowly:

"Another man said that to me. But he was thinkin' of other things. You are a veree ni-ice boy. I am so glad I met you. You see the good in people, don't you? That is the first thing in the world—because there is really not much good in people, you know."

He said, smiling:

"You're a dreadful little cynic!" Then thought: "Well—of course!"

"Cyneec? How long do you think I would live if I was not a cyneec? I should drown myself tomorrow. Perhaps there are good people, but, you see, I don't know them."

"I know lots."

She leaned forward eagerly.

"Well now—see, ni-ice boy-you haf never been in a hole, haf you?"

"I suppose not a real hole."

"No, I should think not, with your face. Well, suppose I am still a good girl, as I was once, you know, and you took me to some of your good people, and said:

'Here is a little German girl that has no work, and no money, and no friends.' Your good people they will say: 'Oh! how sad! A German girl!' and they will go and wash their hands."

Silence fell on him. He saw his mother, his sister, others—good people, he would swear! And yet—! He heard their voices, frank and clear; and they seemed to be talking of the Germans. If only she were not German as well!

"You see!" he heard her say, and could only mutter:

"I'm sure there are people."

"No. They would not take a German, even if she was good. Besides, I don't want to be good any more—I am not a humbug—I have learned to be bad. Aren't you going to kees me, ni-ice boy?"

She put her face close to his. Her eyes troubled him, but he drew back. He thought she would be offended or persistent, but she was neither; just looked at him fixedly with a curious inquiring stare; and he leaned against the window, deeply disturbed. It was as if all clear and simple enthusiasm had been suddenly knocked endways; as if a certain splendour of life that he had felt and seen of late had been dipped in a cloud. Out there at the front, over here in hospital, life had been seeming so—as it were—heroic; and yet it held such mean and murky depths as well! The voices of his men, whom he had come to love like brothers, crude burring voices, cheery in trouble, making nothing of it; the voices of doctors and nurses, patient, quiet, reassuring voices; even his own voice, infected by it all, kept sounding in his ears. All wonderful somehow, and simple; and nothing mean about it anywhere! And now so suddenly to have lighted upon this, and all that was behind it this scared girl, this base, dark, thoughtless use of her! And the thought came to him: "I suppose my fellows wouldn't think twice about taking her on! Why, I'm not even certain of myself, if she insists!" And he turned his face and stared out at the moonlight. He heard her voice:

"Eesn't it light? No air-raid tonight. When the Zepps burned—what a horrible death! And all the people cheered—it is natural. Do you hate us veree much?"

He turned round and said sharply:

"Hate? I don't know."

"I don't hate even the English—I despise them. I despise my people too—perhaps more, because they began this war. Oh, yes! I know that. I despise all the peoples. Why haf they made the world so miserable—why haf they killed all our lives—hundreds and thousands and millions of lives—all for not'ing? They haf made a bad world—everybody hating, and looking for the worst everywhere. They haf made me bad, I know. I believe no more in anything. What is there to believe in? Is there a God? No! Once I was teaching little English children their prayers—isn't that funnee? I was reading to them about Christ and love. I believed all those things. Now I believe not'ing at all—no one who is not a fool or a liar can believe. I would like to work in a hospital; I would like to go and help poor boys like you. Because I am a German they would throw me out a hundred times, even if I was good. It is the same in Germany and France and Russia—everywhere. But do you think I will believe in love and Christ and a God and all that?—not I! I think we are animals—that's all! Oh! yes—you fancy it is because my life has spoiled me. It is not that at all—that's not the worst thing in life. These men are not ni-ice, like you, but it's their nature, and," she laughed, "they help me to live, which is something for me, anyway. No, it is the men who think themselves great and good, and make the war with their talk and their hate, killing us all—killing all the boys like you, and keeping poor people in prison, and telling us to go on hating; and all those dreadful cold-blooded creatures who write in the papers—the same in my country, just the same; it is because of all them that I think we are only animals."

He got up, acutely miserable. He could see her following him with her eyes, and knew she was afraid she had driven him away. She said coaxingly: "Don't mind me talking, ni-ice boy. I don't know anyone to talk to. If you don't like it, I can be quiet as a mouse."

He muttered:

"Oh! go on, talk away. I'm not obliged to believe you, and I don't."

She was on her feet now, leaning against the wall, her dark dress and white face just touched by the slanting moonlight; and her voice came again, slow and soft and bitter:

"Well, look here, ni-ice boy, what sort of a world is it, where millions are being tortured—horribly tortured, for no fault of theirs at all? A beautiful world, isn't it? 'Umbug! silly rot, as you boys call it. You say it is all 'Comrade!' and braveness out there at the front, and people don't think of themselves. Well, I don't think of myself veree much. What does it matter?—I am lost now, anyway; but I think of my people at home, how they suffer and grieve. I think of all the poor people there and here who lose those they love, and all the poor prisoners. Am I not to think of them? And if I do, how am I to believe it a beautiful world, ni-ice boy?"

He stood very still, biting his lips.

"Look here! We haf one life each, and soon it is over. Well, I think that is lucky."

He said resentfully:

"No! there's more than that."

"Ah," she went on softly, "you think the war is fought for the future; you are giving your lives for a better world, aren't you?"

"We must fight till we win," he said between his teeth.

"Till you win. My people think that, too. All the peoples think that if they win the world will be better. But it will not, you know; it will be much worse, anyway."

He turned away from her and caught up his cap; but her voice followed him.

"I don't care which wins, I despise them all—animals—animals! Ah! Don't go, ni-ice boy—I will be quiet now."

He took some notes from his tunic pocket, put them on the table, and went up to her.

"Good-night."

She said plaintively:

"Are you really going? Don't you like me enough?"

"Yes, I like you."

"It is because I am German, then?"

"No."

"Then why won't you stay?"

He wanted to answer: "Because you upset me so;" but he just shrugged his shoulders.

"Won't you kees me once?"

He bent, and put his lips to her forehead; but as he took them away she threw her head back, pressed her mouth to his and clung to him.

He sat down suddenly, and said:

"Don't! I don't want to feel a brute."

She laughed. "You are a funny boy, but you are veree good. Talk to me a little, then. No one talks to me. I would much rather talk, anyway. Tell me, haf you seen many German prisoners?"

He sighed—from relief, or was it from regret?

"A good many."

"Any from the Rhine?"

"Yes, I think so."

"Were they very sad?"

"Some were—some were quite glad to be taken."

"Did you ever see the Rhine? Isn't it beautiful? It will be wonderful tonight. The moonlight will be the same here as there; in Rooshia too, and France, everywhere; and the trees will look the same as here, and people will meet under them and make love just as here. Oh! isn't it stupid, the war?—as if it was not good to be alive."

He wanted to say: "You can't tell how good it is to be alive till you're facing death, because you don't live till then. And when a whole lot of you feel like that—and are ready to give their lives for each other, it's worth all the rest of life put together." But he couldn't get it out to this girl who believed in nothing.

"How were you wounded, ni-ice boy?"

"Attacking across open ground—four machine-gun bullets got me at one go off."

"Weren't you veree frightened when they ordered you to attack?"

No, he had not been frightened just then! And he shook his head and laughed.

"It was great. We did laugh that morning. They got me much too soon, though—a swindle!"

She stared at him.

"You laughed?"

"Yes, and what do you think was the first thing I was conscious of next morning—my old colonel bending over me and giving me a squeeze of lemon.

If you knew my colonel, you'd still believe in things. There is something, you know, behind all this evil. After all, you can only die once, and if it's for your country all the better."

Her face, with intent eyes just touched with dark, had in the moonlight a most strange, other-world look. Her lips moved:

"No, I believe in nothing. My heart is dead."

"You think so, but it isn't, you know, or you wouldn't have been crying when I met you."

"If it were not dead, do you think I could live my life walking the streets every night, pretending to like strange men—never hearing a kind word—never talking for fear I will be known for a German. Soon I shall take to drinking, then I shall be '*kaput*' very quick. You see, I am practical; I see things clear. Tonight I am a little emotional, the moon is funny, you know. But I live for myself only now. I don't care for anything or anybody."

"All the same, just now you were pitying your people, and prisoners, and that."

"Yes, because they suffer. Those who suffer are like me—I pity myself, that's all; I am different from your Englishwomen. I see what I am doing; I do not let my mind become a turnip just because I am no longer moral."

"Nor your heart either."

"Ni-ice boy, you are veree obstinate. But all that about love is 'umbug. We love ourselves, nothing more."

Again, at that intense soft bitterness in her voice, he felt stifled and got up, leaning on the window-sill. The air out there was free from the smell of dust and stale perfume. He felt her fingers slip between his own, and stay unmoving. If she was so hard and cynical, why should he pity her? Yet he did. The touch of that hand within his own roused his protective instinct. She had poured out her heart to him—a perfect stranger! He pressed it a little, and felt her fingers crisp in answer. Poor little devil! This was a friendlier moment than she had known for years! And after all, fellow-feeling was bigger than principalities and powers! Fellow-feeling was all-pervading as this moonlight, which she had said would be the same in Germany—as this white ghostly glamour wrapping the trees, making the orange lamps so quaint and decoratively useless out in the narrow square, where emptiness and silence reigned. He looked round into her face—in spite of kohl and powder, and the red salve on her lips, it had a queer, unholy, touching beauty. And he had suddenly the strangest feeling, as if they stood there—the two of them—proving that kindness and human fellowship were stronger than lust, stronger than hate; proving it against meanness and brutality, and the sudden shouting of newspaper boys in some neighboring streets, whose cries, passionately vehement, clashed into each other, and obscured the words—what was it they were calling? His head went up to listen; he felt her hand rigid within his arm—she too was listening. The cries came nearer, hoarser, more shrill and clamorous; the empty moonlight seemed of a sudden crowded with figures, footsteps, voices, and a fierce distant cheering. "Great victory—great

victory! Official! British! Severe defeat of the 'Uns! Many thousand prisoners!"
So it sped by, intoxicating, filling him with a fearful joy; and leaning far out, he
waved his cap and cheered like a madman; and the whole night seemed to him
to flutter and vibrate and answer. Then he turned to rush down into the street,
struck against something soft, and recoiled. The girl! She stood with hands
clenched, her face convulsed, panting, and even in the madness of his joy he felt
for her. To hear this—in the midst of enemies! All confused with the desire to
do something, he stooped to take her hand; and the dusty reek of the tablecloth
clung to his nostrils. She snatched away her fingers, swept up the notes he had
put down, and held them out to him.

"Take them—I will not haf your English money—take them." And suddenly
she tore them across twice, three times, let the bits flutter to the floor, and turned
her back to him. He stood looking at her leaning against the plush-covered table
which smelled of dust, her head down, a dark figure in a dark room with the
moonlight sharpening her outline—hardly a moment he stayed, then made for
the door…

When he was gone, she still stood there, her chin on her breast—she who
cared for nothing, believed in nothing—with the sound in her ears of cheering,
of hurrying feet, and voices; stood in the centre of a pattern made by fragments
of the torn-up notes, staring out into the moonlight, seeing, not this hated room
and the hated square outside, but a German orchard, and herself, a little girl,
plucking apples, a big dog beside her; a hundred other pictures,too, such as the
drowning see. Her heart swelled; she sank down on the floor, laid her forehead
on the dusty carpet, and pressed her body to it.

She who did not care—who despised all peoples, even her own—began,
mechanically, to sweep together the scattered fragments of the notes, assembling
them with the dust into a little pile, as of fallen leaves, and dabbling in it with
her fingers, while the tears ran down her cheeks. For her country she had torn
them, her country in defeat! She, who had just one shilling in this great town
of enemies, who wrung her stealthy living out of the embraces of her foes! And
suddenly in the moonlight she sat up and began to sing with all her might—"*Die
Wacht am Rhein.*"

The Man in the Next Bed
(from *The Next Man*)

Paul Alverdes

One autumn evening in 1915, while the Allies were delivering a violent attack on the German positions to the south of La Bassée, a raw recruit, who was little more than a boy, was alone in one of his battery's dug-outs. In accordance with orders he had been boiling soup at an iron stove for the other men in his battery outside, who had been loading and firing ceaselessly since the attacks by Moroccan and Indian divisions, which had unexpectedly developed immediately after lunch. He was just about to dish out the steaming fluid with a large ladle into the dixies on the ground, when a bearded face appeared between the tent-flaps, at the entrance to the dug-out, and looked down at him nervously. Directly afterwards the flaps opened completely, and a strange militiaman in coat and helmet, carrying a full pack, slowly descended the steps.

His sudden appearance dismayed and confused the youth for a moment in a manner which he himself could not understand. It was as though he had known the man for a long time and had only been waiting for him to come again, but at the same time it was in vain that he racked his memory as to how he knew him; he could not think what they had had to do with one another. The images which he conjured up passed across his mind's eye with lightning rapidity again and again. Shapes kept on giving place to one another, young and old, handsome and distorted, with which he had run through the misty fields of shell-holes or wandered about in the nightly labyrinth of graves. But this one, which drew him as with the strength of a father's love, with a powerful and mysterious force, was not among them.

When he had reached the bottom of the steps the stranger remained standing before him. He was of gigantic size, so that everything which he had about him seemed like a kind of toy, although he was very heavily burdened. He had thick, straw-colored hair, which bunched out of the rim of his helmet that had slipped to the back of his head, and a broad beard of the same color. His eyes, under their bushy, white brows, were small and of a very light blue. Their glance was searching and uneasy, but not as though he were afraid of any danger, but as though he were in constant expectation of being called upon to perform some duty which he did not wish to refuse. His pack was adjusted very high on his back, and his rifle, the breech of which was carefully wrapped about with rags, hung obliquely across his chest, while six or eight chains of closely packed clips of cartridge cases, which he had disposed about his neck and shoulders, drew his weight somewhat forward. A knotted stick with a long, very flat-polished crook hung from his wrist in a leather sheath.

"I say," he remarked in a tone that was half apologetic and half confidential, as he took off his helmet and dangled it like a hat in his hands—"I say, it's all right here." He gazed at the steaming dixies.

"Yes, you've struck it all right here," answered the youth, and bent lower over his cooking utensils; "they're all good fellows here."

The militiaman now also bent down low and drew his chin in, for at that very moment it seemed again as though one of the naval shells that kept howling over the position in a flat trajectory were poising in the air directly over the dug-out in order the more certainly to hit its objective.

He was coming back from leave, he murmured almost into the youth's ear, after waiting for the explosion, and he had had a long way to march. He belonged to a Prussian militia regiment, which must be somewhere in front. He wanted to rejoin his company that night. He wanted to ask for a dish of soup, because he hadn't had anything to eat.

Without a word the youth passed one of the dixies to him, and the militiaman, grasping this helmet between his knees, raised it with both fists to his mouth. He emptied it in long gulps without setting it down and without taking his eyes off the face of the other. Then he returned the pot, wiped his beard as he passionately murmured, "Many thanks, old boy," and began to look about the dug-out with a kind of polite interest.

"Don't misunderstand me," he then uttered with an insistent look, when he saw that the other did not catch the drift of his meaning—"don't misunderstand me, but I wonder whether I ought to give myself up?" He explained that he was, so to speak, a double size, but could generally only get rations for one. That was terrible, and sometimes he thought that he would not be able to stick it much longer.

The youth filled the dixie again, somewhat reluctantly, and with a nervous glance at the entrance of the dug-out; for at that time provisions were beginning to run short, and the thoughtless sharing of rations with members of strange units had already been punished in some instances by the authorities, as being unfair to one's own.

The stranger refreshed himself once more, then he put on his helmet, fastened the chin-strap, and was about to go up the steps again with an embarrassed "Good luck to you, old boy." But the youth suddenly recollected a box containing cake, which his aunt had sent him a few days previously; he had been keeping it on a shelf at the head of his bunk. He called the militiaman back again, got up an earth-step in front of him, and tied the box to the straps of his pack by a string. The large man remained motionless, looked down at the boy's hands, and shook his head the while, seeming with heartfelt sighs to express his regret at taking away such precious things. Suddenly he looked up, raised his enormous hand to his helmet by way of farewell, and remained for some time in that position, while he smiled at the youth with the purest expression of admiring and devoted love.

The latter slowly blushed all over and returned his smile. Directly afterwards the stranger disappeared through the flaps into the outside world.

A little later, when the recruit also stepped out, carrying in both hands the dixies which were tied together, a cloud of shrapnel was again screaming over the battery, which was still firing madly. The four guns, dug in only up to their carriage axles, were standing fairly close together on the marshy meadow ground over to the left; the bombardiers were massed close up behind the shield, while the telephonists,were dug in further back with the sergeant, who was constantly shouting ranges and fire orders. The flickering lights of the attack showed them all up clearly, now in a red light as of distant conflagrations, and now sharp, black shadows in the white blaze of munition dumps that were going up on the flank, or again bathed in a dazzling brightness as bunches of Verey lights came slowly gliding to earth, illuminating the foliage and grasses so that for seconds they gleamed as green as by daylight. The militiaman was still leaning on his stick in the shadow of the farm ruins under which the dug-out was; he gazed up at the sky, shaking his head, as though he were wondering what the weather was going to do, and plaintively sighing again and again: "O God! O Christ Jesus!" Then he went up once more to the youth, who was just getting his breath before making a dash through the fire zone with the soup, and gazed long in poignant silence at his face. Finally, he turned away, scrambled up the bank of the road to the right of the battery, and, swaying under his load, broke into a double in the direction where the infantry fire was at its hottest. Not long afterwards the battery ceased firing, as the attack seemed to have collapsed. A man remained on guard with the guns; the others threw themselves fully clad and in their boots on the mattresses in their dug-outs, and the youth also lay down beside his fellows. But, although he was utterly exhausted, he could not get to sleep; the memory of his strange visitor began to trouble him, and again he ransacked his memory in vain for a similar voice, face, and form. He is in difficulties, he thought, listening anxiously, as a confused din came across from the trenches; they are doing him in. He had the face of a man who is soon to die, and now I know how I recognized it. Finally, however, in order to hear no more, he drew his thick woollen cap over his ears and fell asleep, but he had a strange dream.

In the grey of morning he saw a monstrous flat field, on which innumerable soldiers were standing next to one another in grey coats and grey helmets. It was surely the whole army; they were ranged all in circles, facing inwards as for a game of ring of roses. The game seemed to be starting, and they raised their hands to their helmets in salutation, and bowed to one another. They all looked just the same, for each one of them had the face of the flaxen bearded militiaman. But suddenly the sky flamed with tongues of light, a terrific thunderclap shattered the air, the groups broke up into a chaotic mass of men swinging their weapons, and in an instant they were changed, each one assuming a different form.

At this moment the dreamer awoke completely, the guard shouted the alarm, the bombardiers rushed cursing up the steps into the open, where the crashing of hand grenades, the rattle of infantry fire, and the confused noise of men shouting words of command already filled the air. As he stumbled along to his gun behind the others, the recruit thought that he detected something like blue sky above the dawn mists of the grey morning; we shall have fine weather again, he thought, and above and about him swarms of birds were singing. But he perceived directly that it was the whistling of rifle bullets. They were coming thick, in a fairly flat trajectory across the hollow, and the top of a willow behind whose trunk he flung himself, waiting until an oncoming shell should have burst, scattered a silent, constant rain of leaves and twigs upon him. Suddenly, as though it had long been settled and decided, and it had merely slipped his mind for the time, it occurred to him that today he was to die. In point of fact he had never thought of such a thing, but had confidently attributed a virtue greater than the force of any bullet to the blessing which his father had given him with his farewell embrace. Now, however, it seemed to him the simplest and most natural thing in the world to die here in the meadow by the ruins of the French farm, and to his own astonishment the idea no longer terrified him, although many and many a time he had not been able to master a wild fear of death. From that moment the day passed in a state of expectation that had no element of fear, but mere curiosity as to when and how his death would occur.

He had taken the place at his gun of the loading bombardier, who had been killed shortly after dawn—with a bullet in his hip the man had staggered a few yards to the side, crouching and pressing both hands to the front of his body. He now lay flat on his back in the grass with slightly parted lips, as though he were only asleep; for there had been no time to carry him away. At his place behind the shield, close to the gun-barrel, the recruit was now standing, wearing a blue woollen jacket, his cap askew on his head, with the sweat pouring down his face and mingling with the oil and gun fumes.

"Get a move on! Same elevation! Another round! Another round!" the sergeant kept shouting again and again, leaping like a man possessed from gun to gun. "Fire!" shouted No. 1 as he sprawled over the sights; the youth bent from his hips and snatched out the detonator by its leather thong. The howitzer leapt with a thunderous report, the thick short barrel speeding backwards deep between the thighs of the limber, as though it would bury itself in the earth, and it was only slowly and with reluctant growling that it reverted to its former position. Even before it had completely done so the youth tore open the breech again. A puff of smoke belched out, driving the empty shell case to the rear; its place was taken by a new one. He raised his free arm and pressed his hand to his ear, and even as the breech was rattled to, the new word of command rang out. This lasted hour after hour until the burnt-out cartridges mounted to hills and the empty wicker baskets for shell cases rose mountain high behind the guns. More and more frequently a high-explosive shell, bursting right among the guns, or a cloud of shrapnel just above the shield, drove them all to the ground, and more and more of the section remained afterwards lying on their faces or ran off suddenly with staring eyes, staggering like drunken men and covered with blood. But nothing happened to the youth.

It was already near evening when the battery had fired off all its ammunition; there were no fresh supplies to be got, and the remnant of the section collected in one of the dug-outs in an exhausted condition, expecting to be taken prisoners or to receive orders to leave the position. But all of a sudden, just as the rattle of machine-gun fire in the immediate vicinity and the shrill shouts of native troops who were attacking again seemed to herald the immediate approach of the end, the recruit was overcome with a wild fit of uneasiness, and he pushed into the open past the sergeant, who was on the lookout for the eagerly awaited munition columns. He observed on the bank of the road to the right of the battery a man crawling back painfully on all fours, whom he believed that he recognized. The man was bareheaded, and his yellow hair hung right down into his eyes. The sergeant had seen him too, and was gesticulating and shouting at him to crawl under the cover of the remains of a wall, which skirted the road there. At the same time, however, he held the youth, who wanted to go across, back by the belt, for the British machine-gun bullets kept pelting across the street, and the battery had already lost several men that day, who had wanted to get across to help the man to make his way back.

The wounded man must have heard the shouts; he stopped moving, raised his head, and stared across in perplexity. Then suddenly he crumpled up and rolled over on his side. Then, with his face turned away, he made a movement with his arms indicating that he badly wanted a drink. The youth wrenched himself free, and got across in great bounds. But while he knelt beside him, and pulled at the stopper of his water-bottle with his teeth, he saw that he had made a mistake. The wounded man was not the militiaman after all; he was wearing the badges of a different regiment. The youth pushed his hand under his neck, and put the bottle to his mouth. Greedily the wounded man smacked his lips like a child and tried to drink; but suddenly an anxious look came on his face, and with his muddy hand he pushed the bottle from him. He seemed to wish to say something, but he only shook his head and looked at the recruit with a wistful embarrassment, as though he profoundly regretted having caused so much trouble, and now to be unable even to drink. His head-shaking changed to a rolling movement; he gave a pathetic sigh, made one gesture of negation with his hand, and lay still with failing eyes. At the same moment a bullet from the flank went through the throat of the young man, who was just going to raise himself, and he flung himself upon the dead man, pressing his face upon his. He got up again, however, at once, staggered back, and collapsed at the feet of the sergeant, who was cursing and lamenting.

By the most extraordinary chance the arteries of the neck had not been hurt, or at any rate they were not bleeding at the moment, and so, breathing with difficulty and at first completely bereft of speech, he was able that very night to reach the nearest field hospital behind that sector of the German position. The doctors immediately took steps to ease his breathing, and were moderately successful.

When he awoke on the following afternoon he found himself in a large room, which had been the wagon-shed of a farm and had been converted into a hospital. Two long rows of rough-hewn beds stood facing one another, and behind each one hung a black board, bearing in white letters the name, unit, and age of its wounded occupant. It was deathly still, as though they were all asleep, or as though they were already dead. The sun shone in obliquely.

When the youth turned over on his side he saw the militiaman sitting in the bed next his own. He recognized him at once, although he seemed very much altered. His hair had been cut in accordance with military requirements and his beard trimmed, no doubt in order to get at his wound more easily, which he, too, must have received in the neck or the lower part of the jaw. Supported by a few pillows he was sitting upright in bed with his neck heavily bandaged and breathing with difficulty; but he seemed to pay no attention to this or to be deliberately concealing it, for he looked straight ahead, not moving his face. His eyes now seemed big and had completely lost all restlessness.

In order to attract his attention, the youth tapped at his bedstead. The other slowly turned his face; he showed no surprise, but just smiled wanly, and as he cast down his eyes, made a soothingly affirmative gesture, as though he had known everything for a long time, and what was going to happen too, and as though the other should just leave things to him. Then he looked straight ahead, laid his finger on his lips, and gazed into the distance again with a clear, resolute expression. The recruit lay back again comforted, and immediately fell once more into a deep sleep.

He did not wake until the middle of the night, when he was roused by a noise, which he could not at once interpret. It was a whistling and hissing and rattling, which was constantly repeated in quick, wild gasps, and he now realized that it was the man in the next bed, fighting with death. In the dim light of the lamps he saw the assistants standing about his bed, he heard the clatter of instruments, and the quiet voice of the doctor giving his instructions. A horrid terror overcame him. I must die, he thought, and I must go off with him; it cannot be otherwise. He wrung his hands and raised them to his face, over which sweat and tears were running; he wanted to pray, but he was unable to do so, for the pious words turned on his lips to desperate railing and cursing. Then he drew the rug over his head and buried his face deep in the pillows; he would have welcomed unconsciousness, even death itself, only to make an end. But it was of no avail. His breath, too, began to rattle, his heart fluttered in his breast, and the room began to sway about him in longer and ever quickening pulsations, and to turn backwards and forwards in a circle. But quite suddenly there was quiet next to him, the light went out, and the figures went away. He listened: the man's breath was coming wholesomely and quietly.

He has got over it, he thought; we have got over it. He stretched himself and closed his eyes. Sleepily, he groped with his hand at his naked breast over the heart. It was going in regular, strong beats.

Next morning, when he awoke, wonderfully refreshed, with a cool skin and a feeling of absolute conviction that he would soon recover, he saw two soldiers taking a long form from the bed next to him and carrying it out. It was wrapped from top to toe in the white bed-cover, and did not stir. He jumped up and stretched out his arms; his lips moved as though he wanted to shout something, but no sound issued from his lips. Then he sat down with burning eyes. When, after a little while, one of the two orderlies returned and began to sponge out the name and regimental number on the board above the empty bed, he sank back and laid both hands over his face. It was now certain that he would return home, and he was ashamed, although perhaps not before men.

He was in due course transferred to a hospital in Germany, where he got well.

One Hundred Per Cent

Leo V. Jacks

Uncle Henry flicked the reins over the black mare, and shifted his quid of Union Leader. "What'd you think of all the speechifyin' at the Crossin'?"

As any dutiful fifteen-year-old nephew would, I said it was good. The Crossing is a town of a thousand inhabitants, and, like many such towns, it takes its Fourth of July undiluted. When there is any Americanism to be dispensed, the Crossing always gulps a liberal dose.

This ideal rural festival had just terminated after a barbecue in the grove, many tubs of pink lemonade, firecrackers till hell wouldn't hold them, and of course some perspiring orators. Now it was sundown, and Uncle Henry and I were on our way home. The yeomen had milled around all day in the hot sun, red-faced, panting, and happy. They enjoyed everything. The chief speaker was the Honourable J. O. Coughlin, our Congressman, and if he didn't twist the British lion's tail, and pull all the feathers out of the Austrian eagle—He gave the French hell for not paying their war debt, and the crowd said he ought to know, for he was there in '18.

He talked at great length about the gallantry of our boys in the War, and he told a story of a very brave secretary who had run out into No Man's Land, or some place, under the fire of eighty-four machine-guns and several regiments of the Bavarian Guard to rescue some wounded soldier. While this story was being related, I heard Uncle Henry swearing under his breath, and I thought maybe a mosquito had bitten him. Mr. Coughlin told none of his own brave deeds. I suppose he was too bashful.

As I studied him, I couldn't help thinking that he would be a dangerous man in a fight, for he was big and heavy, and he looked strong enough to put an awful push behind a bayonet. Then, too, he had an air of embattled virtue which indicated that when he was roused he could be terrible. It was a mighty good thing for our district that we had such a man to protect the public interests. And, yet, he had an ingratiating way; tall, with a fair, full face, and bright, trusting blue eyes, and a great handshake. He dressed very well.

A young boy is a natural-born hero-worshipper. You know how quickly he will construct a heroic character out of any big man he admires, and how badly he feels when he sees the feet of clay. I'll never forget the story of the Chicago White Sox trial, and the newsboy's wail when Joe Jackson fled from the courtroom with his hands over his face: "Say it ain't true, Joe, say it ain't true."

The mayor had introduced Coughlin as a veteran of many battles, who had gone into politics to purify them. I didn't see any medals on him, but he was probably modest and left them at home. The mayor said, anyway, that he had been in some desperate battles, so, like any youngster, I watched the big man with a good deal of admiration and not a little awe. I'd made up my mind that on our way home I'd quiz Uncle Henry about those battles.

Uncle Henry is thin-faced, and always clean-shaved. He has bright grey eyes and a retiring way. He is five feet nine, and he limps a little when he walks. He got a shrapnel bullet in his left foot at the Fond des Meszeires, and didn't go to the hospital.

So, you see, he is an alumnus of the A.E.F., and a clever one, too, and a skilled manipulator of the esteemed *soixante-quinze*. Now, as we jogged along, he hummed gently over the exploits of the mademoiselle from Bar-le-Duc, and the old farm-wagon rattled. Uncle Henry rolled his quid reflectively and ruminated for a moment. Then he spat accurately at a thirteen-striped gopher that darted out of the rut just in time to escape the encroaching wheels.

"Fourth of July speeches don't mean nothin', kid," he observed. "The politicians—and that goes for Coolidge and Coughlin, and ninety-nine per cent of the men holding offices that they got by votes—they don't care a rap for the common people, or the soldiers either, spite of all they talk about battles, and brave boys, and all that."

"Well, if the politicians don't appreciate what the boys did in France, the people did," I said. "They've elected some of these fighting soldiers to good jobs. There's Mr. Coughlin—"

"Yeah? Well, if the people feel that way, they sure show their appreciation of the fighting man in strange ways.

"Now, I recall a fellow in our battery, and he was—But I'll tell you all about him.

"When our brigade started up to the Marne in July, the dope had it that there would be a big battle. It came, too. Well, this fellow, a handsome blond with blue eyes and very fair hair, whom you can call Spicks or Sticks, or some such thing, was a cannoneer." In the middle of the last night, when we were getting close to the front, and we could hear the guns booming and see the red flashes on the sky-line, it began to rain cats and dogs, and what with all the mud and confusion, and the trampling, and the troops jammed up in the cross roads, and the black darkness, Sticks or Wicks lost his way, and went somewhere else. Damned if we didn't have to go into action without him.

"Our brigade was in fighting at Fresnes, and Courmont, and the Croix Rouge Farm, and Chamery, and Dravegny, and old Death Valley, where we buried a lot of our good men, and so on, from July 30th to August 24th. You'd think, now, wouldn't you, that a rabid patriot who was just yearning to kill him a few Germans would have found his way up to the front, and rejoined his regiment in the course of twenty-six consecutive days of hard fighting?

"But Sticks or Bicks couldn't find his way. By day the thunder of the guns could have guided him somewhat, and at night you could see the sky all lit up like the mouth of hell and fiery red for miles around Hangar Claudin, and Fismes, and Fismettes. But he didn't see or hear. From where we lost him it was only a ten-mile walk to Courmont, and many's the time we hiked thirty miles between sundown and sunrise, so the distance couldn't have bothered him much.

"But, anyway, on August 25th we were pulled out of the Aisne-Marne entertainment, and started elsewhere. And our boys went along feeling pretty chirrupy, because they had it that we were bound for a rest-camp. Soldiers are optimistic cusses. They still think a rest-camp means rest.

"Well, sir, second day on the road we ran right into Ticks or Spicks, and there were tears in his big blue eyes as he told First Lieutenant Finnegan, who happened to be our commanding officer because the Captain had been killed by a shell, how hard he'd been hunting for us, and what a rocky time he'd had away from the battery, and, gee! couldn't he have something to eat? He was damn near starved.

"So the Looie rode back to the rolling-kitchen, and he said to the cooks: 'This poor son of something is in an awful fix. Can you give him a little snack?'

"They said they could, and they did.

"For the next three days Spicks or Hicks was one of the most diligent boys I ever laid my two eyes on, and he certainly made some of our prize duty-dodgers look like what they were. He chopped wood for the kitchen, and worked at this and that, and he begged Sergeant Nixon to give him back his old job on the seventy-five.

"On August 27th came a God-awful hike. All day and no letup. Top speed. Night fell. Some of our men began to get pretty leg-weary. The old horses groaned, and panted, and cursed in horse and the Colonel made every son get down and walk.

"The country we were passing through looked tough. Fields all shell-holes, and the houses in ruins. Besides, you don't go to rest-camps on twenty-four-hour forced marches. Finally, about three in the morning we began to see the old red flashes and hear the guns. We didn't know where we were, but we knew there was a hell of a battle going on, and that was the reason for all the hurry. We were slated for a nice juicy job, probably right in the front row.

"Then it rained. Ye gods, how it rained! But at last our column, blistered and tottering and groaning and cursing and starvation-hungry, pulled up under some trees in a meadow to take a final inventory before we stepped in where the water was deep.

"Then somebody discovered that Sticks was missing. Lost again. By God, that boy had tough luck! He always got lost when there was a battle in the offing.

"The great Oise-Aisne drive is all history now. We had a wild time in company with the First Moroccan Division. They're the greatest soldiers in the world. I take off my hat to those North Africans.

"Our division lost a lot of men, but we took all our objectives, and buried our dead, and, finally, our brigade came out on the 6th of September, after about nine days of real big league battling.

"We were marching down the old sunshiny road toward the Forest of Retz when here came Sticks. Lord! he was a sorry-looking mess, but he was sorrier when Lieutenant Finnegan clapped eyes on him. 'Jesus-God!' Finnegan roared. 'Donner und Blitzen! *Sacre nom du chien*! Get me a pair of handcuffs quick!'

"And if he didn't grab that Sticks in a hurry, I hope to spit in your mess-kit.

"Believe it or not, Sticks had had a lot of hard luck. Practically all the hard luck in the A.E.F. There were tears in his eyes while he told about it, and Finnegan couldn't make him shut his mouth. And, believe me, he begged hard, and argued.

"For a while nobody really believed that he got lost the second time, but if you keep at a story long enough you can make some people swallow it. And, of course, we didn't have any handcuffs. What'd you do with handcuffs in a regiment of field artillery?

"So Finnegan had to let him go. But the officers were disgusted, and some of the enlisted men that'd had their friends or relatives killed said Spicks should be made an example of, and they talked about court-martial.

"You'd think, maybe, with all that hanging over his head, Spicks would have deserted in dead earnest. But he didn't. He wore his air of injured virtue day and night. He was humbler than ever, and more diligent. He cut wood, and he didn't have to be told. He worked hard for the cooks, and he stuck to the battery like a leech. And all the time he protested innocence, and swore his disappearance had been an accident pure and simple. He may have been pure, but he was not so simple.

"We went to a damn rest-camp in the Haute-Marne, where we did everything but rest, and before there was time for a court-martial, before there was time for anything but one or two good drunks, the whole brigade was hustled away to Verdun. The underground telegraph said that all the battles fought up to date would shrink into nursery rhymes alongside what was coming. So we tightened our harness, and oiled the guns, and ate everything we could get. We never let the War interfere with our appetites. And every night we went legging it in thirty-mile hikes up through the Bar-le-Duc country, past Eurville-Bienville, and on to Esnes.

"It rained every night, and lots of the boys fell down by the road just plumb paralysed, and every morning our column was thinner than the day before. And all day long the cripples would come staggering into camp, and the cooks fed them, and helped them along. We had good cooks.

"On the morning of September 23rd we limped into the Bois de Brocourt. The rain stopped, and at six o'clock the sun shone. Lord I that was a beautiful morning. Some birds were singing, and the grass and leaves were sprinkled with raindrops shining in the light. There were little sunny meadows all around. Lieutenant Finnegan said that when breakfast was over, and the horses fed and groomed and watered, we could sleep all day.

"When we lined up for mess, there was no Sticks at the kitchen. The head cook, Jones, said that Sticks was with them some time during the night, and then again, all of a sudden, he wasn't there. Just like that.

"Lieutenant Finnegan never said a word, but his face got as hard as a steel trap, and I figured it'd be the firing-squad for Sticks if we ever caught him again. So we went blithely, and from September 26th to November 11th the Meuse-Argonne drive was on, forty-seven days of continuous battling in a country that'd make the Dismal Swamp look like a public playground.

"And our regiment fought in most of that fight, because we saw thirty-nine consecutive days of the fun. When they brought us out at last we could just totter, and that was all. Clothes in rags, equipment busted, guns blown up. Seventy-five per cent of the old horses were dead, seventy-two per cent of the men killed, wounded, or gassed.

"Nobody laughed, or joked, or talked. They just walked along, glassy-eyed. When it was time to rest, they rested, and when the guides said 'Go,' they got up passively, and went. Thirty-nine days in the Meuse-Argonne without a break. Ask anybody that was there.

"After a week or two we'd hobbled down into the neighborhood of Neuville-sur-Orne, and damned if we didn't walk right on to Private Sticks. And, believe it or not, he got lost on that hike to Verdun. He smiled a wan smile when they took him to the guard-house. He said it was tough treatment for a poor boy who was trying to do his duty, and had had misfortunes. But the M.P. snapped him off, and said that the Y. was also doing its duty, and having misfortunes.

"Our regiment wasn't really a hard-hearted crowd, and nobody hated Sticks, though they all despised him. But you'd think we were a lot of Pontius Pilates from the way he behaved toward us. He got six months in the brig, and the guards cuffed him around a lot, but he was damned lucky he didn't get shot.

"When we finally came back to America, old Finnegan said: 'Turn the blankety-blank son of a skunk loose, and let him go.' So Sticks chirked up immediately. I heard he worked 'em for an honourable discharge."

The plodding team was beginning to descend into the old hollow around grandfather's farm, and we could hear the crows cawing in the woods, and some squirrels barking in the great cottonwoods overhead.

"Gee," I said, "that fellow was a dirty yellow coward, and I wouldn't trust him with anything. What made you think of him, Uncle Henry?"

"Oh, I saw him—at the Crossin'."

"You did?" I cried. "Who is he?"

Uncle Henry got rid of his quid of Union Leader, and flicked the reins sharply over the black mare before he answered: "Why, our honourable Congressman, J. O. Coughlin."

Marie-Luise

Karl Wilke

Gehrmann was in charge of the canteen of our war prisoners' company in France. He slept next to me in the tent. He came from Berlin, and was engaged to a girl there, about whom he used to talk to me a lot in the evening before going to sleep. But I was favoured with even more about the girl whom he had in tow at St. Quentin. She was the daughter of Madame Bouffon, who supplied our canteen, and her name was Marie-Luise.

Gehrmann was a merchant in civil life, a wholesale merchant, as he was sometimes wont to emphasize, explaining to me that for this higher grade of commerce it was essential to have matriculated. So he had given this modest evidence of intelligence, and after two years of training had become a *Kriegsfreiwillige*, and had hoped speedily to get his commission—if nothing were to interfere, as unfortunately it did, for he had just got his second stripe when the French took charge of his further destiny by making him a prisoner.

He once showed me a photograph of the girl in Berlin, which had come with a letter, and asked me what I thought of her. It was a beautiful face, frank, but perhaps a little cold; it suggested sincerity and great purity.

"She will be true to you," I said at once.

"She is," he replied; "true as gold."

"Much too good for you," I said, handing back the picture after I had studied it for a while longer, held by this curiously lovely face. The becoming large hat which she was wearing also testified to her good taste.

Gehrmann turned round in his bed so that he faced me; the wire mattress creaked under the weight of his heavy body. He nipped the candle out with his fingers. It was the last candle alight in our tent, and the sentry had already called his familiar "*La lumiere kaput!*" We continued to talk in a whisper, so that the others should not overhear.

"She suits me all right," said Gehrmann, "just because I am rather more easygoing in many ways. Opposites always get on well together; besides, fidelity is not so difficult for women as for us…I've had three years of it, old boy."

"Hence Marie-Luise, I suppose."

He was silent and thoughtful for a while, then he said slowly: "Hence Marie-Luise? No. That's my dilemma—in point of fact, I'm thinking of marrying her."

"You're mad," I exclaimed indignantly. "Fancy thinking of leaving your pretty German girl in the lurch for a French woman."

He tossed about. "Mad? Well—you go to Madame Bouffon and have a look at Marie-Luise, and then say if I'm mad. The Berlin girl can get ten others to take my place."

He had often suggested that I should go round to Madame Bouffon's, but I was not keen on making the acquaintance of my fellow-prisoner's French love. During the following days he grew more insistent. Marie-Luise was a beautiful girl, he said, not at all the ordinary type. In the end I yielded out of sheer curiosity, for I really had not seen a French woman who could be called beautiful.

We belonged to the so-called Town Company; most of us had been taken prisoner at the beginning of the War, we were well dressed and the majority of us could speak French. Apart from the camp staff, to which I belonged, we were engaged by private people in the town as clerks and as interpreters. We were not kept under any kind of surveillance and each man had his pass. Gehrmann's chit, which covered me, was made out from the camp to the Rue Cordelière, where Madame Bouffon lived.

We were not supposed to walk on the pavement; but this regulation did not trouble Gehrmann. He had told a French officer who had wanted to drive him off the pavement that as a man of *kultur* his place was not down where the horses walked. He had put the point suavely in his best French, and the officer had smiled and had let him alone.

Gehrmann's whole manner was expressive of this convinced superiority; that may have been why nobody stopped us. I had often noticed that, as he walked along with his confident stride, it was the French who side-stepped rather than he. He seemed to impress the feminine population especially; he was tall and broad and had bright blue eyes. I could understand that he was a success.

Madame Bouffon's shop contained a medley of every kind of thing that is bought and sold, and everything that prisoners of war might possibly want from a canteen. Gehrmann took me through the miscellaneous stock of goods to the back room, where a few favoured guests were sitting drinking wine. But he did not stop here. "Go through there," he said over his shoulder, "and open the next door." We found ourselves in the kitchen, one corner of which was arranged as a sitting-room. There was a broad sofa behind the table and there was even a piano next to it.

As we passed through the outer shop we had greeted Madame Bouffon. Marie-Luise was not to be seen; a plump little maid was fussing about the stove in the dark background. Gehrmann immediately sat down at the piano and began to play a Strauss waltz. The maid smiled at me invitingly, and Gehrmann winked at me, indicating that I ought to dance with her. I explained that I was not conversant with that art.

Possibly if it had been Marie-Luise—

At that moment she entered. That lucky fellow Gehrmann was right. She was strikingly beautiful; slender and elegant, a thoroughbred, like the kitten which she carried on her arm. There was a warm glow in her cheeks, and she had dark, melting eyes.

I jumped up; Gehrmann continued to play a few bars until I nudged him.

I was interested to see how the two would meet, but there was no special familiarity noticeable. Gehrmann bowed in courtly fashion over her little hand; there was a half smile on the lovely creature's mouth, which vanished as she turned to me.

"My friend," he said, introducing me. I saw only her wonderful dark eyes; like velvet, I thought...

Then the German lesson began. Gehrmann had not told me that he was teaching her German. Marie-Luise seemed rather dense; and she was certainly lacking in concentration. After five minutes she took up the kitten again and went out. Gehrmann sat down to the piano. He did not look at me; perhaps he was ashamed of her stupidity.

The maid took up the carpet. Her skimpy skirt exposed her ridiculously short legs. My friend looked at me and nodded his head in her direction. Then Marie-Luise suddenly appeared behind him; had she noticed something? Her eyes had a surprised or severe expression; they were quite unfathomable.

She tapped the pianist on the shoulder; he subdued his playing somewhat and half turned round to her.

"*Wie heisst Ge-burts-tack*?" she asked in German.

"Birthday."

Marie-Luise reflected for a moment, and then she pressed her dark head into the warm fur of the kitten and disappeared again. As the piano resounded again to the industrious fingers of the prisoner of war I reflected quietly in my sofa corner on the strange relationship between these two persons. It was obvious that nothing sensible would ever come of it. I believe that a Franco-German reconciliation was more likely than a successful union between these two particular representatives of the two nations. I felt I had to argue him out of it. He had once made a point of the fact that Marie-Luise was his eleventh love, so that it was to be hoped she would not be his last. On the other hand, I knew well that he had a strong vein of obstinacy, especially when he felt himself opposed. It was not for nothing that the French had entered on his pass the honorary title, "*Tête carrée*." I could well understand that this strange girl would attract him. She had suddenly entered the room again without a sound, and tapped him on the shoulder with the same swift, confident gesture which had affected me unpleasantly before.

"The Adjutant has forbidden music here," she said. Gehrmann stopped abruptly, and said we had to go, in any case.

"You know who she means by the Adjutant?" he said as we walked along. "That's our friend Boulanger. And he's my rival in her affections. That's how matters stand."

"Well, you're asking for trouble."

"That's just what makes it interesting, my dear fellow. Of course, she doesn't want to have anything to do with him, but he's awfully keen on her. It's a pity that I can't just tell him plainly that he doesn't cut any ice with her...I'm the only one that does. How do you like her?"

"Very well," I said, rather hesitating, "but—"

"No buts about it," he put in at once, "I can't do better than marry her. She's got money; the business is doing splendidly. She wants to marry somebody in the wholesale business if possible. When the War's over I shall be in clover. What's the good of Germany to me?"

"I thought that your main interest in this affair was something rather different," I suggested.

He saw my point. "Well, I don't want to buy a pig in a poke, but I do mean to marry her."

He was as fickle as a child. At one moment he decided in favour of the Berlin girl, the next for Marie-Luise. Every evening I was favoured with an account of his love-pangs until I told him bluntly that he was a cad, and that I had lost all interest in the whole business. He didn't bear me any resentment, and we had indeed told each other plainer home truths. Although he said nothing more about the matter, I thought that was for other reasons. The canteen orderlies, too, noticed the sudden gloom that had descended upon his exuberant nature.

One evening he confided in me: "The Adjutant is on my tracks," he said.

"So he knows that you're the man?" I asked in alarm.

"He doesn't actually know that it's me. He only knows that a prisoner is constantly pursuing Marie-Luise, but he has sworn to shoot him on the spot if he catches him. He watches like a lynx, but he's not yet discovered that I'm the man."

"Let the girl alone," I advised him for the umpteenth time.

"Certainly not now," he answered aggressively. "Of course, I won't be able to be with her so much during the day. I'll have to wangle things a bit. I'll just go there at night, and you will be a sport and say I've gone out to the lavatory if anybody comes to inspect. You will, won't you?"

I promised to oblige him. We were a specially favoured company, and there was no real risk in remaining away occasionally even at night, provided that the German sergeant-in-charge was made wise. He was responsible for defaulters.

The following evening Gehrmann told me that the Adjutant did seem to be suspicious of him. He had been in the back room that day where the customers were sitting, and had looked at him sharply. Gehrmann, however, had refrained from gratifying him by going into the kitchen, and Marie-Luise had pretended complete indifference. No doubt I had noticed on the other occasions how well she could do this.

That evening he crawled through the "mole's alley," which a love-sick prisoner in our tent, who was always abroad at night, had laboriously burrowed. This approach to the outside world started under the shoemaker's bed, and was concealed during the day by a box. It ended on the other side of the barbed wire fence in a mass of litter under an old railway truck. I kept guard, pressed close up against the tent, until the sentry had passed that point, when I tapped the ground several times with my boot. Directly afterwards my friend was scurrying through the trees of the Champs Elysées, unnoticed by the sentry. He came back without my assistance, it being about midnight when he lay down.

"Did it all go off well?" I asked.

"Splendidly. It was a good evening, my lad. A pity the Adjutant couldn't see us, he'd have gone blue with fury. *Sacré nom de Dieu!*"

For a week it worked all right, and then Gehrmann stayed out all night. I didn't worry about this particularly; perhaps he was having a specially good time with Marie-Luise, and had decided not to leave and would come through the gate the next day just like any ordinary man who had been to the canteen. He did come in the next morning immediately after the fatigue parties had left. He was looking deadly pale and immediately sank on his bed.

"What's up?"

He sighed heavily. "Get the medical orderly—with bandages—I have been shot at—but not the doctor," he shouted after me as I dashed off to the hospital.

He had been shot through the upper portion of the right arm. As we carefully took his coat off, he called for the tailor. "Are you good at invisible mending?" he asked. "I want you to deal with my sleeve as quickly as possible. I'll make it worth your while."

It was a clean shot; hardly any blood had flowed. "We won't need the doctor," said the orderly, "but you must take things easy for a couple of days."

"Out of the question," exclaimed Gehrmann, "I must get to the canteen again at once. The Adjutant must know nothing about it. Was there any inspection at night?" I told him there was none.

"Yes, but he might come at any moment; hurry up so that I can get across."

The tailor took some time, and we put a man at the door to warn us if the Adjutant came, in which case Gehrmann would have put on someone else's tunic. "I dare say he won't come at all for the next few days," Gehrmann remarked when the medical orderly had gone and we were left alone for a moment. "I believe I landed him a good one. The night was on my side: I have always gone through the courtyard lately, but he had found that out too, and last night, when I was on my way home, a man was standing outside—I didn't recognize him, but I would bet it was that swine. He collared me and gave me one in the chest; but I was too quick for him and planted my fist in his face. If it was he, he won't be able to show himself in the street for some time. He fell flat on the ground and I was up and off in a moment. Then the swine fired at me; I felt that I was hit and thought I'd better not come back to the camp until the fatigue parties were out, so I hid in a ruined house. Then I crawled in. Give me a drink, old man, I'm feeling a bit faint..."

I got him some wine, which cheered him up, and after that he insisted on going to the canteen. The tailor had mended his tunic so well that there wasn't the slightest trace of the hole. He got a five franc note for his skill. The bandage had also been very skilfully put on so as not to make it too awkward for him to move, and strong-smelling antiseptics had been avoided.

I went with my friend to the canteen. He held himself well and there was no sign that there was anything the matter with him except that his arm hung a little awkwardly. "If the Adjutant should look in I can even move it about a bit," Gehrmann said.

The canteen had a back room, with a sofa which had been requisitioned from the town. By agreement with the other inmates the sofa was left to Gehrmann, who reclined on it while someone was detailed in return for a drink to keep a lookout in case the enemy should come into sight.

I went to visit him at midday and on my way I saw the Adjutant bearing down on the camp. I hurried along, but Gehrmann had already been warned, and he came out of the back room, his face flushed with sleep, as I entered the canteen. The Adjutant was inside already; he looked sharply at Gehrmann and asked him for a drink. I could hardly repress my laughter when I saw the Frenchman's black eye as he turned to the light, and Gehrmann also found it hard to control himself. His lips quivered sarcastically. Apart from this there was nothing to notice about him as he handed his rival a glass of wine and said:

"*Votre santé, mon Adjutant!*"

"*Merci*—you look very pale, Monsieur Gehrmann."

"Had a bit of a binge last night," mumbled the prisoner, and looked meaningly at the other's black eye. He paled noticeably, and I saw that he had difficulty in standing straight.

Thereupon an orderly dashed in and told the Adjutant that he was wanted by the Commanding Officer. The Adjutant went out quickly with an oath. The prison guards told us later that he was severely reprimanded for being seen in the street with a black eye. The interpreters stated definitely that he was put under arrest.

Gehrmann slept himself well, and when his enemy reappeared in the camp he had fully regained the use of his arm. He naturally made for Marie-Luise again, but Madame Bouffon informed him that she had gone away on a visit and was not coming back for some time. Meanwhile, the time for our return home was approaching, and it was not until the evening before we left that he met her again. It seemed that his passion for her had cooled considerably in the meantime.

"How did the farewell go off?" I asked him chaffingly.

"Oh, so-so. I confined myself principally to discussing business with the old woman. I am coming back again as a civilian. I'll get another one in on the Adjutant then."

I advised him not to do anything foolish as it might involve the whole company. He shook his head and said that he would see to it that it happened on the other side of the frontier. Perhaps he would let the Adjutant off, only he would like to tell him that it was he who had given him the black eye, "and then I'll invite him to my marriage with Marie-Luise."

He was not able to carry out his intentions because the French escort marched us back too quickly to Dusseldorf. After we had got home it was a long time before I heard anything further from him. One day he paid a surprise visit and told me that he was engaged to a girl near my home; he showed me her photograph, she was very pretty.

When I reminded him of Marie-Luise he said: "It was sport more than love with her. I only wanted to prevent the Frenchman from winning."

A Raid Night
(from *Waiting for Daylight*)

H. M. Tomlinson

September 17, 1915. I had crossed from France to Fleet Street, and was thankful at first to have about me the things I had proved, with their suggestion of intimacy, their look of security; but I found the once familiar editorial rooms of that daily paper a little more than estranged. I thought them worse, if anything, than Ypres. Ypres is within the region where, when soldiers enter it, they abandon hope, because they have become sane at last, and their minds have a temperature a little below normal. In Ypres, whatever may have been their heroic and exalted dreams, they awake, see the world is mad, and surrender to the doom from which they know a world bereft will give them no reprieve.

There was a way in which the office of that daily paper was familiar. I had not expected it, and it came with a shock. Not only the compulsion, but the bewildering inconsequence of war was suggested by its activities. Reason was not there. It was ruled by a blind and fixed idea. The glaring artificial light, the headlong haste of the telegraph instruments, the wild litter on the floor, the rapt attention of the men scanning the news, their abrupt movements and speed when they had to cross the room, still with their gaze fixed, their expression that of those who dreaded something worse to happen; the suggestion of tension, as though the Last Trump were expected at any moment, filled me with vague alarm. The only place where that incipient panic is not usual is the front line, because there the enemy is within hail and is known to be another unlucky fool. But I allayed my anxiety. I leaned over one of the still figures, and scanned the fateful document which had given its reader the aspect of one who was staring at what the Moving Finger had done. Its message was no more than the excited whisper of a witness who had just left a keyhole. But I realized in that moment of surprise that this office was an essential feature of the War; without it, the War might become Peace. It provoked the emotions which assembled civilians in ecstatic support of the sacrifices, just as the staff of a corps headquarters, at some comfortable leagues behind the trenches, maintains its fighting men in the place where gas and shells tend to engender common sense and irresolution.

I left the glare of that office, its heat and half-hysterical activity, and went into the coolness and quiet of the darkened street, and there the dread left me that it could be a duty of mine to keep hot pace with patriots in full stampede. The stars were wonderful. It is such a tranquillizing surprise to discover there are stars over London. Until this War, when the street illuminations were doused, we never knew it. It strengthens one's faith to discover the Pleiades over London;

it is not true that their delicate glimmer has been put out by the remarkable incandescent energy of our power stations. As I crossed London Bridge the City was as silent as though it had come to the end of its days, and the shapes I could just make out under the stars were no more substantial than the shadows of its past. Even the Thames was a noiseless ghost. London at night gave me the illusion that I was really hidden from the monstrous trouble of Europe, and, at least for one sleep, had got out of the War. I felt that my suburban street, secluded in trees and unimportance, was as remote from the evil I knew of as though it were in Alaska. When I came to that street I could not see my neighbors' homes. It was with some doubt that I found my own. And there, with three hours to go to midnight, and a book, and some circumstances that certainly had not changed, I had retired thankfully into a fragment of that world I had feared we had completely lost.

"What a strange moaning the birds in the shrubbery are making!" my companion said once. I listened to it, and thought it was strange. There was a long silence, and then she looked up sharply.

"What's that?" she asked. "Listen!"

I listened. My hearing is not good.

"Nothing!" I assured her.

"There it is again." She put down her book with decision, and rose, I thought, in some alarm.

"Trains," I suggested. "The gas bubbling. The dog next door. Your imagination." Then I listened to the dogs. It was curious, but they all seemed awake and excited.

"What is the noise like?" I asked, surrendering my book on the antiquity of man.

She twisted her mouth in a comical way most seriously, and tried to mimic a deep and solemn note.

"Guns," I said to myself, and went to the front door.

Beyond the vague opposite shadows of some elms, lights twinkled in the sky, incontinent sparks, as though glow lamps on an invisible pattern of wires were being switched on and off by an idle child. That was shrapnel. I walked along the empty street a little to get a view between and beyond the villas. I turned to say something to my companion, and saw then my silent neighbors, shadowy groups about me, as though they had not approached but had materialized where they stood. We watched those infernal sparks. A shadow lit its pipe and offered me its match. I heard the guns easily enough now, but they were miles away.

A slender finger of brilliant light moved slowly across the sky, checked, and remained pointing, firmly accusatory, at something it had found in the heavens. A Zeppelin!

There it was, at first a wraith, a suggestion on the point of vanishing, and then illuminated and embodied, a celestial maggot stuck to the round of a cloud like a caterpillar to the edge of a leaf. We gazed at it silently, I cannot say for how long. The beam of light might have pinned the bright larva to the sky for the inspection of interested Londoners. Then somebody spoke. "I think it is coming our way."

I thought so too. I went indoors, calling out to the boy as I passed his room upstairs, and went to where the girls were asleep. Three miles, three minutes! It appears to be harder to waken children when a Zeppelin is coming your way. I got the elder girl awake, lifted her, and sat her on the bed, for she had become heavier, I noticed. Then I put her small sister over my shoulder, as limp and indifferent as a half-filled bag. By this time the elder one had snuggled into the foot of her bed, resigned to that place if the other end were disputed, and was asleep again. I think I became annoyed, and spoke sharply. We were in a hurry. The boy was waiting for us at the top of the stairs.

"What's up?" he asked with merry interest, hoisting his slacks.

"Come on down," I said.

We went into a central room, put coats round them, answering eager and innocent questions with inconsequence, had the cellar door and a light ready, and then went out to inspect affairs. There were more search-lights at work. Bright diagonals made a living network on the overhead dark. It was remarkable that those rigid beams should not rest on the roof of night, but that their ends should glide noiselessly about the invisible dome. The nearest of them was followed, when in the zenith, by a faint oval of light. Sometimes it discovered and broke on delicate films of high fairweather clouds. The shells were still twinkling brilliantly, and the guns were making a rhythmless baying in the distance, like a number of alert and indignant hounds. But the Zeppelin had gone. The firing diminished and stopped.

They went to bed again, and as I had become acutely depressed, and the book now had no value, I turned in myself, assuring everyone, with the usual confidence of the military expert, that the affair was over for the night. But once in bed I found I could see there only the progress humanity had made in its movement heavenwards. That is the way with us; never to be concerned with the newest clever trick of our enterprising fellow-men till a sudden turn of affairs shows us, by the immediate threat to our own existence, that that cleverness has added to the peril of civilized society, whose house has been built on the verge of the pit. War now would be not only between soldiers. In future wars the place of honour would be occupied by the infants, in their cradles. For war is not murder. Starving children is war, and it is not murder. What treacherous lying is all the heroic poetry of battle! Men will now creep up after dark, ambushed in safety behind the celestial curtains, and drop bombs on sleepers beneath, for the greater glory of some fine figment or other. It filled me, not with wrath at the work of Kaisers and Kings, for we know what is possible with them, but with dismay at the discovery that one's fellows are so docile and credulous that they will obey any order, however abominable. The very heavens had been fouled by this obscene and pallid worm, crawling over those eternal verities to which eyes had been lifted for light when night and trouble were over-dark. God was dethroned by science. One looked startled at humanity, seeing not the accustomed countenance, but, for a moment, glimpsing instead the baleful, lidless stare of the evil of the slime, the unmentionable of a nightmare...

A deafening crash brought us out of bed in one movement. I must have been dozing. Someone cried, "My children!" Another rending uproar interrupted my effort to shepherd the flock to a lower floor. There was a raucous avalanche of glass. We muddled down somehow—I forget how. I could not find the matches. Then in the dark we lost the youngest for some eternal seconds while yet another explosion shook the house. We got to the cellar stairs, and at last there they all were, their backs to the coals, sitting on lumber. A candle was on the floor. There were more explosions, somewhat muffled. The candle-flame showed a little tremulous excitement, as if it were one of the party. It reached upwards curiously in a long, intent flame, and then shrank flat with what it had learned. We were accompanied by grotesque shadows. They stood about us on the white and unfamiliar walls. We waited. Even the shadows seemed to listen with us; they hardly moved, except when the candle-flame was nervous. Then the shadows wavered slightly. We waited. I caught the boy's eye, and winked. He winked back. The youngest, still with sleepy eyes, was trembling, though not with cold, and this her sister noticed, and put her arms about her. His mother had her hand on her boy's shoulder.

There was no more noise outside. It was time, perhaps, to go up to see what had happened. I put a raincoat over my pyjamas, and went into the street. Some of my neighbors, who were special constables, hurried by. The enigmatic night, for a time, for five minutes, or five seconds (I do not know how long it was), was remarkably still and usual. It might have been pretending that we were all mistaken. It was as though we had been merely dreaming our recent excitements. Then, across a field, a villa began to blaze. Perhaps it had been stunned till then, and had suddenly jumped into a panic of flames. It was wholly involved in one roll of fire and smoke, a sudden furnace so consuming that, when it as suddenly ceased, giving one or two dying spasms, I had but an impression of flames rolling out of windows and doors to persuade me that what I had seen was real. The night engulfed what may have been an illusion, for till then I had never noticed a house at that point.

Whispers began to pass of tragedies that were incredible in their incidence and craziness. Three children were dead in the rubble of one near villa. The ambulance that was passing was taking their father to the hospital. A woman had been blown from her bed into the street. She was unhurt, but she was insane. A long row of humbler dwellings, over which the dust was still hanging in a faint mist, had been demolished, and one could only hope the stories about that place were far from true. We were turned away when we would have assisted; all the help that was wanted was there. A stranger offered me his tobacco pouch, and it was then I found my rainproof was a lady's, and therefore had no pipe in its pocket. The sky was suspect, and we watched it, but saw only vacuity till one long beam shot into it, searching slowly and deliberately the whole mysterious ceiling, yet hesitating sometimes, and going back on its path as though intelligently suspicious of a matter which it had passed over too quickly. It peered into the immense caverns of a cloud to which it h ad returned, illuminating to us unsuspected and horrifying possibilities of hiding-places above us. We expected to see the discovered enemy boldly emerge then. Nothing came out. Other beams by now had joined the pioneer, and the night became bewildering with a dazzling mesh of light. Shells joined the wandering beams, those sparks of orange and red. A world of fantastic chimney-pots and black rounds of trees leaped into being between us and the sudden expansion of a fan of yellow flame. A bomb! We just felt, but hardly heard, the shock of it. A furious succession of such bursts of light followed, a convulsive opening and shutting of night. We saw that when midnight is cleft asunder it has a fiery inside.

The eruptions ceased. Idle and questioning, not knowing we had heard the last gun and bomb of the affair, a little stunned by the maniacal rapidity and violence of this attack, we found ourselves gazing at the familiar and shadowy peace of our suburb as we have always known it. It had returned to that aspect. But something had gone from it for ever. It was not, and never could be again, as once we had known it. The security of our own place had been based on the goodwill or indifference of our fellow-creatures everywhere. Tonight, over that obscure and unimportant street, we had seen a celestial portent illuminate briefly a little of the future of mankind.

Fear

James Warner Bellah

It was a little spot, that fear, but it had ached in his heart for months—ever since his first solo flight at Upavon Aerodrome. It had come suddenly one morning like the clean pink hole of a steel-jacketed bullet—a wound to be ashamed of, a wound to fight against, a wound that never quite healed. Always it was there to throb and to pinch like the first faint gnawing of cancer. It came with him to the theatre and rankled his mind: "Enjoy this—it may be your last play." It crept into his throat at meals sometimes, and took away the poor savour that was left to the foods of wartime.

The fear of the men who fly. Sometimes he pictured it as an imp—an imp that sat eternally on his top plane and questioned him on the strength of rudder wires, pointed to imaginary flaws in struts, suggested that the petrol was low in the tank, that the engine would die on the next climbing turn.

It was with him now as the tender that was to take him up to his squadron jolted and bounced its way across the pave on the outskirts of Amiens. The squadron was the last place he had to go to. All the months that were gone had led up to this. These were the wars at last. This was the place he would cop it, if he was to cop it at all.

He shrugged. Anyway, he had had his four days in London and his ten days idling at Pilot's Pool before the squadron sent for him. He braced one shoulder against the rattling seat and reached in his tunic pocket for a cigarette. Mechanically he offered one to the driver. The man took it with a grubby finger.

"Thankee, sor-r."

He nodded and lighted both cigarettes with the smudge of his pocket lighter. Anyway, he was not flying up to 44. That was one flight saved. Funny, that fear—how it came and went like the throb of a nerve in an open tooth. Sometimes the spot was large, and filled his whole being; then again it would shrink to a dull ache, just enough to take the edge from the beauty of the sunrise and the sparkle from the wine of the moon.

There had been a time when it had jumped in every fibre of his soul. He had been a cadet officer then, with only twelve solo hours in the air, under the old rough-and-tumble system of learning to fly. Spinning at that time was an unsolved mystery to him, a ghastly mystery that had meant quick death in a welter of blood, flecked with splinters. Fred McCloud had gone that way, and Johnny Archambault. For weeks afterward, Johnny's screams had rung in his ears like a stab of pain; until the mere smell of petrol and fabric dope made the fear crawl into his throat and strangle him. Somehow he had kept on with the rest, under the merciless scourge that lashed one on to fly—and the worse fear of seeing cold scorn in the eyes of the men who taught the lore of thin cloud miles. The tender twisted and dodged along the hard mud ribbon that ran like a badly healed cicatrix across the pock-scarred face of the fields. Gnarled and bleak, they were fields that had held the weight of blood-crazed men, still held them in unmarked graves, where they had fallen the year before under the steel flail. He had heard stories from his older brother about those fields—the laughing brother who had gone away one day and returned months later without his laugh, only to go away again, not to come back. He had seen pictures in the magazines—but somehow no one had caught their utter bleakness as he saw it now.

The riven boles of two obscene trees crouched and argued about it on the lead-grey horizon, tossing their splintered arms and shrieking, he fancied, like quarrelling old women in the lesser streets of a village. Close to the roadway, there were a torn shoe and a tin hat flattened like a crushed derby. Poor relics that even salvage could see no further use in. Farther off, a splintered caisson pointed three spokes of a shattered wheel to the sky, like a mutilated hand thrown out in agony. He was seeing it for himself now.

No one could smile at the cleanness of his uniform again and say: "Wait till you get out. When I was in France—" He was out himself now. In a day or so he would go over the line with loaded guns. His instructors at the training 'drome—thin-jawed men with soiled ribbons under their wings—had done no more, and some of them had done less. The thought braced him somewhat.

They had seemed so different—so impossible to imitate those men. Their war had always been a different one from his; a war peopled with vague, fearless men like Rhodes-Moorehouse and Albert Ball and Bishop, the Canadian; men who flew without a thought for themselves.

It occurred to him with a start that theirs was the same war as his now. Twenty-five miles ahead of him, buried somewhere in rat runs, between Bapaume and Cambrai, it went on and on, waiting for him to come—waiting to claw and maim and snuff him out when he did come. It had seemed so far away from him in England. When he was at ground school he had seen it as a place where one did glorious things—he was young, pitifully young a place that one came back from with ribbons under one's wings, with nice clean scratches decently bandaged. And he had been slightly offended at his brother's attitude—at the things his brother had said of the staff. Then he had gone to Upavon to learn to fly. He had soloed for the first time, and the spot of fear had crawled into his own heart.

They were rattling into the broken streets of a tottering town—a town that leered at them and grimaced through blackened gaps in its once white walls. There was a patched-up estaminet with a tattered yellow awning that tried bravely to smile.

"Albert," said the driver.

The new pilot nodded. Some sapper officers were loitering in the doorways of the café. Their uniforms were faded to a rusty brown and reinforced with leather at the cuffs and elbows. Their buttons were leather, too, to save polishing, and their badges were a dull bronze. He looked down at his white Bedford-cord breeches and the spotless skirts of his fur-collared British warm—privileges of the flying corps that men envied. Baths, clean clothing, and better food. The P.B.I.'s idea of heaven. They called flyers lucky for their privileges and cursed them a little bit for their dry beds and the wines they had in their messes, miles behind the line.

The new pilot wondered if they knew what it meant to be alone in the stabbing cold with no one to talk to, no one to help you, nothing between you and the ground save a thin, trembling fabric of cloth and wire and twenty thousand feet of emptiness. That was his fear—emptiness—nothingness—solitude. Those men under the awning could die in company. Not so himself—alone, screaming into the cloud voids, with no one to hear, no one to help, staring with glazed eyes and foam-flecked lips at the emptiness into which one hurtled to death miles below. The price one paid for a bath! He remembered seeing Grahame-White fly at Southport before the War. People had called him an intrepid aviator. The new pilot laughed harshly inside his throat and stared out across the bare fields.

The car topped a slight rise and turned sharply to the left. The driver pointed his grubby finger. "They be comin' in from afternoon patrol," he said. "Yonder is aerodrome."

There were three flat canvas hangars painted a dull brown, and a straggling line of rusty tin huts facing them from across the narrow landing space—like a deserted mining village, shabby and unkempt. As he watched, he saw the last machine of the afternoon patrol bank at a hundred and fifty feet and side-slip down for its landing. In his heart he could hear the metal scream of wind in the flying wires. A puff of black smoke squirted out in a torn stream as the pilot blipped on his engine for one more second before he came into the wind and landed. By the time the tender rolled up to the dilapidated squadron office, the machine had taxied into the row of hangars and the pilot was out, fumbling for a cigarette with his ungloved hands. A thin acrid smell of petrol and carbonized castor oil still hung in the quiet air between the shabby huts. Snow in large wet flakes commenced to fall slowly, steadily. The new pilot climbed down from the tender, tossed his shoulder haversack beside his kit-bag, and pushed open the door of the squadron office. The Adjutant was sitting on his desk top, smoking and talking to someone in a black leather flying coat and helmet—someone with an oil-streaked face and fingers still blue and clumsy from the cold.

"Paterson, sir, G. K., Second Lieutenant, reporting in from Pilot's Pool for duty with the 44th."

The Adjutant raised a careless finger in acknowledgment. "Oh yes. How do? Bring your log books?"

"Yes, sir."

"Chuck 'em down. D' ye mind?"

Paterson laid them upon the desk top, still standing to attention.

The Adjutant smiled. "Break off," he said. "We're careless here. This isn't cadet school."

The new pilot smiled and relaxed. "Very good, sir."

"That's better," said the Adjutant; "makes me feel more comfortable. Just give me a note of yourself now." He reached for a slip of paper. "G. K. Paterson, Two Lt. Next of kin?" Paterson gave his father's name. "Age?"

"Eighteen and four-twelfths."

"Good!" said the Adjutant. "You'll find an' empty cubicle in B Block—that's the middle line of huts. You're lucky. Roof only leaks in three places. I'll have your duffel trekked over shortly."

The man in the flying coat blew upon his numbed fingers and smiled. "I'm Hoyt," he said. "Skipper of C Flight. I'm going to take you now, before A gets after you." He turned to the Adjutant. "That's all right, isn't it, Charlie? Tell 'em I intimidated you." He grinned.

The Adjutant shrugged. "Right-o!"

"Come on," said Hoyt. "I'm in your hut block. I'll show you your hole."

They went out into the snow flurry. Mechanics were fussing in little knots around the five tiny machines that had just landed, lining them up, refilling them, and trundling them into the brown musty hangars.

"Le Rhône Camels," said Hoyt. "We've just been over around Cambrai taking a look-see."

Inside one of the hangars, as they passed, Paterson saw something that drew a thin, wet gauze across his eyeballs. On a rough bench just beside the open flap sat a man with his eyes closed and his lips drawn tightly into a straight bluish line. His flying coat was rolled up behind his head for a pillow, and his tunic had been unbuttoned and cut away from his left shoulder. The white of his flesh showed weirdly in the gloom, like the belly of a dead fish. Just below the shoulder, the white was crumpled and reddened as if a clawed paw had been drawn across it. One man was holding his other hand, while another probed and cleaned and dabbed with little puffs of snowy cotton that turned quickly to pink and then to a deep brown.

Hoyt shrugged. "Lucky man. That's Mallory. He was Number Four this afternoon. We never saw a thing. Just happened. Funny." And he smiled. "That's why I was so keen to get you. Can't tell how long it will be before Mallory gets around again, and I've got one vacancy in the flight already." He shrugged. "You'll see a lot of that here—get used to it. It doesn't mean a thing as long as you get back alive."

Paterson looked at him sharply. He wanted to ask him how many didn't get back alive. He wanted to know what had caused the other vacancy in the flight. But people didn't ask those things. People merely nodded casually and went on.

"I suppose not," he said. They tramped on across the aerodrome.

"Here we are," said Hoyt. He kicked open the hut door and groped down the dark passageway, with Paterson after him. Presently he pushed back another door and yanked at a tattered window curtain.

The new pilot saw a tiny room, with two washstands, a cot, a folding chair, and a cracked mirror. In a corner were his kit-bag and haversack. He pulled out his own cot and chair and set them up; meanwhile Hoyt threw himself down on the other cot and let his cigarette smoke dribble straight upward into the gloom of the pine-raftered roof. Presently he spoke.

"This is a queer war," he said; "full of queer things, and the queerest of these is charity." He laughed in the darkness, and the tip of his cigarette became suddenly pink as he drew the smoke into his lungs. "What was your school?"

"Winchester," said Paterson.

"Right," said Hoyt. "Remember your first day? This is it over again. They've fed you up on poobah at your training 'drome and down at the Pool. They always do. It's part of the system. Just take it for what it is worth and forget the rest. If you want to know anything, come to me and I'll tell you as well as I can. I've been here three months. When I came, I came just as you did today, pucka green and afraid to the marrow—afraid of uncertainty. You get over that shortly.

"Our job is a funny one, and we're not here for ourselves, and we're not here to be heroes or to get in the newspapers. The V.C.s are few and far between." He raised himself upon his elbow. "I'm not preaching self-abasement and a greater loyalty to a cause that is right, mind you. I don't know anything about causes or who started the War or why, and I don't care. I'm preaching C Flight and the lives of five men.

"You saw Mallory over at the hangar. It was teamwork that put him there in his own M.O.'s hands. Not much, perhaps"—the cigarette described a quick arc in the darkness—"just a slight closing in of the formation—a wave of somebody's hand—somebody else dropping back and climbing above him to protect his tail from any stray Huns that might've waylaid him on the way home. That's what I mean. *Esprit de corps* is a cold, hard phrase. Call it what you like. It's the greatest lesson you learn. Never give up a man." Hoyt laughed. "They call me an old woman. Perhaps I am. Take it or leave it.

"Slick up a bit and come into my hutch while I scrape off the outer layer of silt. Dinner in half a tick and I'm as filthy as a pig." He vaulted up from the cot and punched his cigarette out against the sole of his boot. At the door he paused for a moment.

"Ever have wind up?" he asked casually.

Paterson stiffened against the question and the small spot of fear danced within him. "No," he said firmly. Hoyt shrugged. "Lucky man." And he went out into the passage-way.

At dinner he met the rest of the squadron and the other men in C Flight. Mallory, very pale, with his arm slung in a soft pad of bandages, sat beside him. They were coming for him later to take him down to the base hospital. Phelps-Barrington sat on the other side of Mallory, mourning the fact that the wound was not his, that he might get the inevitable leave to follow. Phelps-Barrington took Paterson's hand with a shrug and asked how Marguerite was in Amiens. "What? You didn't meet Marguerite on your way through? 'Struth!"

MacClintock sat across the table beside Hoyt—MacClintock, too young to grow a moustache, but with a deep burr that smelled of the heather in the Highlands and huge pink knees under his Seaforth kilts, muscles like the corded roots of an oak. The other man in the flight, Trent, was down with mild flu. He was due back in a week or so from hospital.

There was a wild argument on about the dawn patrol the next morning. Paterson listened to the fragments of talk that flew like sabre cuts across the glasses:

"He's in a red tripe. I don't give a damn for Intelligence. Saw him this morning myself. Same machine Mac and I had that brush with down at Péronne."

"The next time they'll get an idea for us to strafe a road clear to Cologne for them. What are we—street cleaners?"

"So I let go a covey of Coopers and turned for home. They had it spotted for a battery over at 119 Squadron. I saw the pictures. Right pictures, but wrong map squares as usual. That crowd can't tell a battery from a Chinese labour-corps inclosure. I'd rather be a staff officer than a two-seater pilot."

"Steward, a whisky-soda for Mr. MacClintock and myself. Have one, Hoyt? You, Paterson?"

Cruel, thin, casual talk clicking against the teeth in nervous haste; the commercial talk of men bartering their lives against each tick of the clock; men caught like rats in a trap, with no escape but death or a lucky chance like Mallory's. Caught and yet denying the trap—laughing at it until the low roof of the mess shack rumbled with the echo; drowning it in a whisky for the night.

Afterward, Hoyt came down the passage with him to his room—Hoyt, with his face cleaned of the afternoon's oil and his eyes slightly bright with the wine he had taken.

"We're relieved tomorrow on account of casualties," he said. "I'll tick you out early and we'll go joy riding—see what we can teach each other." He smiled. "'Night."

Paterson undressed slowly and threw back the flap of his sleeping bag. He ran his fingers softly down the muscles of his left arm. Automatically they stopped at the spot Mallory had been hit. He stretched his thumb from the arm to his heart—seven inches. He shrugged. Nice to go that way. Clean and quick. He sat upon the edge of his cot and pulled on his pyjama trousers. Oh, well, this was the place—the last place he had to go to. This was the cot he would sleep his last sleep in. If it weren't a lonely job! That chap in the mess who wouldn't be a two-seater pilot for anything. If he could only fed like that. If he could only feel Hoyt's complacency. Hoyt, with his calm smile and the two little ribbons under his wings. Military Cross and the Legion of Honour, and three months before he had been green—pucka green!

Paterson blew out the light and turned in. Hoyt was a good fellow—damned decent. Outside he could hear Phelps-Barrington's voice muffled by the snow: "Come on, snap into it! Tender for Amiens! Who's coming?" The yell died in the roar from the car's engine.

Paterson lay for a moment thinking; then suddenly he reached for his pocket flash, snapped it, and stared nervously at the empty cot across the room. There was no bedding on it, nor any kit tucked under it; only the chair beside it, and the cracked mirror.

He got up and padded over in his bare feet. Stenciled on one corner of the canvas there was a name—J. G. H. Lyons. There had been no Lyons introduced to him in the mess. Perhaps he was on leave. Perhaps he had flu with Trent and was down at the base. The spot of fear in his heart trembled slightly and he knew suddenly where J. G. H. Lyons was. He was dead! Somewhere out in the snow, miles across the line, J. G. H. Lyons slept in a shattered cockpit.

The door behind him opened softly. It was Hoyt, in pyjamas.

"Got a cigarette?" he asked casually.

Paterson turned sharply and grinned. "Right-o," he said. "There on the table."

Hoyt took one and lighted it. "Can't sleep," he said. "Come in and take Mallory's cot if you want to. I've some new magazines and I can tell you something about our work here until we feel sleepy."

Hoyt was a good fellow—damned decent.

The cold wet mist lay upon the fields like a soft veil drawn across the face of an old woman who had died in the night. Mechanics, with their balaklavas pulled down across their ears, were running about briskly to keep warm—kicking chocks in front of under-carriage wheels, snapping propellers down with mighty leaps and sweeps until the cold engines barked into life and settled to deep concert roaring. Dust and pebbles, scattered by the backwash, swept into the billowing hangars in a thin choking cloud that pattered against the canvas walls. Hoyt's machine trembled and crept out of the line, with Phelps-Barrington after it. Trent, who had come back from the base the day before, taxied out next.

Paterson waved to the mechanics to pull out his own chocks. They yanked mightily on the ropes, and he blipped his motor with his thumb. Behind him and to the left came Yardley, the new man who had come up from Pool to fill Mallory's place. Then MacClintock, sitting high in his cockpit, rushed out with a roar and a swish of gravel. MacClintock was deputy leader.

Hoyt waved his hand in a quick nervous sweep, and the flight started. Through the mist they roared with their engines howling into sharp echo against the hut walls. A moment later tails whipped up and wheels bounced lightly upon the uneven ground. Then Hoyt's nose rose sharply and he zoomed into the air in a broad climbing turn, with the five others after him in tight formation.

Paterson glanced at his altimeter—five hundred feet. He looked ahead and to the left. There was Bapaume in its raggedness, half drowned in the mist. Suddenly Phelps-Barrington's machine burst into rose flame and every strut and wire trembled like molten silver—the sun. He could see the red rim just peeping up ahead of him and he was warmer for the sight of it. Below, under the rim of his cockpit, the ground was still wrapped in its grey shroud. They were climbing up in close formation. The altimeter gave them four thousand feet now. He glanced to the left. Yardley waved. Yardley was going through the agony of his first patrol over the line—the same agony he had gone through himself the week before. Only Yardley seemed different, somehow surer of himself—less imaginative. He was older, too. Behind them, MacClintock, the watch-dog, was closing in on their tails and climbing above them to be ready to help if the Hun swooped from behind unexpectedly.

There were clouds above—grey blanket clouds that came together in a solid roof, with only a torn hole here and there to show the blue. Bad clouds to be under. Hoyt knew it and kept on climbing. Almost ten thousand feet now. The ground below had cleared slowly and thrown off most of its sullen shroud. Here and there, in depressions, the mist still hung in arabesque ruffles like icing in a confectioner's window or the white smoke of a railway engine. The line was under them now, running south and east like a jagged dagger cut, in and out, in and out across the land, not stopping for towns, but cleaving straight through their grey smudgy ruins with a cold disregard and a ruthless purpose. The first day he had seen it, it had seemed a dam to him; a breakwater built there to hold something that must not flow past it; a tourniquet of barbed wire twisted and held by half the world that the blood of the other half might not flow. Some day something would break and the whole thing would give way for good or evil. Curiously, now, like Hoyt, he didn't care which. And suddenly he knew how his older brother had felt, on that last leave, and he had called him unsporting in the pride of his youthful heart!

Hoyt was still climbing. Thin wraiths of cloud vapour groped awkwardly for the six tiny Camels, like ghost fingers, trying desperately to stop them and hold them from their work. Paterson glanced again at Yardley. He had been glad when Yardley came. He was still green himself, but Yardley was greener. It helped buck him up to think about it.

The line was behind them now. Hoyt turned south to pass below the anti-aircraft batteries of Cambrai, and presently they crossed the tarnished silver ribbon of the Somme—Scheidt Canal. Mechanically, Paterson reached for his Bowden trigger and pressed it for a burst of ten shots to warm the oil in his Vickers gun against the bite of the cold air. Then he clamped the joy-stick between his knees and reached up for the Lewis gun on his top plane.

His throat closed abruptly, with a ghastly dryness, and his knees melted beneath him. The wing fabric beside his gun was ruffling into torn lace and he could see the wood of the camber ribs splintering as he watched! For a moment he was paralysed, then frantically he whipped around in his seat and swept the air above him. Nothing. There was the torn fabric and the staring rib and nothing else. MacClintock was gone. Yardley was still there, lagging, with the smoke coming in puffs and streaks from his engine. Then Hoyt turned in a wild climb to the left. Phelps-Barrington dipped his nose suddenly and dived with his engine full on, and at once, where there had been only six Camels, the sky was full of grey machines with blunt noses and black crosses.

Blindly he pressed his Bowden trigger and fired into the empty air, blindly he dived after Phelps-Barrington. Somewhere to the left he saw a plume of black smoke with something yellow twisting in the sunlight on its lower end. A blunt nose crossed his propeller—into his stream of bullets. He screamed and banked wildly, still firing. He saw Hoyt above him. He forgot the machine in front and reached for his Lewis to help Hoyt. He tried to wait—something about the outer ring of the rear sight—but his fingers got the better of him and he fired point-blank.

As quickly as it had begun it ended. There was Hoyt circling back, and two other Camels to the left and below him—four of them. They closed in on Hoyt and he wondered where the two others were. He looked for them—probably chasing after the Huns. He could see dots to the southward—too far away to make out the markings. Hoyt had signalled the washout and they were headed back across the line. Funny those two others didn't come. He wondered who they were. Probably Phelps-Barrington and MacClintock, hanging on to the fight until the last. They worked together that way. He had heard them talk in the mess about it. They'd be at it again tonight, and tonight he could join them for the first time. He'd been in a dog fight! Shot and been shot at! The spot of fear shrank to a pin-point.

The brown smudge of the aerodrome slid over the horizon. He blipped his motor and glided in carefully. No use straining that top wing—no telling what other parts had been hit. No use taking chances.

Hoyt was standing beside his machine with his glove off, staring at his finger-nails. Phelps-Barrington was climbing out. Paterson taxied in between them. The man in the fourth machine just sat and stared over the rim of his cockpit. Phelps-Barrington walked slowly across to Hoyt and laid a hand on his shoulder. Hoyt shrugged and stuffed his bare hand into his coat pocket. Paterson sat with his goggles still on and his throat quite dry. The man in the fourth machine vaulted out suddenly, ripped off his helmet and goggles and hurled them to the ground. It was Trent.

He climbed out of his own machine and walked over toward Hoyt. Phelps-Barrington, who had a wild word for all occasions—Phelps-Barrington, who led the night trips to Amiens—was silent. When Paterson came up he shrugged and scowled ferociously.

"Is it you, Pat?" said Hoyt. "Thought it was Yardley."

"'Struth!" said Phelps-Barrington. "Let's go and have a drink."

Paterson thrilled as the man slipped an arm through his. For one awful moment he had thought—

"Well," Hoyt said, "those things will happen." And he shrugged again.

"I saw dots to the southward," said Paterson. "Maybe they'll be in later."

"No, little Rollo," said Phelps-Barrington. "They won't be in later or ever. I saw it with my own eyes—both in flames. I thought it was you, and until Trent landed I thought he might be Mac. But I was wrong. Let's shut up and have a drink!"

Then suddenly he knew, and his mind froze with the ghastliness of the thought. If he'd been quicker—if he'd turned and climbed above Yardley when he saw him lagging, with the smoke squirting from his hit motor—he could have saved him. If he had kept his eyes open behind instead of dreaming he might have saved MacClintock, too. In a daze, he stumbled after Phelps-Barrington. That's why Trent had hurled his helmet to the ground and walked off. That's why Hoyt had shrugged and said: "Those things will happen." It was his fault—his—Paterson's. He'd bolted and lost his head and fired blindly into the empty air. He hadn't stuck to his man. He had let Yardley drop back alone to be murdered.

"Look here, P. B.," he muttered, "I'm not drinking." He wanted to be alone—to think. So quick it had all been.

Phelps-Barrington grabbed his arm and pushed him stumbling into the mess shack. Trent was slumped down at the table with his glass before him, thumbing over a newspaper. He raised his head as they came in. "Two more of the same, steward—double." They sat down beside him, and Phelps-Barrington reached for a section of the paper.

"It says here," said Trent, "that Eva Fay didn't commit suicide. Died of an overdose of hashish she took at a party in Maida Vale the night before."

The steward brought the glasses. Trent raised his and looked at Paterson. "Good work, son."

Paterson stared at him in amazement. Trent sipped his whisky and went on reading as if he had never stopped. Some time later, Paterson left them and went down to the flight office to find Hoyt. The thought of the morning still bothered him, in spite of Trent's words, and he wanted to clear it up. Hoyt smiled as he came in."Washed the taste out in Falernian?" he asked.

"Some. Look here, skipper—this morning—what about it?"

"What about it?"

"My part—I was fast asleep. I saw Yardley lagging, and I had a moment to cross above him, but I lost my head, I'm afraid, and went wild."

The smile faded and Hoyt laid down his pencil. "Do you really think you could have saved him?"

"He was behind me already when I saw him lagging, just as you climbed and P.B. dived."

"Then you couldn't have helped him, because Mac was done for when I saw him and climbed, and half a tick after I climbed, P.B. saw Yardley burst into flames. There you are."

"But if I'd kept my eyes back instead of trusting to Mac?"

"Look here," said Hoyt, "no man can keep his eyes on everything. Something always happens in the place he isn't looking. Bear that in mind and forget this morning. You've seen a dog fight from the inside and lived. Take it easy. You're not here to do everything. You're here to stick to us. You might have run away. Remember that and be afraid of it. Remember if you get away by leaving a pal— he may live to come back. Then you'll have to face him, and engine trouble is a poor excuse.

"Trouble with you youngsters is that you've been fed up on poobah. And the myth of the fearless air fighter. Put it out of your mind. There's no such thing. Some are less afraid than others. Some are drunker—take your choice. Class dismissed." Hoyt grinned. "Go get cleaned up. We'll jog into Amiens for tiffin. Tender in half an hour. Tell Trent and P.B."

They spent most of the afternoon at Charlie's Bar with some of the men from the artillery observation squadron. For dinner they went to the Du Rhin and the glasses flowed red. Afterward, in another place, there was a fight, as usual, and chairs crashed like match sticks, until whistles sounded outside and the A.P.M.'s car, siren screaming, raced up the street. They poured out into the alleyway and ran, leaving the waiter praying in high, shrieking French.

Trent had a bottle with him. They rode all the way home singing and shouting to high heaven, forgetting that there were two empty chairs in the mess and that there might be more tomorrow.

> Take the cylinders out of my kidneys,
> Take the scutcheon pins out of my brain,
> Take the cam box from under my backbone
> And assemble the engine again!

They were good fellows—Billy Hoyt, P.B., Pat, and Ray Trent. Have 'nother li'l' drink.

They roared along like a Juggernaut, with the exhaust splitting the night air. Sometimes they were on the road and sometimes they were off. No one cared so long as they kept hurtling into the darkness.

Phelps-Barrington was fast asleep. Pat woke him up at the aerodrome and tumbled him into the hut.

They stumbled over a kit-bag in the doorway. P.B. straightened up suddenly. "Good-bye, Mac, old lad, sleep tight."

Trent kicked the bag out of the way. "Damned Adjutant! Take P.B. in with you, Pat. I'm bunking with the skipper. Might have the decency to take Mac's kit over to squadron office and not leave it lying around the passage. 'Night."

Paterson was quite sober. He tumbled P.B. into bed and stood for a moment at the open window, staring out across the ground mist that billowed knee high in the faint night breeze. He rested his elbows on the sill and hid his face in his trembling hands. If he could only be like the others—casual—calloused. If he had less imagination—more sand—stamina—something. MacClintock had planned this night himself, at breakfast. Yardley had left a letter addressed and stamped on his window sill. Paterson's mind jumped miles to the eastward. He saw the two blackened engines lying somewhere in the bleak fields beyond, ploughed into the ground, with their mats of twisted wires coiled around them in a hideous trap.

Their families would get word tomorrow. "Missing," it would read. And then later: "Previously reported missing, now reported killed in action." And tomorrow—perhaps his own family. Why can't it be quick?

There was a noise behind him. Someone fumbling at the door latch—Hoyt. "Had this bit left. Bottoms up! Quick!" He took the glass and drained it. The liquor bit into his veins and burned him. Hoyt set his own glass down on the washstand with a sharp click. "Get into bed now, you idiot. Good-night."

Spiked drink. Hoyt was a good fellow—damned decent. Do anything for Hoyt. Never let Hoyt go. Like my brother—before the War. Good old Hoyt. And he sank suddenly into a dreamless fuddle of sleep.

The weeks crawled on slowly. Paterson felt like a man climbing a steep ladder. Each day was a rung behind him. Each new rung showed an infinite number still ahead, waiting for him to go on, luring him with their apparent safety, waiting for him to reach the one rotten rung that would do him in. Some day he would reach it, and it would crack under him, or his fingers would slip and hurtle him into the abyss under his charred engine.

Offensive patrols and escort for the artillery observation squadron filled their time, with sometimes a road strafe to vary the monotony. These he liked best, for some quaint reason—perhaps because there was less space to fall through. Sometimes there would be a battalion on those roads—a battalion to scatter and knock down like tin soldiers on a nursery floor. Quite impersonal. They were never men to Paterson. Like dolls they ran and like dolls they sprawled awkwardly where they fell.

P.B. and Trent and Hoyt carried him through somehow. Mallory was back again, but Mallory never counted much with him. P.B. and Trent and Hoyt were a bulwark. They meant safety. It was good to wake up at night and hear P.B. snoring on the other cot, to know that Hoyt and Trent were asleep in the next cubicle. It was good to see them stamping to keep warm before the patrol took off in the half light of early morning. So different from one another and yet so alike underneath. Hoyt was nearer his kind than the two others. Tall and spindly like his brother, with a straight, thin nose that quivered slightly at the nostril when he was annoyed. Hoyt, who smiled and sanctioned the childish depravity of little P.B., but never quite met it with his own, although always seeming to, on the night trips to Amiens. Trent, glowering and quiet, with a keen hatred for everything political that he learned in the offices of the London and South-Western before the War, when the Army to him had meant young wastrels swanking the Guards' livery in the boxes of theatres—wastrels who had died on the Charleroi Road three years before.

Suddenly, from one of his mother's letters, he found that he had been in France almost three months. He stiffened with the thought and remembered what Hoyt had told him that day he had come: "I've been here three months. When I came, I came just as you did today—pucka green." He knew then that all his hopes were false. He was the same today as he had been that first day. He would always be the same. The spot of fear would always be with him. Some day it would swell and choke him and his hands would function without his frozen brain. He should never have tried to fly. He should have gone into the infantry as his brother had. Too much imagination—too little something. In three months he had learned the ropes, that was all; how to fire and when to fire, where the Archie batteries were near Cambrai, how to ride a cloud and crawl into it—nothing more.

The weeks went on, creeping closer and closer to the twenty first of March—the twenty-first of March—and with them the feeling crept into Paterson's heart—a feeling that something frightful was to happen. Things had been quiet so long and casualties had been few. C Flight hadn't been touched in weeks. He brooded over the thought and slept badly. He went to Amiens with P.B. more frequently. If it was to be any of the three, he knew he wouldn't be able to stand it. His bulwark would crumble and break and he would break with it. On the dawn patrols, those few minutes before they climbed into the cockpits and took off were agony: "This will be the day. It must be today. We can't go on this way. Our luck will break."

One day when they were escorting us, four dots dived on them from behind and he knew suddenly what he would do. Stark, logically, the thing stood before him and beckoned through the wires of his centre section. If a shot hit his plane, he would go down. They were far over the lines, taking no on a bombing show. He would wobble down slowly, pushing his joy-stick from side to side in a slow ellipse as if he were out of control. Then he would land and run his nose into the ground and be taken prisoner. The others would see him and swear that he'd been hit and he wouldn't do it until his machine had been hit. That for his own conscience's sake and for the years he would have to live afterwards.

But A Flight, behind and far above, saw the dots and scattered them, and the chance was gone.

Then day by day he waited for another. He knew now that he would do it at the first opportunity. He slept better with the thought, and the minutes seemed shorter now while he waited at dawn for his bus to be run out. All the details were worked out in his mind.

If any one of the three were close to him, he'd throw up his hands wildly before he started down. They'd see that and report it. Then when he landed he'd pull out the flare quick and burn his machine so that they would think he had crashed and caught fire. It was so easy!

He spent less time with P.B. now. Somehow the old freedom was gone. Somehow Hoyt wasn't the same to him either. He was working with three strangers he had never really known—three casual strangers he would leave shortly and never see again.

On the morning of the fourteenth of March the caller turned C Flight out suddenly, without warning, about an hour after P.B. and Trent had returned from Amiens. A special signal had come in from wing headquarters. B Flight had the regular morning patrol, but there was to be an additional offensive patrol besides. A Flight had morning escort and the dusk patrol. That meant C for the special. Paterson could hear Hoyt swearing about it next door. P.B., across the room, uttered a mighty curse and rolled over. Paterson got him a bucket of cold water and doused his feverish head in it. Trent and Hoyt were still cursing pettishly in the next cubicle.

Sleep-stupid, the four of them stumbled into the mess for hardboiled eggs and coffee. Mallory and the new man, Crowe, were already eating, white-faced and unshaven. They slumped down beside them in silence.

In silence, they trooped across the dark aerodrome, buttoning their coats and fastening helmet straps against the cold wretchedness of the March wind. The machines were waiting for them in a ghostly line like staring wasps that had eaten the food of the gods and grown to gigantic size.

They climbed in and taxied out mechanically. B Flight had already left on the regular dawn patrol. They blipped their motors and roared away, leaving their echo and the sharp smell of castor oil behind on the empty 'drome.

Hoyt led them south to the crumpled ruins of Péronne and out to the line, climbing high to get the warmth of the sunlight that began to tint the clouds above them. They were going over to Le Cateau and beyond. Intelligence wanted pictures to confirm certain reports of new Hun shell dumps and battery concentration. The photographic planes were to go out and get them under escort as soon as there was enough light. As additional precaution, offensive patrols were to be kept up far over the enemy's lines to insure the success of the pictures. They passed the sullen black stain that was Le Câtelet and turned to the eastward. The ground was already light and the camera busses would be starting.

Hoyt took the roof at eighteen thousand feet and skirted the cloud wisps, watching below for customers. Paterson watched P.B. anxiously. He had been roaring drunk an hour before. Groggy and drunk still, probably. He closed in a trifle and climbed above him, but P.B. waved him down and wiggled his fingers from the end of his nose.

He looked ahead and down at Trent. Trent had been drunk, too, but he was steady now, sawing wood above and slightly behind Hoyt.

Then, suddenly, beyond Trent and far below, he saw a Hun two-seater alone. The old stunt. Hoyt shifted and pulled up his nose to climb above it and wait. Trent followed him up. Somewhere above that two-seater, and a half-mile behind, there would be a flight of Hun scouts skulking under the clouds, waiting to pounce on whoever dived for the two-seater. Hoyt knew it for a decoy. Paterson knew it. They would climb above the cloud edge, circle back, and catch the Hun scouts as they passed underneath.

Paterson trembled slightly. This was his chance at last. There'd be a long dive and a sure fight from behind, and in the mix-up he'd wobble down and out of the War via Lazaret VI in Cologne. He glanced around to see if Mallory was above him, and suddenly, out of the corner of his eye, he saw P.B. shove his nose full down and throw himself into a straight dive for the decoy bus.

He gazed and shouted "No!" into the roar of his engine, P.B., in a nasty temper and half fuddled, didn't smell the trick. There was one awful second, while Crowe closed up into P.B.'s place and Hoyt banked to wait above for the Hun scouts to pounce down on the Camel.

P.B. fired, pulled up, and dived again, far below them. The Hun two-seater banked sharply and came up and over in an Immelmann turn to get away. P.B. caught it halfway over and a trickle of smoke swept out from its engine. Then in an instant Hoyt dived, with the rest of C Flight after him.

The next thing Paterson knew there were two Huns on his tail and a stream of tracer bullets pecking at his left wing. He pulled back on his stick and zoomed headlong up under Mallory. So close he was for a second that he could see the wheels turning slowly on Mallory's undercarriage and almost count the spokes glinting in the sunlight where the inside canvas sheathing had been taken off.

Mallory pulled away from him in a quick climbing turn and the Huns passed underneath, banking right and left. Paterson picked the left-hand one, thundered down on him in a short dive, and let go a burst of ten shots into the pilot's back. He saw the pilot's head snap sideways and his gloved hands fly up from the controls. Then Mallory dived over him after the other one. He turned in a wild split-air and followed Mallory.

There were more Huns below him and to the left, with two of the C Flight Camels diving and bucking between them. He raced furiously into a long dive, picked the nearest, and opened fire again in short, hammering bursts. His Hun wobbled and started down awkwardly in long sweeps. He picked another, still farther below, and pushed his stick forward until the rush of air gagged him. Wildly he fired as he ploughed down on it, and the chatter of his guns stabbed through the roar of his engine. He yelled like a madman, shot under the Hun, pulled up sharply, and fired into its grey mud-streaked belly. There was a fan of scarlet flame and a shock that tossed him to one side. He stalled and whipped out into a spin. Far below him he could see the decoy two-seater trailing a long plume of reddish smoke and flopping, wings over, toward the floor.

Then, suddenly, he saw his chance to wabble down and get away. He ruddered out of the spin and ran his stick once through the slow ellipse he had planned. But somehow he had to force himself to do it. There wasn't the relief he had expected. He looked back. Three C Flight machines were still above him, fighting madly—P.B., Trent, and Hoyt. No—not this time. He pulled his stick back and climbed up. There were five Huns circling the Camels. It was a long shot, but he fired at the nearest and came up under the tail just as one of the Camels hurtled into a nose dive, twisted over, and snapped off both wings. He saw the pilot's arms raised wildly in the cockpit and no more.

Blood streamed into his mouth. He had torn his lips with his teeth in the excitement. The warm salty tang mounted to his brain.

His goggles were sweat-fogged. His fingers ached with their pressure on the joy-stick, and his arm was numb to the elbow. In a spasm of blind hatred, he fired. Tracers raced across his top plane and struck with little smoke puffs that ripped the fabric into ribbons. His own bullets clawed at the Hun above him and fanged home.

He threw himself up and over in an Immelmann turn and came under the next, still firing. He let go his stick and jerked his Lewis gun down its sliding mount on his top plane. It fired twice and jammed. He yanked madly at the cocking lug, but it stuck halfway. He hurtled down again in another spin. The ground swept around in a quick arc that ended in clouds and more Hun busses. He caught at his thrashing joy-stick. Again the ground flashed through his centre section struts in a brown smudge, with the blaze of the sun hanging to one end of it. Then there was a Camel above him and a Camel below him. He closed in on the one below and squinted at the markings. Hoyt. He looked up at the other Camel, but the numerals on the side of its fuselage were hidden with a torn flap of fabric. Together, the three turned westward and started back.

Presently, near the line, the bus above him wabbled and dipped its nose. He stared at it. It went into a long, even glide that grew slowly steeper as he watched. He looked down for Huns. There were none. The glide became a dive, the dive twisted into an aimless spin, like the flopping of a lazy swimmer turning over in shallow water. The spin flattened and the Camel whipped out upside down, stalled, snapped out again, and again spun downward in that ghastly slow way. Over and over, only to whip out, stall and spin again. It was miles below him now. Nothing to do. Fascinated, he watched it as he followed Hoyt's tail. It was a mere dot now, flashing once or twice in the sun as it flopped over and over. Close to the ground now—closer. Then, suddenly, a tiny sheet of pink flame leaped up like the flash of a far beacon. That was all.

Hoyt was side-slipping below him, and he saw his own aerodrome under the leading edge of his bottom wing. He followed Hoyt down. They landed together and taxied slowly in toward the hangars. They stopped side by side and climbed out stiff-legged. Paterson looked down and saw that his right flying boot was torn and flayed into shreds across the outer side. There was a jagged fringe on the skirt of his coat where the leather had been ripped into ruffles. Dumbly, he looked back into his cockpit. The floor boards were splintered and the wicker arm of his seat was eaten away. He shrugged and walked over toward Hoyt. There was blood on the rabbit fur of Hoyt's goggles, blood that oozed slowly down and dripped from his chin piece in bright drops.

"Cigarette?"

Paterson gave him one. They walked into the flight office and slumped into chairs. Hoyt ripped off his helmet and dabbed at the scratch on his cheek. "I'm glad you got out, Pat," he said absently.

Then the fear spot broke and spattered into the four corners of Paterson's soul. He sprang up trembling, with his fists beating the air.

"The dirty lice!" he screamed. "They've killed P.B.! They've killed Trent! D' y' hear me, Hoyt?—they've killed 'em! They're gone! They'll never come back! They've—"

Hoyt's voice came evenly, calmly, through his screaming. "Steady, boy! Steady! You can't help it. No one can. Steady, now!"

A mat of white oil-splotched faces stared at them from the open doorway that led into the hangar. The boy turned wildly. "Clear out!" he shrieked. They vanished, open-mouthed. Hoyt drew him down into a chair. "No, Hoyt, no! Can't you see? P.B. and you and Trent have meant everything to me. I can't go on. I've fought this thing till I'm crazy." Hoyt reached quickly and slammed the door. "I've fought it night and day!" He threw up his arms hopelessly and covered his face with his shaking hands.

Hoyt put his hand on his trembling shoulders and patted them.

"Steady, now! Steady! None of that!" he said awkwardly.

Paterson's head whipped down across his sprawled arms on the desk top and the sobs tore at his throat in great gusts that choked him. "Oh, God!" he sobbed. "What's it all about, Hoyt? What's the use of it?"

"Steady, son! I don't know. Nobody knows. It just happened, as everything happens. It's much too late to talk causes. We're here and we know what we have to do. That's enough for us. It's all we have anyway, so it must be enough." He took his bloodsoaked cigarette from his mouth and hurled it into a corner. It landed with a soft spat.

Someone knocked at the door. "Come in." It was the runner from squadron office. He saluted. "Yes?" said Hoyt.

The man glanced at Paterson's face and snapped his eyes quickly back to the Captain's.

"Beg pardon, sir," he said. "Squadron's just been signalled through wing. One of the C Flight machines came down near B Battery, the 212th."

"Who was it?" asked Hoyt.

"Lieutenant Mallard, they reported it, sir. That'll be Lieutenant Mallory, sir, won't it?"

"Yes." Hoyt's voice was quite flat. "Thank you."

The man saluted again and shut the door. Hoyt dabbed at his cheek and reached into his desk drawer for another cigarette. Paterson stood up suddenly and grabbed his arm. "Listen, skipper!" Hoyt's eyes met his calmly. "I'm going to tell you something. I'll feel better if I do. I've been a weak sister in this flight. I've planned for days to go down and let myself be taken prisoner—to get out of it all. I've been sick of it—sick of it, d'y' hear, until I couldn't think straight. I wanted to get out alive. I wanted to get away in any way I could. This morning I broke. I let go and started down—"

Hoyt smiled. "Your trouble, Pat, is that you think you're the only person in this jolly old war."

Paterson stared at him. "But I did! I started down, out of it, this morning!"

"How'd you get here?" asked Hoyt.

"But if I hadn't broken for that moment this morning—"

"That's a lie!" snapped Hoyt. "You're talking poobah! I know how those things happen. If P.B. hadn't gone down after the twoseater they'd all be here now; and by the same reasoning, if my aunt wore trousers she'd be my uncle. The important thing is that it's you and me now and nothing else matters. We'll have four brand-new men to whip into shape tomorrow, and whatever you think of yourself, you've got to do it. I can't do much, for I'll be ahead, leading. You'll be behind them and you'll have to do it all. They'll be frightened and nervous and green, but the job's to be done. Understand? You've got to goad them on and get them out of trouble and watch them every minute, so that in time they'll be as good as P.B. and Trent—so that when their turn comes they can do for other green men what P.B. and Trent did for you. Do you see now what this morning has done for you?" He paused for a moment, and then, in a lower tone: "Afraid? Who isn't afraid? But it doesn't do any good to brood over it."

C Flight did no duty the next day, nor the day following. Hoyt went up to the 212th and identified Mallory for burial, while Paterson flew back to the Pool for the replacement pilots and a new Camel for Hoyt.

In Amiens he heard the first whispered rumors of what was going to happen. Intelligence was ranting for information. Everybody had the story and nobody was right. The hospitals were evacuating as fast as possible. Fresh battalions were being hustled up. It wasn't a push. Anyone could tell that with half an eye. Something the Hun was doing. The spring offensive a month earlier this year. G.H.Q. was plugging the gaps frantically, replacing and reinforcing and wondering where the hammer would fall and what it would carry with it. Hence the pictures that had cost the lives of P.B. and Trent. The air itself trembled with uncertainty, and rumors flew fast and thick.

Paterson flew back with the four new pilots and brought the rumors with him. Hoyt had more to barter in exchange. The talk ran riot at dinner.

"It's a Hun push, all right, but where, nobody knows. We'll have word in a day or so, but it'll be wrong whatever it is, mark what I say!"

And then on the evening of the twentieth things started. A signal came for the Major just as they sat down to mess. He went out and presently called out the three flight commanders. When they came back they took their places thoughtfully. Silence trembled in the room like the hush that precedes the first blasting stroke of a great bell in a cathedral tower. The Major swept his eyes down the board.

"You will remain at the aerodrome tonight, gentlemen, and remain sober. Officers' luggage is to be packed and placed on lorries which Mr. Harbord is providing for that purpose." He paused for a moment. "This is a precautionary move, gentlemen. We are to be ready to retire at a moment's notice. Flight commanders have the map squares of the new aerodrome. You can take that up later among yourselves." He leaned back in his chair and beckoned to the mess sergeant. "Take every officer's order, sergeant, and bring me the chit."

The talk broke in a wild flood that roared and crackled down the length of the table. The tin walls trembled with the surge of it and the echoes broke in hot discord among the rough pine rafters. Offensive patrols for all three flights, to start at five minutes to 4 a.m. Air domination must be maintained. Wing's instructions were to stop everything at all costs. Go out and fight and shut up. Somebody presented the Adjutant with the sugar bowl and asked him if he had his umbrella for the trip back. The Adjutant had spent eighteen days without soles to his boots in 1914. He and the medical officer stood drinks for the squadron.

About ten o'clock, Hoyt called the five men of C Flight into his hut. "Tomorrow, something is going to happen, I'm afraid, and you've got to meet it without much experience. What I want you to understand is simply this: You've got Pat and you've got me. Follow us and do what we do. We won't let you down so far as it is humanly possible. If the flight gets split up in a dog fight, then fight your way out two and two—and go back to the new 'drome two and two. Don't go separately. Further"—he paused—"if anything happens to me"—Paterson looked up at him quickly and something tugged sharply at his heart; Hoyt went on quietly—"take your lead from Mr. Paterson. You'll be Number 5, Darlington. You'll climb up as deputy leader. And if anything happens to Pat, then it's up to you to bring the rest home." He smiled. "There is a bottle of Dewar's in this drawer. Take a snifter now, if you want it, and one in the morning. It's for C Flight only. Oh yes, one more thing: The fact that we're moving back to a new aerodrome seems to indicate that staff thinks nothing can stop the Hun from breaking through. The fact that nothing can stop the Hun seems to indicate that, for the nonce, we are losing our part of the War. If the thought will help you—it's yours without cost."

The caller rapped sharply and threw back the door. Paterson leaped to his feet half asleep and pushed back the window curtains.

The clouds were down to about four hundred feet, lowering in a grey mass over the mist on the aerodrome. He went into the next cubicle and turned Hoyt out. Hoyt sat up on the cot edge and ran his hand across his forehead.

"Stop the caller," he said. "Let's see what's what before we turn everybody out." They shrugged into their flying coats and groped down the passage to the Major's cubicle in the next hut block.

"Let 'em sleep," said the Major. "Can't do anything in this muck. Turn out one officer in each flight to watch for the break and to warn the rest. Send Harbord to me if you see him wandering about."

They woke up the skippers of A and B Flights and told them the news. Paterson took the watch for C. He turned up his coat collar and went out. It was cold and miserable in the open, and the chill crept into his bones. The smoke from his cigarette hung low about him in the still air.

Presently to the eastward there came a low roar. He looked at his wrist watch. The hands pointed to six minutes to four o'clock. The ground trembled slightly to the sound of the distant guns and the air stirred in faint gusts that pulled at blue wraiths of his cigarette smoke. The push had started. His muscles stiffened at the knees as he listened. The first shock of the guns was raw and sharp in the quiet air; then it settled into a lower, full-throated rumble like the heavy notes of an organ growling in an underground basilica. Now it rose again in its greater volume—rose steadily, slowly, as if it were a colossal express train hammering down the switch points at unthinkable speed. Presently it soared to its highest pitch and held the blasting monotony of its tone. The minutes ticked off, but the guns never faltered in their symphony of blood. At 4:35 one pipe of the organ to the south-eastward cut out suddenly and almost immediately began again, closer than before. Again it broke as he listened, and crept nearer still.

He walked down the line of huts, thrashing his arms and blowing on his cold hands. An impersonal thing to him, yet he shivered slightly and stared upward at the low clouds. Men out there to the eastward were in it. The suspense was over for them. And suddenly he found himself annoyed at the delay, annoyed at the fog and clouds above, that kept him on the ground. He wanted to see what was going on—to know. He turned impatiently and went into the mess. The sergeant brought him coffee, and presently Muirhead of A Flight came in with Church of B.

"It's on," Church said absently. "I suppose this fog means hell up the line."

They drank their coffee and smoked in silence. The sound of the guns crept nearer and nearer, and one by one the rest of the squadron drifted in for breakfast.

Hoyt sat down next to Paterson. "I don't like it," he said. "Something is giving way up there." He went to the window and looked out. "Clouds are higher," he said, "and the fog's lifted a bit. What do you think, Major?"

They crowded out of the mess doorway and stood in an anxious knot, staring upward. It was well after six o'clock.

"All right"—the Major turned around—"get ready to stand by."

C Flight collected in a little knot in front of Hoyt's Camel, smoking and talking nervously. Paterson kept his eyes on Hoyt and stamped his feet to get the circulation up. A strange elation crept into his veins and warmed him. In a moment now—in a moment. Awkward waiting here. Awkward standing around listening to Darlington curse softly and pound his hands together.

Somewhere behind him on the road, a motor-bike roared through the mist, and then to the southward a shell crashed not a thousand yards from the 'drome, and the echo of it thumped off across the fields. Darlington jumped and stared at the mushroom of greasy black smoke. A moment more—a moment now. Paterson reached over and tapped Darlington's sleeve. "Keep your guns warm, old boy." Darlington nodded fiercely.

The Major climbed into his cockpit and a mechanic leaped to the propeller. The engine coughed once and the propeller snapped back. The mechanic leaped at it again. It spun down and melted into a circle of pale light. Everyone was climbing in. Hoyt flicked his cigarette away sharply and put a leg up into his stirrup.

They were taxi-ing out into the open ground, with the mechanics running after them. Presently they could see the road. Paterson stared at it in amazement. It was brown and crawling with lorries and troops. Something had happened! A Flight, with the Major, sang off across the ground and took the air together in a climbing turn. B Flight waited a brief second and followed. Out of the corner of his eye Paterson could see the mess sergeant climbing up on the lorry seat beside Harbord, the equipment officer. Then Hoyt waved his hand. Mechanics yanked at the chock ropes and waved them off. They blipped their motors and raced out after Hoyt.

At five hundred feet they took the roof in the lacy fringe of the low clouds. Bad, very bad, Paterson thought. He ran his thumb across the glass face of his altimeter and his globe became wet with the beaded moisture. He could hardly see Darlington's tail. Ahead of them the clouds were a trifle higher. Hoyt led them up and turned northward. Murder to cross the line at that height, with the barrage on. Darlington was lagging a bit. Afraid of the clouds. He dived on Darlington's tail and closed him up on Number 3. Darlington glanced back at him and ducked his head.

Hoyt was circling back now in a broad sweep. Over there somewhere was Cambrai. He looked up for an instant just in time to see the underside of a huge plane sweep over him. He ducked at the sight of the black crosses, but the plane was gone before he could whip his Lewis gun into action. Almost immediately one corner of his windshield ripped away and the triplex glass blurred with a quick frosting of a thousand cracks. He cursed into the roar of his motor and kept on.

They were higher now, but the visibility was frightful—like flying in a glass ball that had been streaked with thick, dripping soapsuds. Here a glimpse and a rift that closed up as soon as you looked; there a blank wall, tapering into tantalising shreds that you couldn't quite see beyond. He fidgeted in his cockpit and turned his head from Hoyt, below him, to the grey emptiness behind. Nothing.

Presently Hoyt banked around, and following him, the compass needle on Paterson's instrument board turned through a half circle. They were going back toward the south again and climbing still higher. An even thousand feet now—just under the rising, ragged clouds. He felt a drop of rain strike his cheek where his chin piece ended. It bit his skin like a thorn and stung for seconds afterward. His goggles were fogging. He ran a finger up under them and swept the lenses.

Then, in a breath, it happened. A grey flash swept down out of the clouds in front of the formation. Hoyt zoomed to avoid it. The Hun zoomed, and they came together and melted into each other in a welter of torn, rumpled wings and flying splinters. Something black and kicking rose out and disappeared. The cords stood out in Paterson's neck and his throat closed. Somewhere his stomach leaped and kicked inside of him, trying to get out, and he saw coffee dripping from the dials of his instruments.

In a second he had thrown his stick forward and gone down into Hoyt's place. He didn't dare look—he couldn't look. He was screaming curses at the top of his voice and the screams caught in his throat in great sobs. His goggles were hopelessly fogged. He ripped them off. Behind him the four new men closed in tightly, with Darlington above them as deputy leader.

There was blood again on his lips. He pulled back his stick and climbed. There, somewhere in the clouds, were the men who had done it! All right! All right! His eyes stung and wept with the force of the wind, and his cheeks quivered under the lash of the raindrops. With his free hand, fist clenched, he pounded his knee in stunned anguish until his muscles ached. Hoyt! Hoyt! Then he saw what he wanted, and dived down furiously at the shape in the mist. Bullets tore at his top plane and raked across the cowling behind him. He closed on the Hun and sent it spinning. There was another—three—five—nothing but Huns. He dived in between them. Fine! He was screaming again and firing. He forgot he was flying. The joy-stick thrashed crazily between his knees, and the ground and the clouds were a muddy grey scarf that swept from side to side across his eyes. Guns were the thing. Once, in a quick flash, he saw tiny men running upside down through the ring sight of his Lewis gun—the gun on his top plane—funny.

His wrists ached and his fingers were quite dead against the Bowden trigger. No, not that; that's a Camel-Darlington. He grabbed at his joy-stick and pulled it back. Funny how hard it was to pull it. Another Camel swept in beside him, and another, with startling suddenness. It had been a long time now—a long time. Somebody had been afraid once and there had been a man named Hoyt. No, Hoyt was dead. Hoyt had been killed days before. Must have been P.B. P.B. was probably in Amiens by now. He'd left in the tender at six o'clock. And always his guns chattered above the roar of his engine.

Abruptly, the cross wires of his centre section raced up to him from a great distance and stopped just before his eyes. He wondered where they had been all this time. He stared past them into the light disc of his propeller, and again the rain lashed into his face and stung him. He caught at the kicking joy-stick and held on to it with both hands—but one hand fell away from it and wouldn't come back. With an effort he pulled back his stick to climb up under the clouds again. Must be up under the clouds. Must wait and get more Huns. Funny things, Huns. Clumsy, stupid grey things you shot at and sent down. Go home soon, rest a bit, and get some more. He laughed softly to himself. Joke. Funniest thing in the world.

The centre section wires clouded up before his eyes and started to race away from him. Here! That's bad! Can't fly without centre section wires. He chuckled a bit over that. Absurd to think of flying without centre section wires! Come back here! You come back!

Just as his eyes closed, he saw a streak of roadway flicker through the struts of his left wing. There were faces on it quite close to him—faces that were white and staring; faces with arms raised above them. Funny. He whipped back his joy-stick with a convulsive jerk, and then his head crashed forward and he threw up his arm to keep his teeth from being bashed out against the compass.

It was very dark—dark except for a dancing blue light far away. He moved slightly. Something cool touched his forehead.

"All right," he muttered; "that's all right now. You just follow me." Someone whispered. He opened his eyes and stared into the darkness. "No," he said quite plainly. "I mean it! Hoyt's dead. I saw him go down."

He felt something sharp prick his arm. "You've got the new aerodrome pinpointed, haven't you?" he asked.

A soft voice said: "Yes. Sh-h-h!"

"No," he said, "I can't. Darlington's alone now, and I've got to go back. They're green, but they're good boys." He moved his legs to get up. "There's a bottle of Dewar's———"

"No," said the voice beside him.

"Oh yes," he said quietly. "Really, this is imperative. I know I crashed."

A stealthy languor crept across his chest and flowed down toward his legs. He thought about it for a moment. "I ought to go," he said pettishly. "But I'm so tired."

"Yes," said the voice. "Go to sleep now."

"Right-o," he said. "You call a tender and wake me half-an-hour." He was quiet for a moment more and then he chuckled softly. "Tell 'em it's poobah," he said sharply.

"All right," said the voice. "It's poobah."

His breathing became quiet and regular, and footsteps tiptoed softly down the ward away from his bed.

Among the Trumpets

James B. Wharton

"He paweth in the valley, and rejoiceth in his strength: he goeth on to meet the armed men. He mocketh at fear. . . He saith among the trumpets, Ha, Ha; and he smelleth the battle afar off, the thunder of the captains, and the shouting. The glory of his nostrils is terrible." — Jos xxxix.

The morning was well advanced; that is to say, it was some time after nine o'clock. Westward the high-banked clouds that were the remnants of those that had deluged the countryside with rain the night before were still black and menacing, but eastward the sky was blue, and the sun already gave promise of unpleasant heat later on.

From the black woods on the right, gloomy and sinister beneath the clouds, to the rolling hills of the horizon stretched a wavy band of newly ploughed earth. It was wide, it was irregular, it ran up and down hill and squirmed along the side of crests as if the man that had furrowed it had been either drunk or blind. That wavy band of earth, though made with steel, had not been ploughed. It marked the German front line in front of Richecourt; it showed where the defense system that the French had crowned with such names as the Trench of the Goths, Trench of the Vandals, and Trench of the Barbarians had once frowned on Seichprey and Jury Wood. The system was no more. Parapet and parados had been flattened into one uneven heap of mangled earth; the wire had been plucked up by shells, tossed about, rolled up, and flattened again by the passage of tanks. Dug-outs and strong-points that had defied assault for four years had gone as the snows of yesteryear. The American attack that had begun at dawn had crossed this band of ploughed ground in one jump, found no resistance, and had gone on across the fields to the north, where they were already out of range.

The American artillery, most of its guns outranged, and the others unable to direct the barrage at such a distance from the target, had ceased firing. The Germans, their guns abandoned or in retreat, had done likewise. Deep silence had fallen where so short a time before thunderbolts had crashed, and the ground had trembled with the recoil of a thousand guns. Where all had been smoke and shouts and frantic rockets were now only peaceful fields and quiet, shady woods, except for that long, waving, sinister gash that was like a wound that had killed this countryside.

From a hollow suddenly appeared a group of horsemen. They drew rein before their silhouettes cut the skyline and hurriedly examined the ground to the right flank with their field-glasses. The fields, through a field-glass, were not at all deserted.

The leader of the horsemen, a Captain of United States cavalry, could see men stringing telephone wire, prisoners in groups of three and four coming back, ambulances being loaded with wounded, and, far away northward, white puffs of smoke that came from bursting grenades, and that showed where the American advance was bombing its way toward an objective it had not hoped to reach until the morrow.

"We're through the first line," said the Captain decisively; "the road will be about there." He pointed to his left front, then looked curiously at Mont Sec, a sugar-loaf hill that rose abruptly a thousand feet from the surrounding plain. Its summit was crowned with smoke, from which came the continuous flash of bursting shells. "I doubt if any Boche up there can see us," said the Captain. "We'll assume not. Can you make out the road, Lieutenant? We'd better locate it before we start across."

The officer addressed wore the blue of the French Army. He had a round, bullet head and moustaches that were much too long. He polished his field-glasses with a white handkerchief, breathing upon them, wiping them carefully, and holding them to the light to see if they were clean.

The Captain tightened his lips impatiently. Behind him he heard the stamping of a horse, and, turning about, saw a sergeant who had just ridden up.

"Where the hell have you been?" barked the Captain.

"Sir, I had to come in from the extreme left, and this horse ain't much of a horse."

The sergeant panted slightly. It was apparent from his flushed countenance that he had been having difficulties with his mount.

"Well, if you can't ride him, turn him in," snapped the Captain, and turned back to the French officer.

An enlisted man, his legs seemingly lost behind the high pommel of his packed saddle, under-slicker, gun boot, sabre, saddle-pockets, blanket roll, and two days' grain ration, moved his horse over next to the sergeant's.

"Hey, goldbrick!" he whispered. "Where yuh been?"

The sergeant turned. "Hey, Mac!" he cried. He suddenly paused. He noted that the other wore a trumpet slung across his shoulders, and on the sleeve of his blouse, plainly discernible, was the scar of recently removed chevrons.

"You been busted?" went on the sergeant. "Huh? Drunk? A.W.O. loose? A guy with your service! Yuh oughta know better!"

"Naw, naw," grinned the trumpeter, "I got caught with a pair o' leather putts on. 'N' by the corps commander, too, no less. Don't worry; I got a better job blowin' horn. Why dinyuh join up with us at Mandrees? Where yuh been, anyway, the last three months?"

"At Besançon, learnin' machine-rifle. I'm commandin' the machine-gun troop. How come else I got invited to a council of war? Whaddyuh think, kid? See any other sergeants around?"

The trumpeter grinned a slow grin, then ejected tobacco juice.

"Machine-gun troop, huh? You an' them two machine-rifles! Well, if you get from here to them woods with 'em I'll buy yuh a drink."

"You think that's the entrance then?"

The Captain's voice came clearly in the silence that followed.

"Very well; I think I'll move them across there in echelon of double columns. I don't think we'll meet any resistance yet. The infantry would never have got by the woods if there were any square-heads in a fighting mood there.

"Troop commanders! You will cross the open space by troops, in echelon of platoons in double column. You will regulate the gait according to the nature of the ground and the circumstances, without attempting to maintain the regularity of the squadron formation. On arriving at the woods we'll again resume column formation. I will be with 'H' troop's first platoon. Understand? Posts!"

"Boy," whispered the trumpeter, "if any o' them take up the gallop he won't have a man left in the saddle."

"How come?" demanded the sergeant. "What yuh been doin all summer?"

"Diggin' a sewer for the Q.M. corps at Gievres," grinned the trumpeter. "Ninety per cent o' this here 'raggedy pants cadet' outfit ain't never been on a horse before in their lives."

"No kiddin'."

"No kiddin'. If we meet up with any Boche that's on the peck any, there'll be a hot time in the old town, know, what I mean."

"Sergeant Lee!"

"Sir!"

"Where are your machine-rifles?"

"In rear of 'H' troop, sir."

"Good. Ride with me so that I can give you orders for their employment. Off we go!"

The troop commanders—there were but two, and one of them a Lieutenant—rejoined their troops, there was an arm signal, a few moaning whistle blasts, then the squadron, in a formation very similar to that which old-timers used to style "column of bunches," topped the skyline, and, hurriedly descending into the hollow beyond, proceeded at a fast trot toward the distant woods. A fast trot. Too fast, for the slower horses began to canter, whereat the faster ones, hearing tremendous clatter and thumping of hoofs, wanted to canter too; and here and there a bolter began to go from rear to front of a platoon column, to the accompaniment of squeals and kicks from the other horses, and untrammelled language from the riders, who had received a blow from a rifle butt on the thigh, a cinch ring on the knee, or who had been nearly torn from the saddle by the impetuous rush of the bolting horse.

"They'll get over that," observed the trumpeter sagely. "They been fillin' 'em with oats. They won't prance very long under them full packs."

"They didn't waste any oats on mine," panted the sergeant. He had, by dint of voice, heel, and a dub he carried, urged his horse into a shambling trot.

"Nor on that Frog Looey's either."

The French officer's horse was one of those who are averse to traveling alone, and who will not leave ranks or picket line for any persuasion. This steed was proceeding at a sort of drifting gait, going sideways like a yacht with no centre-board, and making always toward 'H' troop's second platoon. The French officer kept the horse's head firmly toward the woods, so that the steed could not see his companions; but he knew they were there, and kept ever an ear turned in their direction. Spur and whip prevailed for a time, but the moment the Lieutenant stopped to draw breath or rest his tired leg the drifting began again, accompanied by head tossing and lightning—like thrusts of the neck, which attempts had the effect each time of nearly unseating the French officer.

"That's a nice horse for an officer to ride," observed the sergeant. "You'd think he'd know better than to bring a goat like that with him."

"We give it to him. It's an 'H' troop horse. 'Sidewinder,' they call him. He's like Coke Gillis. He ain't gone straight since he was born."

"We give it to him!" protested the sergeant. "That's a great way to treat an officer and an ally. Give him a star-gazin' goat like that!"

"Huh!" grunted the trumpeter, helping himself to another chew. "The French give him to us in the first place. Let 'em see now how they like their own horses."

They arrived, finally, at the edge of the woods. No sign of life. Not a shot fired. There was a narrow field there, along the edge of which ran a rough track, an old cart path, but now beaten flat by many feet. Beyond, across the field, were more woods, into which this cart path led. There was a trench along the edge of the woods, but empty, and the hurdle that barred the road where it went through the wire had been so hastily put in place that the advance guard had been able to unwire it and drag it clear before the main body had come up.

Across the field went the squadron, skirting a communication trench, then the advance guard was seen to halt, troopers galloped out to left and right, and some indecision was manifested.

"What the matter?" demanded the Captain, riding up.

"There's four roads here," replied one of the troopers of the advance guard.

"Which road, Lieutenant?"

The French officer pulled up his horse and dragged forward his map-case.

"You're not going to look at a map, are you?" demanded the Captain. "I can look at a map myself. I thought you knew this country. Do you realize that I've got a squadron of horse standing here in a field that runs from Apremont halfway to Metz? Do you suppose the Boche are going to sit down and wait for us to cut them off? They're running so fast now we won't catch up with them before night."

"The other end of this field is held by French troops," replied the French Lieutenant. "They won't fire because they have been warned not to. There will be plenty of Boche very soon, don't worry." He bent over his map.

"Very well," snapped the Captain. "I'll make my own decision."

"If you do," replied the other, lifting his long moustache in a sneer, "you are liable to come into an area that is under our own artillery preparation, in which case the responsibility will be yours."

The Captain flushed, but said nothing. After all, this French officer had been sent for just that purpose, to keep this squadron out of areas that the French were pounding. It would not advance the situation to have the squadron destroyed by friendly artillery fire.

The French officer put away his map, took out a cigarette-case, extracted one, and lighted it.

"The road to the right," said he.

The trumpeter tossed his chin meaningly in the direction of the French officer.

"Ah, don't worry about him," replied Sergeant Lee. "The French are probably just as proud of him as we are of some of the mail order wonders we got. Boy, they got 'em in all armies, like coots."

Thick trees but no underbrush, huts, scattered grey overcoats, then, suddenly, long lines of wagons and empty picket lines. Loose horses, many of them wounded, could be seen among the trees, some trotting and whinnying at the sight of the advancing troops, others bounding away, and one or two limping in their direction, as if to ask for help from others of their kind.

Suddenly, at an alley that crossed the main track, the Americans saw men. The Captain, the trumpeter, an orderly, and Sergeant Lee saw them almost simultaneously. There was a group of ten or fifteen that had probably heard the advance guard thud by and had come out of their holes to see what it was all about.

The Captain swung his horse, whipped out his pistol, and charged. "H" troop's leading platoon followed him. Pistols barked, and Sergeant Lee's horse, that up to that time had given but the faintest signs of life, bolted, and, having gotten a firm grip of the bit before the sergeant had recovered himself, was well away into the trees.

It was impossible to circle the runaway in the trees, but the sergeant saw before him an opening in the woods, into which the horse presently tore. Here was the place to reach out, seize the head-stall, and by main strength drag the horse's head around so that he must run in a circle and eventually stop.

Bark!

"Cut out shooting, you damned fool!" shouted the sergeant. "Can't you see this horse—"

Bark! bark!

There was another man there, on a black horse. Flame spat from his hand. It was a German. Lee whipped out his sabre, and, instantly stopping all attempts to control his horse, let him go headlong for the black. The black, however, did not wait for the attack, but leaped aside, and its rider shot at Lee, as he tore by, at point-blank range.

But Lee had pinked him with the sabre. Not badly, he knew, but he had felt resistance as he had lunged out. If only now he could pull this goat down!—but they had crossed the glade and were again amidst the trees.

Bark! Again! The man on the black was pursuing him! Swiftly through the sergeant's mind passed the realization that he was very probably drawing his last breath. The German was behind, hence Lee would have to either sheathe his sabre—impossible at that gait—let it hang by the sabre-knot while he drew his pistol impossible, because he had not put his hand through the wristloop when he had drawn it—throw it away, and then engage in a pistol combat with the German—impossible, because if he turned around the horse would undoubtedly dash headlong into the first tree—or just lay on the horse's neck, say a prayer, and pour the hooks into him.

How many shots? The German's gun must be nearly empty now. Ah, no, the German pistol held ten. Before him suddenly loomed wire—a parapet. Would the horse jump it? He was done now, anyway.

The horse bucked to a halt. Lee dropped his sabre, tore out his pistol, and, swinging around in the saddle, had one wild shot with it, anyway. He shouted and fired again, more shouts, crashing, then the black horse tore by, saddle empty, and came to a rearing halt at the belt of wire, like a horse that has thrown his rider before the barrier in a riding hall.

There were Americans there—the trumpeter, pistol in hand, two privates of the advance guard.

"Hey, Lee!" cried the trumpeter. "We come down the road! I got that guy on the black!"

He and the two privates rode back to look at the German. He was on his face, but when one had dismounted and turned him over, they saw that he was dead. He was a private, with the black medal that indicates one wound and the light blue and yellow shoulder-straps of a *Jaeger zu Pferde*, or mounted rifleman.

"Striker, probably," decided the trumpeter, "because this here horse looks like an officer's."

"I'll say," agreed Sergeant Lee. He had ridden over and taken the black's bridle, and then led him back to the others.

"Well, let's go," said the others hurriedly. "This ain't no place to match pennies. These woods are full o' Boche."

"Right!" agreed Lee. "Where's the rest of 'em?"

"On the road. Whachuh dismountin' for?"

"I'm goin' to mount up on this black horse."

"You are?" cried the trumpeter. "Why, if anyone mounts him, I do! I knocked the guy off his back with a 45."

"How do you know?" demanded the sergeant, picking up the sabre he had dropped. "I had two or three shots at him myself."

"No, it was the trumpeter got him," said one of the privates, looking nervously about him. "We better be gettin' back. I see the Captain out there. No, the trumpeter got that kraut. I seen it."

"Well, this horse is mine," said Sergeant Lee, mounting, "because I'm rankest man. What's the good of having three stripes if you can't rank somebody out of a bunk or a horse or something?"

"What are you men doing in there? See anything?" called a voice from behind the trees.

All wheeled their horses and went out. The alley down which they had charged curved, and the Captain with the rest of the platoon had halted there.

"The trumpeter shot a German, sir," said Sergeant Lee. "He was chasing me. I've captured his horse."

"Nice horse that," remarked the Captain. "Better change saddles the first chance you get. We'll be able to use all the extra horses we can get before we're through. Trumpeter, ride back and tell Lieutenant Bennett to push a patrol forward on the road. I'm going to prospect around in here a little to see what we've run on to, to see if there is any sign of a force here, if this is just a bunch of wagoners and stable orderlies that we've run into. See that that French officer knows what's going on.

"Corporal Petersen, take your squad and see if there are any Germans left in those huts. Write down any regimental numbers you see on the wagons.

"Sergeant Lee, take a set of fours and follow along that trench to see what you find. When you hear three blasts of the whistle, rejoin."

He blew a short blast on his whistle. "Foragers, ho-o-oh!" The platoon, in line of foragers, at "raise pistol" moved off among the trees.

Sergeant Lee, riding the black and leading his own horse, led his four men along the line of the trench that had stopped the runaway rush of his horse. The trench was shallow, and had been newly dug. They found shortly after a small house, a sort of shelter for foresters or shepherds, very strongly built of stone. The trench was evidently part of an attempt to make a strong point out of this house, to prevent, perhaps, the flanking of positions farther back in the woods by attack from the road. The house, however, seemed to be abandoned, for its door hung open.

Sergeant Lee, his pistol ready, rode up, but there was nothing in the interior but scattered bed-clothing and the disorder of boots, belts, and equipment that told of hasty flight.

"Number One," said the sergeant, "take this horse. Don't turn him loose, whatever happens, because he's got everything I own on him. I'm going to ride on a little. Listen for the three whistles and repeat them if you hear them."

He turned over his own horse, and being now free could enjoy the feel of riding the black. The horse was a thoroughbred. Lee had never been on one like him before. It was like sitting on a dynamo. He could feel beneath him the nervous energy and the power of those steel muscles running up and down. A touch of the spur, a flexion of the wrist, and the black was cantering. A turn of the shoulder, a shift of the left leg, and the black had changed leads. What a horse! Schooled, intelligent, powerful. Lee, without pressure on the reins, closed his legs and leaned slightly back. The horse slowed his gait. He leaned farther back. The black halted.

"Ah, boy! That's a horse!" breathed the sergeant to himself. What couldn't a man do with a mount like that? He saw himself leading a charge, outstripping Lieutenants, Captain, everyone, hurling himself upon the enemy, capturing their commander, their flags, raging about among them on that black horse—

"Hey, sergeant! Three whistles!"

There was, alas—a war on. The sergeant, taking one last look about him, moved his hand ever so slightly to the left, and the black, coming around beautifully, cantered back to the others. The sun, higher, began to glitter through the trees. No sign of the enemy, no crash of shell, no crackle of machine-guns.

"Come on with that set of fours!" called someone faintly. "Rejoin! Rally! Ralle-e-e!"

Lee gathered his four men and, trotting through the underbrush, rejoined the platoon, which the Captain was leading back in the direction of the road they had left. They came out, in a minute or two, into the sunlight, and found there the head of the column, the trumpeter, and the French Lieutenant.

"What did you see, sergeant—anything?" demanded the Captain.

"No, sir, only blankets and stuff lying around. That trench hadn't even been finished."

"We're losing time," said the Captain quickly. "There was no force in there. We'll probably be seeing stragglers and orderlies and first-aid men and all sorts of goldbricks running loose in these woods, but that's not what we're here for. Now then, we'll push forward vigorously. Pass the word back that if any isolated enemy are seen to shoot at them, but not to delay the advance to try to capture them. Leave that for the doughboys. That agree with your thoughts, Lieutenant?"

The French officer nodded. "Quite right, Captain," said he. He did not turn his face, however, in the Captain's direction. His eye was upon the black horse that Sergeant Lee rode. "Captain," he went on, "I think I shall have to ask you to give me that horse that man is riding."

"Huh? Give you that horse? That's a German horse. He captured it."

"I see that by the equipment, but it is a much better horse than mine. I want it."

"Perhaps you do," said the Captain, gathering his reins, "but we don't take horses away from noncommissioned officers in this man's army."

"Do you mean to say, sir," cried the French officer, "that you will not give an officer of an Allied army a captured horse simply because some soldier found it first? Which is the most important for the success of our mission—that he should be well mounted, or that I, who am the guide and the officer of liaison and the interpreter, should have the best horse? I think that Higher Authority would not take very long to decide the question."

It was in the Captain's mind to make no reply but to order the advance to be resumed. But then this French officer would make a report of it when he returned, which report would come drifting down from corps headquarters, gathering endorsements and bitterness like a descending snowball, until it came into the hands of the squadron commander's immediate superiors. He would get Hades. And he would get no more details to command provisional squadrons.

"Give him the horse, sergeant," ordered the Captain.

The sergeant's face hardened, and for just a second his blazing eyes met the Captain's, whereat that officer's jaw muscles stood out like cords.

"Dismount!" he barked.

The sergeant obeyed, as well as some half-dozen troopers, who thought that the captain had meant them, too. In the slight confusion attendant on these men being cursed back into their saddles by their respective corporals, Sergeant Lee was able to turn over the black, go to Number One and get his own horse, and mount. The column moved forward again, at a rapid trot.

Sergeant Lee and the trumpeter were once more side by side, Lee muttering under his breath his opinion of some nameless person. His language was picturesque, for he decorated it with idioms learned in bar-room, barrack, and camp, from Jolo in the days of the Sultan of Sulu to the Camp de Valdahon at the present moment.

"You talkin' about that French Looey?" inquired the trumpeter.

"Well, who the hell else would you think?" demanded Lee.

The trumpeter spat expertly between his horse's ears. "Well, I dunno. You ain't got any kick against him. He was just rankest man. What's the use o' bein' rankest man if you can't rank someone out of a bunk or a horse or somethin'?"

The sergeant's reply was horrible, whereat the trumpeter grinned so widely that he lost his chew.

There were signs now of distress from the squadron. The gait of the head of the column was too fast for that of the rear, so that the last third was at a slow gallop. The smothered admonitions of platoon leader, sergeant, and corporal to "Keep that horse back!" or "Four feet from head to croup, you—you know what that means?" or "Tully! you ridin' that horse or is he ridin' you? Git him into ranks!" were becoming louder and more frequent.

The pack of a man in the second set of fours had come undone, so that the shelter half trailed behind him like an old-fashioned caparison, and his blankets he was carrying over his free arm in a most unsoldierly manner. Finally, a poorly cinched saddle turned, the rider was thrown, and the horse, the saddle under its belly, went the length of the column, kicking and squealing, until it caught one foot in the trailing stirrup, fell, and had two men hurl themselves from their saddles and sit on its head. The column perforce halted, for one of the men was the acting troop commander of "H" troop and the other Sergeant Lee.

"And the rest of the dash blanked Johns sitting in their saddles looking at us!" exclaimed Lee.

"Get the saddle off him!" ordered the squadron commander. "Who's horse is it? Take his name, sergeant. Give him a month in the kitchen and all the spare horses to saddle up. Maybe he'll learn to cinch properly. Have 'H' troop dismount and look over their equipment. When they've finished, have 'I' troop do the same. This will be your last chance. I'm not going to stop again until I run into the enemy. Time flies. They'll all be in Berlin if we don't show more progress than this."

Sergeant Lee took the opportunity to have a look at his machine rifles, riding in rear of "H" troop. He met, on his way there, the French Lieutenant, prancing along on the black horse. Lee ground his teeth. He had not ridden a McClellan saddle for a long time, and stirrup-buckle and gun-boot were beginning to rub sores on his unaccustomed shins.

How much more pleasure he would have had riding the beautiful officer's saddle on that black! Saddle! That wasn't the half of it! He would have ridden that horse bareback! It grinds a man to have his horse taken away from him. The mildest man will fly into a murderous rage. Lee thought of a man he had known with a clear record during three enlistments that had deserted because his horse had been taken for the polo team. Well, that bird had the right idea. When the march was resumed, Lee still thought of him. He, Lee, would go "over the hill." He would find an outfit where a guy was appreciated.

"Forget it," said the trumpeter finally, wearied of Lee's silence. "Don't worry about it no more. The Frog's gone an' good riddance."

"He's not gone," replied Lee, spurring his horse savagely. "He's riding with 'I' troop."

"What for?"

"How the hell should I know?"

"Well, cheer up, anyway. Maybe we'll run into somebody that'll rank that horse away from *him*."

They continued the march through the silent woods. They passed collections of huts, then a rustic village built about a tiny lake that was obviously a recreation centre, a narrow-gauge railway yard, more wagons, more loose horses, and one or two isolated wandering men that took to their heels, pursued by random pistol bullets, as soon as they had identified the nationality of the horsemen.

The column crossed hurriedly a surfaced road that cut through the forest from east to west. At one end, in the hazy distance, they could see the roofs and steeple of a town, and to the west, against the foot of the forest-covered hills, another. But in between all was deserted. Across this road they found fewer huts, then, after a while, nothing. The brush grew thicker on both sides.

The Captain suddenly reined up his horse. Lee, startled out of his black thoughts, raised his head. The advance guard had halted where the road came to the edge of the woods. It was only a grove, because Lee could see the trees where the road entered the forest again farther on. But two of the advance guard had dismounted, and one was wildly pumping his rifle up and down above his head in the old army signal that means "Enemy in large number."

"Hold the squadron in readiness!" ordered the Captain hurriedly. "Trumpeter, Sergeant Lee, follow me!"

The three of them went down to the advance guard as swiftly as their horses could carry them. They did not need to have the enemy pointed out to them.

There was a wide circular cut in the woods here, made by an open field, across which the road they were on took its way to enter the forest once more. This field sloped sharply down on the right, and at the bottom of the slope was another road, wide and surfaced, with a narrow gauge track running along.

On this road was a column of infantry, perhaps a battalion, marching steadily along, in good order, and with their rifles slung, German fashion, across their breasts. In front were two mounted officers. Behind the infantry, rapidly approaching, was a truck column, eight, ten, perhaps more—they could not see the end of them. There were eight hundred Germans there at least, and they were not to be charged with one-quarter that number.

"Bring up the auto-rifles, trumpeter," whispered the Captain, "and fast. Everyone dismount. Put the led horses in the brush. Now, sergeant, where shall we put the guns?"

"They've got to be fired prone," said the sergeant hurriedly. "The grass—now that will be all right." He threw himself on the ground. "You can't see over the slope here," he decided. "They'll have to be moved downhill—maybe along the edge of the woods. I'll have a look."

"Don't let any of those square-heads spot you. Don't waste too much time, now."

The German infantry continued to advance, unsuspecting. They had no advance guard out, no flankers. The Captain's heart swelled. The classic role of the cavalryman was to be his, to drive far behind the enemy's lines and fall upon unsuspecting troops . That truck column should be his, too, and the smoke of its burning would spread terror and alarm! On the heels of this panic the squadron would be on to Vigneulles, destroy the railway-station there, and cut off the retreat of all the mass of troops along the heights of the Meuse. But first, destroy this infantry.

"Hold the rifles here," ordered the Captain, as the gunners with their ammunition bearers appeared. "There's no rush. We'll site them together, let the column pass, and then each gun take half with traversing fire. Now damn those trucks! They'll get here at just the wrong time."

The trucks, however, did not pass the infantry, but halted. Perhaps the road was too narrow, perhaps those trucks contained the battalion's baggage. The Germans came on, while the Americans watched with beating hearts, holding their breath so that the enemy would not hear them. The Germans would pass at less than a hundred yards!

"When I give the signal," hissed the Captain, "rush out, flop, set up the guns, and turn loose."

The column drew near, and the dismounted Americans flattened themselves in the brush. The enemy marched by, boots slumping, bayonets rattling, the harsh coughing of the men coming clearly to the ears of the watchers. Wagons creaked past, one of the drivers idly cracking his whip. Then, the second company.

There was a thud of hoofs from behind the Americans. The Captain swung around. Who was this that had left the squadron without permission? It was the

French officer, on the shining black, galloping up from "I" troop to see what the halt was about.

"Get off that horse!" husked the Captain. "Get him back out of sight!"

The black halted. He was alone. Far behind him the squadron waited impatiently. The black tossed his head. He smelled the concealed horses of the advance guard and the machine-rifle men in the brush, or did he see an old stable fellow down there on the road? Did he smell his countrymen? He tossed his head again, then neighed shrilly. The horses in the brush and another in the squadron answered him.

White faces from the marching troops looked up the hill, curious at the sound. Not many, but enough. The Captain, wordless, but thinking many things, rose out of the bush and leaped for the black's head. The black, like all thoroughbreds, was nervous. The sudden rush of the officer from the bushes frightened him. He reared and bolted, and in two jumps was in the meadow. His rider flung himself clear, but too late. The Germans below, open-mouthed, had first heard horses neigh in those woods, and had then seen, clearly against the dark background, a figure in the horizon-blue uniform of the French Army hurl itself from the saddle and run back into the woods again.

"Out with the guns!" shouted the Captain. "Action front! At enemy in road! Fire at will!"

The guns spat, but the road was already half empty. Two seconds more, and the whole column had taken refuge in the ditch on the other side. Wagons, mounted officers, all disappeared.

But the blast of firing that had begun could not have come from the machine-rifles alone! The air crackled, the ear drums rang with the sudden pound of heavy firing. Astonished, the Captain turned about. From the alley in the woods came a thunder of hoofs. Horses reared, others were down and kicking. Dismounted men ran about. There was smoke and the flash of pistols, but the noise was so great that the Captain could not hear the bark of the 45s.

He looked behind him at the road below. The machine-rifles roared, but the road was empty. There were packs there and bundles that the marching troops had dropped in their haste to get to cover, but the Captain could see no bodies.

The German infantry were now in position behind the road. The only thing for two troops of cavalry in front of a battalion of entrenched infantry is to withdraw. The squadron seemed to have already made up its mind to this.

In just the three seconds that the Captain had spent in looking at the road his men had stampeded. They were going, tails high, saddle-bags flying, hell for leather down the road. Even as he watched, dark figures in bucket-shaped helmets appeared from the woods, shot down a dismounted trooper, and began to plunder the saddle-pockets of the dead horses.

There still remained to him, however, the auto-rifles. He leaped back, threw himself down beside the gunners, and shouted in their ears:

"Cease firing!"

The gunners heard and complied. With the roar of the autorifles stilled, a sudden hush seemed to fall.

"You! Number One gun! Action rear. Searching, in those woods, two clips! Commence firing! Number Two gun—" He stopped.

Below and to the left, in the centre of that white road, head high, tail outstretched like a plume, stood the black horse. Rifles cracked, men shouted, machine-guns roared, but the horse paid no attention. He pawed the ground, and the Captain could have sworn that he neighed again the shrill, proud shriek that had alerted the Germans and ruined the squadron. That was the horse that had been frightened by the Captain's rising from the brush! Never! He had bolted purposely! He was a German horse; he had known!

"Number Two gun!" ordered the captain. "Get me that horse on the road, damn his black soul!"

He was not himself, for he had seen his men butchered from ambush, his squadron destroyed, and he knew that the span of his own life could be measured in minutes.

The muzzle of the gun shifted ever so slightly, and the gunner's body thumped the ground as he wiggled himself into his new position. The gun roared. The horse tossed his head quickly, for he must have heard bullets crack by. A German dashed from the shelter of the ditch to seize the trailing bridle, but he seemed to slip in the mud and then fall, a flat, shapeless, motionless heap.

"The horse!" cried the Captain. "Never mind the men; get the horse."

Another burst. Tchk! Silence. "Gimme another clip," panted the gunner.

"Hey, for crysake, bring up that other gun!" shouted Sergeant Lee. "We got an opening here."

"Take up your rifle!" ordered the Captain. "Fall back and report to Sergeant Lee!"

Then the Captain, drawing his pistol, dropped on one knee, and, supporting his right hand on his left arm, took aim at the black horse.

"Hey, Captain!"

The shout in his ear disturbed the officer's aim, and the bullet went skyward.

"What the hell is the matter with you?" he snarled. But it was Sergeant Lee.

"They had machine-guns in the brush," panted the sergeant. "We put one of 'em down. They don't seem to be firin' now. If we're ever gonna get out of here we better go."

From the road below came a deep shout, "Hoch!"

On the heels of it a thin line of the enemy leaped up and, crossing the road, took shelter in the grass at the lower edge of the field.

The Captain emptied his pistol at them, then rose and reloaded. The Germans saw him, for fire crackled along their line.

"Let's get the hell out of here!" said the Captain.

The black horse had turned and, trotting down the road, now faced the German infantry, as though he carried on his back an officer who urged his men on. The Captain would have taken one more shot at him, but bullets whispered about his ears, or cracked overhead like whips. At the edge of the woods the men had already mounted. The Captain, stifling a curse, rejoined them.

Poorly fed horses in full pack, even when stampeded, will not run far, and the Captain, riding off down the woods with his chin on his breast, like Napoleon retreating from Moscow, found the squadron at the cross roads, from whence they had been able to see the two towns.

It had been a rear or flank guard that had ambushed them, and there had been no pursuit. Non-commissioned officers were already displaying their vocabularies, saddles were being transferred from wounded horses to well ones, men were binding up each other's wounds or refilling empty pistol clips.

Into this scene arrived the Captain like an avenging angel. He was a man of few words, but those to whom he addressed himself would remember his remarks to their dying day.

Sergeant Lee, having the care of his auto-rifles first in mind, withdrew them to one side, questioned the gunners, overhauled the ammunition supply, and inspected the horses. His own mount was nearly foundered. Seeing at a little distance a man holding three horses, he went in his direction, thinking he might make an exchange. The other man was the trumpeter, ruefully examining his trumpet that had been punctured by a bullet.

"It'll blow," said the trumpeter, as Lee approached, "but I have to keep my finger over the hole. It don't look military to blow a trumpet that way."

"How's chances on one o' those horses?" demanded Lee. "Mine's about outta breath."

"Naw. One's mine, one's the skipper's, and one's for the Frog Lootenant. He's goin' back."

"Goin' back?"

"Yuh. The Old Man says to him: 'What was the grand idea to gallop out in front where all the Boche would see you? Want them to admire your horsemanship or something?' And the Looey says: 'We rode into an ambush. We went too far without reconnaissance. We haven't lost any ground because this here is the Heudicourt-Nonsard road that we're on now, and we weren't supposed to be here for half an hour yet.' 'Awright,' says the skipper; 'you know the country so well, you go back and report our progress and where we run into the enemy.' 'But I'm your guide!' says the Looey. 'Well, we'll try to struggle along without you!' bites the Old Man. So then—psst!"

The French officer, his bullet-shaped face like a thundercloud, strode toward the two men. They paid not the slightest attention as he took his old horse, mounted, and rode off.

"You mighta held his stirrup for him, at least," observed the trumpeter.

"Who was his dog-robber last year? Anyway, I'm a sergeant. I don't hold nobody's stirrup."

The trumpeter hitched his pistol-belt higher and tilted his helmet just a little farther over his left eye.

"John Lee," said he, "did it ever occur to you you owe that Looey a whole lot? Suppos'n he hadn't ranked you off that black horse? Wouldn't he nickered just the same and give us away to the Boche?"

"Hey?" gasped the sergeant.

Wouldn't the horse have nickered with him? Oh, man! Yes, he would have. And then what would the skipper have done to Lee? He was not an officer but a buck sergeant. He choked at the thought. If it had been his horse that had nickered—well, the least they would have done would have been to hang him. His name would have been a mock and a disgrace throughout the mounted arm of the United States Army from that day forth. Gone would be his stripes! Gone his pistol and sabre! He would wield nothing but a dish-rag for the rest of his military career!

"Naw," said he to the trumpeter, "that black wouldn't have done it with me. I'd ha' *ridden* him."

"Uh-huh!" remarked the trumpeter. "Well, if you're lookin' for a horse, try Corporal Scully's. Scully's hit. That's a good horse for a sergeant."

"No," said the sergeant, "I guess I'll stick to the one I got. He ain't much on looks, but he's no nickerer."

No Quarter

W. Townend

Most ruthless of all fighting men is the soldier who goes into action having in his heart a deep and burning hatred of the enemy. To such a man killing is no mere duty, performed in blind obedience to the orders of his superiors, but the direct expression of his whole being, the one immediate aim in life.

MacCorbin, who was twenty and came from the South, hated the Germans, individually and collectively, as a Kentucky mountaineer might hate the slayers of his kinsmen in a family feud.

This is the story of his first engagement.

It was evening once more—July and hot. The sun had set. The sky was still flushed with pink.

There was no actual front line, but in rifle pits and shell holes and hastily dug trenches, on the fringe of a shattered wood of pines and beeches, men in steel helmets and khaki crouched and waited for what fresh horrors the night might bring. Their faces were tanned and lined, plastered with white chalk and sweat; their eyes were strained and anxious; their mouths hard; their uniforms torn and slovenly.

In front of the wood they held was a wide stretch of white, sandy ground, covered with patches of sparse brush, sloping upward gradually to another wood, through which before morning they would have to force their way or die, as those others had died who now lay in the open where they had fallen.

For a time the fighting had lulled. On either side the guns were silent, save where far off, miles distant to the north, the men waiting could hear the dull throb of drum fire and knew that another attack was being launched.

In one end of a stretch of dry ditch that had been deepened into some semblance of a trench were six privates.

Four of them, MacBride, Hennessey, Bridger, and Thompson, survivors of the original platoon that had left New York in the fall, squatted on the trunk of a young birch-tree that had toppled into the ditch and had been trimmed of its branches. They talked listlessly in low voices. Their rifles, with bayonets fixed, rested against the parapet, handy in case there might emerge from the wood opposite men in grey whom they would proceed to kill, without undue waste of energy or ammunition, killing being their business. Another of the six, Marshall, a boy of nineteen, stood in the extreme corner of the trench, shielded from observation by the limbs of a tree and a tangle of broken branches and brushwood. He watched the German position intently.

At a point where the trench twisted back at an angle of about 135 degrees, skirting the front of the wood, the sixth man, Bates, knelt and adjusted a puttee that was loose. He was a fair, sallow man with thin features, a moustache, and sleepy eyes that seemed to miss nothing of what happened. From time to time he glanced to his left at the four men on the tree trunk and smiled to himself. MacBride, a long, lank Texan, yawned.

"Could sleep fer a month, I guess, if I had the chanst!"

"After I'd had some chow, me too!" said Bridger, who was Middle Western, from Iowa.

Thompson, a hard bitten, red-headed Californian from the desert country up Ludlow way, grinned and then sighed:

"Gosh! Any sign them damn' ration carriers gittin' up thisaways tonight, hey?"

"Nary a sign," said Hennessey; an ex-sergeant, with a fondness for whisky, he was Boston Irish. "We're Reg'lars—we don' wanna eat; they says we fight!"

"Et me iron ration two days ago, Gawd help me!" said McBride. "Nawthin' yesterday, as I'm a livin' sinner; nawthin' today! Three dawgone nights without sleep."

"Guys," said Thompson, "I gotta eat."

"To hear you bums talk," said Bates, "you wouldn't think there was a war, nawthin'."

The four men on the tree trunk regarded him in silence. They did not like Bates. He talked too much.

"To hear you talk, Bates, you'd think you owned the dawgone war!" said Bridger. He broke off quickly. "Say, listen to this what's comin'!"

The boy, Marshall, ducked.

Overhead there was a high, wailing sound that grew louder and louder, passed, and ended in the loud *crump* of a heavy shell bursting back where the supports would be awaiting orders to move up.

"S'long as the ol' Boche keeps that range I ain't worryin' none," said MacBride.

Marshall was smiling uncertainly, his face white in the twilight.

"Thought it was nearer," he said.

"No need to apologize," said Bates. "Considerin' you wasn't taught that disappearin' movement on no parade ground, you done it right smart!"

"Fellers," said Thompson, "war ain't all it's cracked up to be! I got cooties breedin' all over me, I ain't had a wash since Pete knows when, nor nawthin' to eat. I ain't slept in a bed so long I can't remember if you put yer head or yer feet on the pillow. An' top of everythin' else, I got the chanst o' gain' to Kingdom Come any minute, expeditious."

"Bo," said MacBride, "you said a heap o' sense! They ain't bad soldiers, the Heinies, what I've seen of 'em!"

"I'll say they ain't! Brave as you'd find anywheres."

"Sure they're brave! Too damn' brave, some o' them guys! D'ye mind that feller we bumped off coupla days ago? Stuck to his machine-gun, he did, an' knocked out Gawd only knows how many of us chaps, an' wouldn't surrender, though we was wishin' him!"

"That's so! Good fightin' man, the ol' Boche!"

"Kinda feel sorry for 'em sometimes," said MacBride. "Gittin' it in the neck good an' plenty, ain't they?"

A voice that was new to the men in the trench said "What made you say that?"

They turned their heads quickly and saw a thin, boy's face and angry eyes under a steel helmet.

"It's an orf'cer," said Hennessey. "Beg pardon, sir."

"That's all right," said the officer. "Don't get up!"

At that the four men on the tree trunk grinned.

Behind the officer was the platoon sergeant, old Culbriddy, with the row of medal ribbons on his blouse and the scar of a bolo slash across his cheek.

"This salient is the most advanced part of our position, isn't it, Sergeant?"

"It is, sir," said Culbriddy.

"H'm! You're keeping a good lookout, I hope."

"Yes, sir," said Marshall.

"I've taken over the platoon," said the young officer gruffly.

He looked not much more than a lad, younger than Marshall, even: a little self-conscious and embarrassed, possibly, but friendly and apparently eager to do the right thing.

"My name's MacCorbin. Perhaps you'd better tell me yours!"

Rather startled by the request, they told him.

MacBride, Hennessey, Bridger, Thompson. Each spoke in turn. The officer who had given his name as MacCorbin nodded toward the man crouching down at the corner where the trench twisted back along the front of the wood.

"Yours?"

"Bates, sir."

"Yours?"

He spake to the boy next him.

"Mine, sir—Marshall."

"Been out long?"

"Two weeks, sir. Two weeks with the regiment, sir."

"I see. Getting on all right?"

"Yes, thank you, sir," said Marshall.

"We tote him along as a kinda mascot," said Bates. "He's ornamental, if he ain't nothin' else."

MacCorbin glanced at him with a frown and spake to MacBride.

"What made you say you felt sorry for the Germans?" he said.

"You can't expect to win battles if you're sorry for the crowd you're up against, can you?"

He gazed toward the German position, silent and sinister in the dusk, the shattered pine-trees, dark against the sky, the hillside and the first dead he had ever seen. He shivered suddenly, though the night was hot, and then turned and studied the grim and tired faces of the men who were with him in the trench. Hennessey, Bridger, Thompson, and MacBride, unshaven, bronzed, covered with the grime and muck of three days' fighting, were, he felt, soldiers—men who would push on to the bitter end, against odds, or hold on, with no thought of retreat.

Bates, the narrow-faced, sallow man with the fair moustache and the cruel, sleepy eyes and the tigerish mouth, puzzled him. He did not trust him. Yet Bates, too, was a soldier; perhaps the best soldier in that short trench. In battle, where other men might show mercy, Bates would kill for the lust of killing. The man was a killer. Brave, of course; cruel, no doubt; but worth a dozen of young Marshall. Glancing at Marshall's angular profile under the steel helmet, MacCorbin was suddenly doubtful. He knew instinctively, watching him, that Marshall was scared. He gave the impression of being broken in spirit by what he had suffered.

And tomorrow these men were some of the men he must lead across the open into the wood. And they were sorry for the Germans. God Almighty!

"I want to tell you about my brothers," MacCorbin said. "My eldest brother was in Paris when war broke out. He joined up with the French and became an airman; he was shot down and crashed behind the German lines in the spring of '15. He died in hospital. They treated him badly, neglected him, didn't forward his letters home, didn't let anyone know where he was. Maybe you'd say that wasn't the fault of the Germans. Well, it was the fault of one damn' German, anyway. That we know for a fact. He died of neglect. Right, that's the first of 'em!

"The second brother crossed to England in the autumn of 1914 and joined the Gordon Highlanders. He was with the Gordons in the advance after the German retirement on the Somme last year. He went down into a dug-out with a couple of other men because they heard a cat crying. They found the cat tied so that it could hardly move. My brother cut the string and set off a mine that blew him to bits. That makes two.

"The third brother was killed in No Man's Land in the spring down Verdun way. He was with the Marines. He was out on patrol at night and was helping a wounded German who'd been lying between the lines a couple of days and a German sniper put a bullet through his head. All right, then, that's the lot! But maybe you understand now how I feel about the Germans. I've got a personal interest in this War because of what I've told you. I'm the last of the crowd and I want to get even. Maybe I'll go the same way as the others, maybe I won't; but I want to do some damage or see some damage done first.

"Anyhow, that's why I don't like to hear you fellows talking about feeling sorry for the Germans. We've got to fight tomorrow and fight like hell!"

"We have the reputation, sir," said Sergeant Culbriddy.

The men grinned.

"I know that, Sergeant," said MacCorbin, "but what I'm trying to impress on you all is, don't stop to take any prisoners! This war's going to be won by killing. Understand what I mean, MacBride? It is MacBride, isn't it? You can't kill if you feel sorry for the man you're fighting. That's why I don't like to hear you say you're sorry for the Germans! That's why I don't want you to take prisoners. Killing's your job, MacBride, and everyone else's job, too."

Bates laughed.

"Killing's what we come out for, ain't it?"

"Killing!" Marshall uttered a harsh noise, deep in his throat. "Sure, that's what we come out for, killing!"

"Who in hell's the fool talking about killing?" said another voice.

Darkness was falling but MacCorbin could see the lean, haggard face and dark eyes of the man who had just made his way through the brush into the trench.

"What are you?" he asked sharply. "Where've you been?"

"Mr. Searle took me off, sir, to help bring up some ammunition that had been dumped at the reg'mental P.O., sir."

"I see. What's your name?"

"Rutherford, sir." The man spoke respectfully enough, but roughly, as if impatient at being questioned. "I didn't know there was an orf'cer here, sir."

"That's all right," said MacCorbin.

This man, Rutherford, was of a different type from the other men in the trench. He was powerfully built, not tall but lean and wiry; capable, probably, of enduring any amount of hardship without harm, yet from his manner not such a good fighter as Bates. He seemed sullen and morose, bitter almost—a man likely to be sensitive to shell fire or the sight of death and not so cheerful when things went wrong as MacBride or Hennessey or Thompson or Bridger; but a sound man, notwithstanding; best, perhaps, fighting with his back to the wall, in defense, not in attack. This, at least; was the impression he gave in those first few minutes. MacCorbin continued—

"You were saying something about killing!"

"Didn't mean nawthin', sir," said Rutherford.

"He's another that wants the War over," said Bates.

"Mebbe the War'll be over soon enough for most of us," said Rutherford, "without a hero like you sayin' so!"

"I ain't trying to be killed," said Bates. "You are."

MacCorbin, feeling rather perplexed, spoke to Culbriddy.

"Let's be going on, Sergeant. And you men, remember what I said. We've got to kill if we want to win the War, so don't you birds worry your heads about taking prisoners!"

He moved along the trench, followed by Culbriddy.

"Who's he?" said Rutherford presently.

"Dunno," said MacBride. "He blew in durin' the heat of the combat to teach us the meanin' of love yer enemies!"

"No prisoners, hey!" said Rutherford. "Who in hell wants to take prisoners? Better be killed straight off than be took prisoner, too!"

"What d'you know about it, hey?" said Bates. "Ever been in prison yet,

Rutherford, or is that a pleasure to come?"

Rutherford spoke without heat or emotion.

"One o' these days, Bates, you'll git a bullet through you and it won't be a German bullet, neither."

"Say," said Hennessey, "you guys cut it out! Rutherford, you talk too much for the good o' yer health!"

In all battalions there will be men who are mysteries to other men. Rutherford was one. An old soldier, who had rejoined his regiment at the outbreak of war, he was a silent, sombre man. Queer tempered, likely to fly into fierce rages without adequate cause, a heavy drinker, yet in spite of MacCorbin's hasty summing up, as fine a soldier as there was in the company. At the best of times a man who had little to say, he had of late been silent, more unapproachable than ever before. He seemed to be suffering, physically as well as mentally. His face was drawn and peaked, his eyes were worn. Although he said himself that nothing could ever tire him, he had the appearance of being exhausted. Uneasy and restless and quarrelsome, he was most composed and cheerful when under shell-fire or in an attack.

Men respected him but did not care for him. Like Bates, he had no friends in the company. Unlike Bates, however, he made no attempt to be friendly.

"Whadja make of the little Loot?" said Thompson.

"Nice boy, I dare say," said MacBride, "but wait till tomorrer an' see what he does when we gits to movin' up ag'in' that wood!"

"Talk about gall!" said Hennessey. "Well, say! Seen nawthin' an' comes along talkin' just like a grown man! Take no prisoners, says he! Wish the ol' Colonel could 'a' heard him!"

Marshall spoke to Bates over his shoulder.

"What did you wanna say that about me for?"

"I said nawthin', kid," said Bates.

"You did. I won't stand fer much more yer damn' kiddin'!"

"Say, tomorrer, don't you git to hangin' back same as last time!" said Bates. "No lettin' other fellers do your fightin' for you, young Marshall, an' don't you forget it!"

"Seems to me I heard someone talkin' about a twisted ankle only yesterday," said Rutherford. "Bates, where was you when we got into that wood? An' last week you was sick an' takin' pills! Doggone funny how many times you been out of it, ain't it?"

"I don't understand what in hell you think you're drivin' at!" said Bates.

"No," said Rutherford. "No, mebbe not. But you will understand if you're anywheres near me tomorrer, Bates, which you won't be! You're a helluva talker, sure, but I've gotta see yet what kinda fighter you are!"

"Damn funny!" said Bates. "That kind o' bein' funny don't cut no ice with me. Listen, fellers…"

Sergeant Culbriddy crept through the thick undergrowth at the back of the trench.

"You birds gotta cut out the yappin'! Next thing you'll have someone turnin' a machine-gun on you to quiet you."

"Don't believe there's no one left in that wood at all," said Bridger. "We ain't had so much as a chirp outa them since long 'bout four o'clock. They've gone back, I bet."

"Mebbe you'll have the pleasure later o' crawlin' out on combat patrol to investigate," said MacBride.

"Mebbe not," said Culbriddy. "That bit o' wood's goin' to git hell mighty soon now; all the guns they can lay their hands to."

"No chanst of any chow before next week, is there?" said Thompson.

"Yeh. Seen the ration carriers on their way up."

"Thank Gawd fer that!" said Bridger.

"Huh! I bet five bucks they forget us stuck here, anyways!" said Hennessey. "Say, Sarje, what about sendin' one of us with our canteens an' mess kits fer our coffee an' slum, hey?"

A flare lit up the sloping, brush covered ground between the lines, making the dusk brighter than midday; but with queer, blue-black shadows; it waned gradually and faded into twilight once more.

"An' now fer business," said Rutherford.

The short summer night was passing. In the east the first faint sign of dawn was visible between the dying down of one flare and the upward flight of the next.

At other times men might have gloried in the freshness of the air, the peace and beauty of the countryside, the stars, the clear sky, the scent of the pine-woods. Now, with the reek of death and high explosive in their nostrils, their ears deafened by heavy gunfire, they crouched in their shelters and watched the great shells bursting with flashes of flame and black clouds of smoke in the shattered wood opposite.

MacCorbin, once more in the section of advanced trench held by Sergeant Culbriddy and the seven privates, MacBride, Hennessey, Bridger, Thompson, Marshall, Bates, and Rutherford, peered through the screen of brush across the open ground at the German position and shuddered.

There were men, perhaps, in that hell, dying, being maimed, torn limb from limb. It was terrible, yet he had no pity. They must pay the price, just as he, too, and the men with him, might pay the same price at any instant.

Marshall, by whose side he stood, groaned.

"Is anything the matter?" said MacCorbin.

No one was near enough to hear what he said.

"I'm scared," Marshall whispered.

"The Germans?"

"Scared of myself, sir. Scared I'll turn and run. I wanted to ask you, sir, if I can't face it, if I run, or anything, I'd like you to promise this, sir—" his voice was so low that MacCorbin could scarcely hear him—"I'd like you to put a bullet through me. I would."

MacCorbin was troubled. What he had felt earlier in the night was true, after all.

"You'll be all right, Marshall, I'm sure."

"You've not been over yet, sir. I have. Last time I just managed to keep going. Tomorrow I won't be able. My God I I hate this War. It's jus' killin' me."

"You're making things harder for yourself by thinking you're bound to fail. Marshall, there isn't a single man of us who isn't afraid at heart. Do you mean to say you're not so good a man as"—he was going to say Rutherford, but changed his mind—"as anyone else? You are. What's the absolute worst that can happen? Turning back, isn't it? Well, suppose you don't! What's the next worst? Being killed! What's that amount to, anyway? You've acknowledged that much, haven't you, by what you asked me to do! You're not afraid of being killed; you've proved it!" He patted his shoulder. "You'll be all right, Marshall, I know."

"I wish I knew it, too, sir."

MacCorbin, despairing of bringing him any comfort, moved along the trench.

MacBride was leaning over the parapet, watching the wood opposite and the bursting shrapnel and high explosive.

"Everything all right, MacBride?"

"They're catching it over there, sir, ain't they?" MacBride stroked the stock of his Springfield. "Maybe they'll all 've gone before we can git to grips with 'em!"

Thompson, the lean, red-headed Californian, said:

"This time tomorrer, wonder what the company's gonna look like! The quicker we git across the open the better."

"The bayonet's the only way," said Hennessey.

"You need the helluva long bayonet to reach them guys from here," said Bridger. "It's the gittin' so you can use the bayonet hurts most."

"You'll get there all right," said MacCorbin. "And when you do, remember what I said—no prisoners. You've got to kill."

And then he heard above the crash of the shells opposite a high wailing sound approaching through the air, growing louder and deeper in note, roaring like a heavy train emerging from a tunnel, rushing straight down at him from the sky.

His heart felt weak and empty. Fear choked him.

The men had flung themselves down into the bottom of the trench.

There was a crash like thunder, worse than thunder, the crash of the end of the world, a flash of yellow flame. The earth shivered and rocked with the concussion. MacCorbin was hurled back and then forward again, against the parapet of the trench. He clawed with his finger-nails at the chalky soil and bent his head. His steel helmet was tilted over his face. Stones and earth fell on him. A tree toppled to the ground. The air was filled with the pungent reek of hot metal and high explosive and smoke.

When presently he straightened himself up he laughed.

"Nothing in that," he said, and shuddered.

"Nothing in that, did ye say, sir?" He saw by the light of a flare Sergeant

Culbriddy by his side. "It's the like o' them nine inchers can lose ye the number of yer mess, just by the blast of its passing, without it so much as touching yez!"

MacCorbin knew that Culbriddy had reproved him and he was annoyed and ashamed. He felt that the reproof was justified.

He moved on to the bend in the trench.

Rutherford, leaning back, his rifle on the parapet, pointing toward the German lines, chewed solemnly. MacCorbin had an impression that he alone of all the men in the trench was unaffected by the shell that had burst so near. He felt that he had kept his feet and waited for death and was startled that he was still alive.

Almost without intention he asked him the question he had asked Marshall.

"Anything the matter, Rutherford?"

The man glanced at him quickly and then turned once more and gazed toward the wood.

"Big shell that, sir."

His voice was harsh and stern.

"There's something worrying you," said MacCorbin.

"It ain't this, then," said the man.

And then he brought his face very near the officer's and whispered—

"Ever been drunk, sir?"

"Drunk!" said MacCorbin. He was indignant. "Is that how you talk to an officer?"

"Guess I didn't mean that, exactly, sir; no. But I was drunk last week, back at Maubray-le-Petit before we come into the line again. I got a girl at home—Baltimore. If I'm killed tomorrer that's the best way out for all of us, her an' me, both! I'm going to be put under arrest as soon as we're through with the fighting."

"For being drunk?"

"No," said Rutherford. "There was trouble in one of them estaminets. Little place, kept by an old woman and her grownup son who was a half-wit and not in the Army. A U.S. soldier, one of our crowd, stole the old woman's money. The son give the alarm just as he was gittin' away an' he turned and hit him. Seems I'm the man."

"But were you?" said MacCorbin.

"No. I wasn't. But I was in the estaminet that evenin' an' next day they found a letter on the floor, addressed to me an' postmarked Baltimore."

"That's no proof," said MacCorbin. "It'll be easy enough to clear yourself, won't it?"

"No," said Rutherford. "I was drunk somewhere's else. No alibi. I got back to my billet early in the mornin'. Where had I been? Asleep in a field. I'm for arrest, if I come out of this alive. It wasn't me stole the money, I swear, but I can't prove it. And then sometimes I wonder. Was it me? I'm mean when I get two three drinks in me. No dawgone good. I oughta quit. Well, that's my weakness—booze. They say the half-wit's dead."

MacCorbin was startled by his placidity.

"Who told you?"

"I heard when I was fetchin' that ammunition up. One of the headquarter crowd heard it from someone who'd come up from Maubray-le-Petit with the transport. Maybe it ain't true. More likely it is. I'm the guy what's responsible. I didn't do it, I swear! But did I? Queer the things a man will do when he's drunk, ain't it?"

MacCorbin sighed. It was terrible that just when all his energy should be directed toward killing Germans he should have had this other problem thrust on to him.

"All they've got against you is that envelope," he said.

"One of our fellers seen me comin' out the estaminet, he said, at the time the money was bein' stolen. I didn't ask if he give me away to the M.P.s; that's nawthin' to do with me. But he seen me, he said, an' spoke to me."

"Who was it? Anyone I've met?"

"Yes, sir. Bates."

Dawn was at hand. The shells still pounded the wood.

"There can't be none o' them left alive!" said MacBride.

"Them poor fellers layin' out in the open," said Marshall softly, "are mebbe waitin' on us. Last night I felt today there'd be a full company to march in with 'em."

Bates cackled a shrill laugh.

"Hear him! Say, kid, you oughta be paid for talkin'!"

"What d'you make of it, Mac?" said Hennessey.

"They've gone," said MacBride. "We'll have the first part of our *pasear*, mebbe, in peace an' comfort with time to admire the view!"

"They're still there," said Marshall. "I know they are. An', my God, you'll know it, too, soon enough!"

"Feelin' bad, son?" said Thompson.

"He's scairt," said Bates. "Didn't I say so?"

"You want the butt of a rifle shoved down your ugly trap; or what?" said Bridger.

MacCorbin, alone in the trench with Culbriddy and the seven men, one of whom was a murderer and one a coward, prayed that he would do them credit, the murderer and the coward no less than the others.

But did the men he was going to lead across the open understand what he understood? It seemed to him that men who could talk so lightly of what lay before them, who treated the War as merely an episode in their lives, of less importance than the food they craved, who sympathized with the enemy, it seemed that such men were not the men to push home an attack and kill.

And yet these men had reputation enough as fighters, God knew! He thought of his three brothers—David, with his laugh and his ready wit, dead in a German prison hospital, neglected, alone, broken; Andrew, the Gordon Highlander, killed by that senseless piece of cruelty that brought tears to one's eyes and hate to one's heart; Stewart, killed on patrol, helping the wounded German. And then he thought of himself, the last of four brothers, so soon perhaps to follow them!

Tired of inaction, he walked the full length of the trench held by the platoon, spoke to the two corporals and one or two of the men and presently turned and walked slowly back to the nose of the salient where he stood between Rutherford and Sergeant Culbriddy and tried to distinguish in the dim light the route he would have to take across the open to the wood still shrouded in smoke and the flashes of bursting shells.

He glanced at the faces of the men in the short stretch of trench near him, just as he had done the evening before. Culbriddy, the grizzled sergeant with the medal ribbons on his blouse. MacBride, the long, lank Texan, who was sorry for the Germans. Thompson, the red-headed, hard-bitten Californian, who thought more of his chow than he did of winning the War. Bridger, the burly Middle Westerner with the nasal drawl. Hennessey, the ex-sergeant, short and thick-set and stern. Bates, the fair haired, sallow man with the cruel eyes, a fighter from the toes up. Marshall, the boy, white faced and afraid. And Rutherford, the man who perhaps had killed the half-wit, grim, tragic, and silent. To his right, other men, who had made less impression on his mind, whose names he had scarcely memorized—Smith, MacBeith, Harrison, Prentiss, Malone. There weren't so many of them. The platoon was only a skeleton of its full war-time strength.

He realized that the Germans were showing signs of life. Shells were whistling overhead and bursting behind the wood where they were, back among the supports.

In five minutes, he reflected, he would clamber out of the ditch where he stood and, cane in one hand, pistol in the other, walk across the open toward the German machine-guns.

He wondered how it would feel to be shot at. He wondered whether he could hide the fear he knew would creep over him. He smiled grimly. He thought once more of his dead brothers. He must kill or he would never again know peace. He felt coldly efficient. A little impatient; a little nervous—but not very.

He looked at his watch again. God, how time did fly!

"Thirty seconds more!" he said.

The hands crawled slowly on. God, how time did drag!

"Twenty seconds!"

If he lived long enough to reach the wood and set his men an example he would be satisfied.

"Fifteen seconds!" he said.

His voice shook. He wasn't afraid, surely. He reached for his pistol. The feel of the butt steadied him.

"Ten seconds!" he said.

The men began to count.

"Nine, eight, seven, six, five, four, three, two, one!"

"Up you go!" he said, and scrambled out over the sandy, crumbling parapet of the ditch that had served them as a trench. The guns had lifted. For a moment the wood in front, the sinister, shattered wood, was silent, still shrouded in smoke already drifting away on the light morning breeze.

MacCorbin, glancing quickly right and left, saw the assault waves deployed, long lines of infantrymen in khaki, tramping stolidly across the open, laden like beasts of burden, with rifles and equipment, steel helmets, chaut-chaut automatic rifles, bandoleers, gas-masks, grenades, two hundred and twenty rounds of ammunition each man.

He saw the dead, the white sandy soil, the scattered brush, the broken trees with their green foliage wilted. He saw beyond the wood the flashes of shells bursting. He heard his own husky voice saying—

"Don't bunch there!"

He heard someone laugh; Rutherford, he thought; but was not sure. He heard, next, a burst of sound, like thunder, a cataclysm of sound, the roar of a typhoon, a sound not to be compared with any sound his ears had ever heard. Machine-guns massed, hundreds of machine-guns, their individual *tocka-tocka-tocka-tocka-tocka-tocka* blended into a devastating roar. He heard the bullets whipping over his head; he saw men dropping, stumbling, lying still; he saw the bayonets.

He was alive still. Christ! But for how long! His neck and back were damp with sweat. His throat was parched. There was a tightness in his chest, a burning pain across his forehead. His limbs were without strength. He shouted:

"Come on! Come on!"

He bent his head and quickened his pace.

Men, he noticed now, were running, intent on reaching the wood whence came the storm of bullets. The ground was rough, scarred with dry rain channels and gullies, pitted with shell-holes.

It was difficult to keep going without tripping.

He heard above the machine-guns' roar Rutherford's voice.

"Get on, you, Bates, or I'll bayonet you!"

"Come on!" he yelled. "Come on! Into 'em!"

God Almighty! how they were falling!

He was afraid now, in grim earnest; not of being killed—he would be killed, he was sure—but of being killed too soon.

"Get on, you, Bates, damn you! Get on!"

Rutherford again. What the devil was the man up to?

MacCorbin turned his head and saw Culbriddy's honest, red face at his elbow; Marshall, pale and distressed, but moving ahead quickly; Rutherford, still alive, fierce looking and hard and angry; Bates, white like Marshall, stumbling, gasping for breath, whimpering; Hennessey, Bridger, MacBride, Thompson. He saw them all. Others of the platoon as well—Harrison, Prentiss, Jacobs, Bradley, Smith, Hughes, Robinson, Malone. He saw Jackson, the company commander—Jackson! What in hell was he doing so far ahead? And his orderly, away on the left. He saw the commander fall and the orderly, bending over him, fall, too.

Nearer, Thompson, the red-headed Californian, hurled his rifle away from him, doubled up, his hands clasped to his belly, and rolled over like a shot rabbit.

Damn those machine-gunners! Damn them! Wouldn't they ever let up?

"Come on!" he shouted. "Come on!"

And then MacCorbin knew that the attack was breaking down.

All impetus had gone. Too many men had been killed.

His foot caught in a hole; he tripped and pitched forward.

Culbriddy threw himself down by his side.

"Stay where ye are, sir! Wait!"

"We've got to get on," he said, panting.

"Give them time, sir. If it wasn't fer the dip in the groun', sir, that's saved us, we'd none of us be here now!"

They lay on a flat sandy piece of ground, sheltered by a steep bank a yard high. With them were Marshall and MacBride, Bridger, his face smeared with blood, Hennessey, smiling a tight lipped smile, and others.

It was full dawn at last. The sun had risen, but the open space across which they had struggled was still in shadow. In front of them, behind the wood, the sky was pink. Back of them, the German shells were crashing, sending up huge masses of smoke and earth, smashing down big trees. The bullets of the massed machineguns whistled overhead .

"Damn them!" said Hennessey. "Damn them to hell!"

He sprawled at full length to the right of the bank that sheltered them, cuddled his cheek against the stock of his rifle and began firing.

"Helluva lot o' good, that!" said Bridger.

There was a strangled cry. MacCorbin turned his head and saw Bates crawling toward him, his face livid, damp with sweat and lined and old looking, stark terror in his eyes, bareheaded and with his fair hair plastered over his forehead. Rutherford, bleeding from a wound in the neck, his lips parted in a grin, crawled after him.

"I'll git you into the German line, you white livered skunk, if I have to bayonet you every yard o' the way!"

"For Gawd's sake, let me be!" Bates whimpered. "I'm sick."

"Yeller from the toes up. Tripped he did, fellers, an' lay on his face, so he wouldn't be made to move! Git up this livin' minute, Bates, or I'll make you!"

He prodded him with the point of his bayonet. Bates shrieked.

"Damn you, lemme be!" He wept. "I can't, I tell you."

He reached across and dragged at MacCorbin's arm. "Sir, make him stop! I'm hurt. Can't you see I'm hurt, damn you! I ain't fitten to die, neither! Let up, Rutherford, fer Gawd's sake!"

He squirmed and screamed. The survivors of the platoon, dirty, tired men, huddled under the bank, watched in silence.

Rutherford caught hold of Bates by the back of his neck.

"What's that you say? You ain't fitten to die! Believe me, you ain't, sweetheart! No more ain't I. But if I can die, guess you can. Up you git, dearest! We two gonna reach the Germans, if the others ain't. D'jer hear me? Up with you!"

"I can't. Christ, lemme get outa this! I'm gonna give myself up, damn you! I stole that money, I tell you. Rutherford, I gotta give myself up. It was me took that money. He fought, damn him! I didn't mean to do him no harm, but he took a knife to me, an' fought."

Rutherford let go of his neck and twisted him about and stared at him with a look of blank amazement in his eyes.

"What's he yappin' about?" said MacBride.

"God!" said Rutherford. "You seen me comin' out that estaminet, you said. You dawgone liar! You killed that poor halfwit an' let me be blamed!" He clenched his fist and struck him on the face. "You Judas!"

"That'll do," said Culbriddy. "Are yez crazy?"

"Do you hear what he said, Sarje?"

MacCorbin, sickened, roused himself from the stupor that had held him and said gruffly:

"Cut it out, Rutherford! We've got to be moving on."

Bates turned and on hands and knees began to crawl down the slope, bareheaded still, without his rifle, toward the wood from which they had advanced.

Suddenly he screamed, rose to his feet and began to run, then leaped in the air, dropped, and lay still.

"I hope he's got some kinda excuse when they git him on to the carpet where he's gone to," said Rutherford. "He'll tell 'em a pack o' lies, I bet, but they won't listen! He blamed me for what he done. but cleared me in front of all you fer witnesses! I don't care now if I die or live!"

"Look!" said Culbriddy. "Look there, sir!"

From the trees that were being shelled by the Germans long lines of men in khaki deployed in combat groups were advancing.

"The supports are up," said MacBride. "Look, the poor fellers are gittin' it! Lookit! God! See them fallin'!"

From the left there came a roar of cheering.

"We're in on 'em over yonder!" said Bridger through bandaged jaws. "Good ol' roughnecks!"

"You're damn' right," said Culbriddy, "we're in the wood."

"How we gonna stop them machine-guns in front of us, hey?" said MacBride.

MacCorbin wriggled forward and lay near where Hennessey was shooting at the right of the bank which sheltered them and peered through a tangle of brush at the wood.

A voice called to him

"Sir, Mr. MacCorbin!"

He turned his head and to his surprise saw Marshall in a shallow gully farther still to the right and some four or five yards in advance of where he lay.

"Sir," he said, "I can see the gunners workin' that gun jus' ahead, plain as anythin'. If someone could knock it out it would clear the way, like, fer the rest of us."

"All right, Marshall, we'll do our best right now."

"Believe I got one them guys!" said Hennessey. "Two, mebbe." He fired again. "Believe they got a sniper layin' out somewhere in front."

MacCorbin shouted to the men sheltered by the bank:

"You fellows ready! When I jump to my feet, follow!"

He glanced back at the waves of men moving up the slope. They were very near now. There was something, he felt, majestic, almost stately, in their advance. But, Lord! To see men drop forward and lie huddled up and know that they were dead!

He waited. Another minute and he and the platoon would join in their final rush.

"Mother o' God!" said Hennessey. "Look!"

MacCorbin turned and saw Marshall crawling on hands and knees up the dry rain channel between sparse and scattered bushes toward the wood.

A lump rose to his throat. Marshall, of all men!

He jumped to his feet.

"Up!" he yelled. "Up, the lot of you!" He scrambled over the edge of the bank and ran forward through the brush.

Only another fifty yards and he would reach the machine-guns.

Fifty yards, but the worst fifty of all. Would he last? God, just to have one chance at them. Alive, still.

"Up! Up!"

Rutherford was by his side, red faced, grinning.

"Not so dawgone fast, that orf'cer!" someone shouted.

"Come on, then! Come on!"

A bullet snicked the edge of his steel helmet; he staggered, recovered himself and plunged forward.

He saw Marshall in front of him rise out of the ground, race up the side of a steep slope of white earth and, poised for an instant, arm uplifted, fling a grenade. There was the crash of an explosion, black smoke, screams. And then Marshall fell and slid down the slope into the brush.

"They got him!" said Rutherford.

MacCorbin pushed on. His heart was thumping fiercely. He was close up to the machine-guns now and he was not yet dead. One gun had been put out by Marshall; that was why he was still alive, perhaps! Another gun—he could see the blunt ugly snout-swung about. He was finished. How could they miss him at so short a range? There was no burst of firing. He could see the rounded helmets of the gunners. Jammed perhaps, or out of ammunition! He heard himself yelling:

"Come on! Come on! Give 'em hell!"

Rutherford thrust himself in front of him.

"Out of it, you!"

His bayonet flashed. There was a wild scream from a rifle pit almost at his very feet.

"Got him!" said Rutherford.

He grunted and lurched forward across the body of the German he had killed.

MacCorbin cursed. Rutherford gone. He scrambled up the last steep slope. He could hear the yells of the men who followed. Nothing could stop them now, he knew.

He reached the crest of the slope. He saw before him broken tree trunks and dead Germans. He smelt high explosive and raw, fresh blood. A cold rage possessed him. He was alive and could kill. He gazed down into the broken machine-gun emplacement and raised his pistol.

And then, before he could shoot, before he could avenge the first of his dead brothers, there rose out of the ground in front of him dead men—dead men with yellow, corpse-like faces, and red eyes and hollow cheeks; men in round steel helmets that came down over their ears; men in dirty grey uniforms that stank of sweat and dirt and wet cloth; men in an agony of fear; dead men; corpses whose faces were the faces of men who have lived in hell and torment.

"*Kameraden! Kameraden!* Mercy! Surrender!"

They held their hands above their heads and whimpered. The machine-guns were silent at last. A deathlike stillness had settled on the wood. The yells of the advancing infantrymen sounded thin and unreal.

"*Kameraden!*"

MacCorbin hesitated, stunned, horrified. He wanted to shoot. He had his chance. Why didn't he shoot, then?

How could he shoot poor broken devils like these!

They had surrendered. Damn them! They had kept fighting their damned guns to the very last, pouring their bullets in on the men attacking them across the open, and then when they were cornered they held their hands up! Damn them!

MacCorbin turned.

He saw the men in khaki racing forward; he saw the long bayonets glinting in the first rays of the sun; he heard the wild yells; he saw MacBride, Culbriddy, Bridger, Hennessey. He saw men he did not know, men from the 2nd Battalion; hard, sunburnt faces, streaked with sweat and white dust.

"Kill them! Let me git at them!"

MacCorbin heard himself shout:

"Stop that! You, MacBride, put that rifle down! Hennessey, Bridger, damn you! They've surrendered! They're prisoners!"

He raised his pistol. There was no other officer living, only himself.

"Get back!" he said hoarsely. "Sergeant Culbriddy, these men are prisoners! We must get them sent back at once! "

He saw men surging up the slope toward him. He saw as through a must angry faces, flushed faces, scowls, jeering grins, eyes that expressed hate and resentment, the faces of soldiers who have endured much punishment and are robbed of their right to kill. He had defrauded them, he felt. He had gone back on his word. He had saved the Germans from the death they deserved. He had done what was right.

"The first man that tries to kill these prisoners, I'll shoot!" he said. "Stop where you are!"

"The fact is," said a voice, "he's gone bugs!"

There was a shout of laughter and something, a clenched fist, the butt of a Springfield—he did not know what—crashed against his chest. He had an impression that he was falling from a great height, down and down and down. He passed into unconsciousness easily, peacefully.

"Hello! He's comin' to. Look at him!"

MacCorbin lay on his back and stared at the blue sky above him. With an effort he raised his head. Near him were men he knew. Bridger, his face bandaged; Culbriddy, with a shattered arm, smoking a cigarette, his face grey; MacBride, the Texan, sullen and tired looking! Hennessey, his eyes closed, leaning forward, bareheaded, breathing heavily; Prentiss, Harrison, Malone, a corporal whose name he did not know, two other men of the platoon, Jacobs and Bradley—or was one Hughes?

He saw they were watching him. He saw no pity in their looks. He saw contempt and suspicion and rage.

"You're a pack of damned cowards!" he said. "You shot them down after they'd surrendered! What kind of men are you?"

They looked at him uneasily.

"Who shot 'em down!" said Culbriddy. "They're prisoners."

"Lucky stiffs!" said MacBride.

"We got 'em rounded up, the dawgone lot of 'em!" said Bridger. "They're on their way to the cages now."

MacCorbin felt very weak.

"But I thought," said Culbriddy, "you told us not to take any prisoners! Wasn't that the gospel you was preachin' last night, sir?"

"My God!" said MacCorbin, and thought of his dead brothers and shivered. "I'm no damn' good, am I?"

"You're as damn' good as anyone," said Culbriddy. "Where would we be now, sir, if it wasn't for you leadin' us up that draw in the ground where them machine-guns couldn't rache us an' restin' us there by the bank under cover till the supports come up? The Colonel's pleased with you, sir. He's afther goin' past not tin seconds ago!"

And that needed thought, too.

"Well," he said after a time, "whoever it was knocked me out did the right thing. Only—only you see how it was, don't you? They'd surrendered. And now, we've got to be pushing on to our objectives!"

They laughed.

"You'll stay where you are, sir," said Culbriddy.

"We've got to go on!"

"There's about thirty left out the whole battalion," said MacBride.

"We're bein' taken out the line," said Hennessey. "The attack's gone on the best part of half an hour!"

"An'," said Bridger, "nobody knocked you out!"

"Someone hit me!"

"Git away with you, sir!" said old Culbriddy, smiling at him.

"You're makin' fun of us. The nose cap of a shell ricocheted an' took you in the breast-bone. You're for hospital an' across the water!"

Souvenirs

W. F. Morris

I

A Maltese cart drawn by a chestnut horse, harnessed in the military fashion without a collar, was jogging along one of the straight, tree-bordered roads of France. Side by side on the plank seat under the canvas tilt sat a young officer and a private soldier. Behind them in the back of the cart was an unsoiled Wolesley valise resembling a huge brown roly-poly.

The private soldier, who had been a country postman in civilian life, was holding forth disparagingly on French agricultural methods, and the young officer was murmuring "quite" and "really" appropriately and even inappropriately in a manner which suggested that on this sunny afternoon in June, 1916, his interest lay in things other than agriculture.

Secretly he was experiencing much the same feelings of excitement and solemnity as he had known on his first day at school not so many years before. He was on the threshold of what the illustrated papers at home in England called "The Great Adventure," and to this youth of eighteen, who found himself, after six months training on his way to join a battalion in the field, the War *was* a great adventure. It was *the* great adventure.

It was not surprising, therefore, that he was not very interested in his companion's disquisition on roots and lucerne and binders; but politeness and that new-boy feeling of not knowing precisely what was "done" and what was "not done" restrained him from interrupting to ask questions about that in which he was interested.

The little Maltese cart jogged unhurriedly on its way. Lorries passed in low rolling clouds of white dust, and G. S. wagons, whose drivers dropped their arms and jerked their heads in salute like mechanical dolls. The road switch-backed uncompromisingly across the low, corn-covered hills of Picardy; and its bordering trees, whose blue shadows lay diagonally across the white surface, could be seen ahead and behind cresting the rollers of the hedgeless country like the wake of a ship. From each crest the road fell away to a valley, and then ran tape-like up the slope beyond; and from each crest the young officer looked eagerly ahead for some change in the landscape that would announce that he was nearing the barrier that stretched from Switzerland to the Channel.

His eagerness was rewarded when the surmounting of a slope showed the road ahead swooping over a low, intermediate crest towards a tall, ruddy church tower that rose from a medley of roofs and chimneys glimmering in the heat haze beyond. There seemed to be something odd about this little town, though at that distance it was difficult to say what it was.

The driver broke off a one-sided discussion on artificial fertilizers to point with his whip at a glittering bar of light that appeared to jut almost horizontally from the top of the tower. "That's the 'Anging Virgin of Albert," he announced, "what the 'Uns can't knock down. They say when it do come down that'll be the end of the War. And," he added cynically, "if that's true, it's a perishin' marvel to me that some bloke 'asn't been up there afore now and pulled it down."

The young officer seized the opportunity to ask a question that had been uppermost in his mind for the past hour. "How far away are the trenches?"

"Up on them hills beyond the town—about four kilos."

The young officer stared eagerly at the low skyline dimly visible through the haze above the roofs.

A long-drawn whistle on a descending note rose suddenly above the klipity-klop of the horse's hoofs. "'Ark at Jerry!" exclaimed the driver.

The young officer was trying to account for the sound when suddenly a reddish-black cloud bellied out in the town ahead. A sound like a blow on a huge brass tray followed.

"Was that a shell?" he asked. His voice betrayed the excitement he was trying to conceal.

The driver nodded. "And here we come again!" he exclaimed, as that long-drawn, descending whistle rose again out of the distance.

The young officer watched the town with galloping pulses. The seat beneath him gave a little jump. He saw a red fountain spout suddenly by the distant church tower and that black, bellying cloud materialize in the clear air. A long, rumbling roar, like coals being tipped down a chute, followed.

"Five-nine," diagnosed the driver professionally. "In the square."

The young officer nodded. His eyes were very bright. He had seen a shell burst, and the experience had been more thrilling and far less terrifying than he had anticipated. Really, it was rather fun to hear that curious whistling sound and then try to guess where the black, rolling balloon of smoke would appear. He would see if he could guess the next one correctly by the sound. But to his regret no more came.

As the cart crossed a bridge above weed-grown railway lines and approached the outlying houses, he saw what it was that had appeared odd about this town. It was a mere shell. Roofs were full of holes or tileless, and windows were without glass. Dark brick walls were pitted with star-shaped hollows as though splashed with red paint. Here and there a roof had collapsed and a ragged hole gaped in a wall. On the right, where a factory had once stood, was a tangle of rusty metal like a huge bramble bush. Weeds sprouted between the stones of the pavements, and circular holes in the pavé of the road had been filled with brick ends.

The church, seen close at hand, was a ruin. The nave was roofless and gutted; the great tower gaped like a broken cardboard box, its ornate brick and stonework gashed and pitted as though slashed by the hammer of a frenzied giant; and the huge gilded figure of the Virgin on top was bent downwards, so that the child she had held aloft now spread its flashing arms like a diver above the shattered houses.

It reminded the young officer of those silent, ruined cities of the jungle that had captured his boyish imagination, and he would have liked to have gone exploring through these brick-littered streets; but he caught only a tantalizing glimpse of a shattered, shell-pocked square before the cart turned off down a street that led back to the open country.

Regret, however, was soon forgotten in the interest evoked by his surroundings; for instead of the green corn that had formerly flanked the road, rank grass and weeds grew on the unhedged fields, and here and there, marked by the yellow weed which seemed to choose them for its home, were holes of varying circumference and depth which even his inexperienced eye recognized as shell craters. Signs of military occupation were now abundant. Horse lines, huts of various kinds, and dumps were scattered about the slopes or tucked snugly away in the tributary valleys, and when the driver left the road for a rutted track between two gentle slopes, the sudden turning of a corner brought into view an amphitheatre crowded like a fair ground. Every inch of the barren ground on either side of the dusty track was occupied by horse lines, wagon lines, forage dumps, and tarpaulins; and the surrounding slopes were terraced with huts, shacks, and bivouacs of every shape and size.

The driver pulled up by a large tarpaulin filled with water.

"That's A Company office up there, sir," he said, pointing towards the slope. The young officer, in all the panoply of revolver holster, field-glasses, water-bottle, and haversack, climbed down to the dusty, sunbaked track and mopped his face with a khaki handkerchief. The driver hoisted the valise on to his shoulder and led the way between a tarpaulin shack and a huge mound of trusses of hay. He dumped his burden between a Stevenson hut and a shack built of ammunition boxes. "In there, sir," he said, with a jerk of his head towards the shack. "You'll find the Captain inside."

The young officer stooped and went through the narrow doorway. Three or four rope-handled ammunition boxes, a blanket-covered table, and a black japanned despatch box with A Company painted on it in white letters, occupied nearly all the space inside. A dark moustached young man wearing captain's badges of rank sat on an upturned box at the table. The young officer pressed his left arm as close to his body as his bulging equipment would permit, clicked his heels, and saluted.

The young Captain looked up and exclaimed: "Hullo! What can I do for you?"

The newcomer, standing stiffly to attention, said: "I have been ordered to report for duty, sir."

The other leaned back on his box and took up a long-stemmed pipe that lay on some papers before him. "Oh, I see. You're a reinforcement." He put the pipe in his mouth and felt in his pocket for a match. "That's good. What is your name?"

"Eastwell, sir."

The Captain nodded as he drew at his half-smoked pipe. "Eastwell—I see." He threw away the match and held out a hand.

"Mine's Jervis. I run A Company. Been out before?"

"No, sir," answered Eastwell.

Jervis nodded towards the other's cumbersome equipment. "I expect you would like to get rid of that junk, anyway. Dump it in the corner there."

Eastwell slipped off his harness and rebuttoned his shoulder straps.

"Got your kit with you?"

"It's outside, sir."

"Good." Jervis glanced at his wrist-watch and stood up. "Well, I'll just show you where to put your kit and then we'll have some tea. Come along."

II

Tea, consisting of bread, butter, and jam, was spread on a box outside the Stevenson hut. "We always feed on the 'terrace,'" grinned Jervis. "You don't eat so many flies."

A young officer wearing a web belt was introduced as Stokes. "Mouldy jam," he growled as he fished a purplish mass out of the tin and inspected it on the end of a knife. "Do you know, Charles, I have dark suspicions that Daddy keeps back all the strawberry for headquarters."

"You don't know our canny Quartermaster, do you?" he added to Eastwell.

"Is he the grey-haired Scotch officer with a lot of medal ribbons?"

Stokes nodded with his mouth full. "That's him—round and ruddy like a haggis."

"I saw him at battalion headquarters," said Eastwell. "Do you know, I—I thought he was the C.O., and—"

"I know," laughed Jervis. "His grey hairs and Piccadilly ribbons are rather imposing. But he's quite harmless unless you lose your disc identity with string, or some damn thing; then he talks backwards at you and eats his young."

"Just come out?" asked Stokes.

"I crossed last night," admitted Eastwell.

"Just in time for the big push."

"Really!"

Jervis nodded. "At seven-thirty ack emma tomorrow the band begins. But of course it's a secret."

"Yes, of course," said Eastwell seriously.

Stokes nodded emphatically with his mouth full of bread and jam. "Rather! Why, we only heard it officially last night when a chit came in labelled all over 'Secret and Confidential' and 'Very Urgent,' though, of course, we had it from the civilians weeks ago."

"It is to be the real thing this time," put in Jervis. "Non-stop to Berlin."

"Same as Loos," grinned Stokes.

"Shut up, George. It's going to be a good show. The cavalry are all up ready and bags of reserves." He pointed towards a rectangular barbed wire enclosure on the opposite slope. "See that gadget? That's for prisoners."

"I say, is it really?" exclaimed Eastwell.

"And do you see all that water down there?" asked Stokes solemnly, pointing with a jammy knife at the tarpaulin water reservoir below them. "Well, that's for the German Navy."

Eastwell grinned. "I say, what on earth is that?" he exclaimed suddenly. Something huge, glistening, and yellow was slowly rising from behind the opposite slope.

Jervis cocked an uninterested eye upon it over the top of his mug of tea. "That's the old sausage balloon going up. Spotting for the heavies. Gets good visibility this time of day with the sun behind."

Eastwell watched the huge yellow bag rise slowly till it hung far above, glistening in the sun like a bloated slug.

"I say, it's—it's awfully interesting about tomorrow," he said presently. "What do we do, sir? Or is it all a secret?"

"Oh, we are just waiting for the Boche collapse to push through. We are not in tomorrow's show. The platoons are all on detachment—O. Pips and things. George here lives in a hole on the Peronne Road—like the night watchman. That is, when he's not catching fish in the Somme."

"Is he a great fisherman?" asked Eastwell conversationally.

"Well, you see, he's the company bombing expert," said Jervis.

And then they both laughed at Eastwell's mystified face. "He drops bombs in the river," explained Jervis, "and stuns the fish so that they float to the top. Then he collects the poor miserable little blighters before they come round. Not my idea of sport—still!"

"Still, his sportsmanship does not interfere with his appetite," put in Stokes drily.

Suddenly it seemed to Eastwell that an express train was tearing across the sky above them. He looked up, but there was nothing to be seen. And then the sound ended in mid-career with a stunning thunderclap right overhead, and he saw a thick woolly black cloud materialize as if by magic in the clear air.

"Jerry sniping the old sausage," commented Jervis.

"What about the fellow in the basket?" asked Eastwell, who had his eyes on the black speck that swung below the glistening yellow bag.

"He is probably wishing he had joined the Navy," grinned Stokes.

"Here we come again!" exclaimed Jervis, as the train-like roar hurtled out of the distance. "Ah, that's a nasty one!" The thick woolly smoke which just preceded the stunning thunderclap was just above and in front of the balloon.

"Thought that would shift him," commented Stokes, as the balloon swung round and moved slowly back.

Eastwell turned his eyes back to the coming and going of horses and wagons and men in the motley town below him. "All this is awfully interesting!" he exclaimed.

Jervis was pressing tobacco into the bowl of his pipe. "War is damned boring really, but you have come out just at the most interesting time. Tomorrow in that cage you will probably see more Germans in half an hour than I have seen the whole eighteen months I've been out."

"But in the trenches surely—" began Eastwell.

Jervis grinned and shook his head.

"It's—it's all rather different," said Eastwell. "I thought that one always—"

"I know," broke in Stokes. "But one doesn't. I was out months before I saw a Hun. And then it was only a little twirp of a fellow washing his neck in a bucket. It was one morning when the mist lifted suddenly, and then it came down again before I could have a pot at him.

"You know, Charles, it's my belief we could walk into Fricourt any time we liked. I don't believe there is anybody there except a machine-gun or two and a fellow running up and down putting up lights and firing a round occasionally. I believe Fritz keeps all his troops back in support. Millington and I went over one night, and we walked along his parapet for a hell of a distance and never saw a Boche. I don't believe there is anyone there."

"Well, we shall know tomorrow, anyway," said Jervis.

"Where are the trenches?" asked Eastwell.

Jervis waved a hand over his shoulder. "Over there. What time are you going back to your hole, George?"

"Not till dusk."

"You might take Eastwell up as far as Bronfay Farm and show him where the communicating trench begins. What do you say, Eastwell?"

"Oh, I—I'd like to awfully, sir."

"Right-o, then. He can find his own way back, or perhaps Stockton will give him a lift back to Sapper Corner in his car."

III

Excitement and a sobering sense of the solemnity of the occasion were the conflicting feelings that possessed Eastwell later on that evening as he struggled into his equipment in the Stevenson hut, where his valise had been spread out by his newly appointed servant. He was going up to the trenches; perhaps even into them. A veteran like Stokes might regard such a journey with bored indifference, but it was not to be expected that a newcomer could contemplate it without a little flutter of the pulses. Though nearly everyone might be a soldier nowadays, there were, after all, varying degrees of soldiership, and the trenches was the summit of those stages of efficiency and experience which one begun to climb with one's first clumsy efforts at forming fours. This was the end of one's apprenticeship; one was about to be initiated into the final mystery.

"Good God! you look like Ragtime Cowboy Joe with all that revolver and stuff hung round you!" was Stokes' greeting as Eastwell emerged from the Stevenson hut.

Eastwell blushed to the roots of his fair hair. "What do I take?" he asked.

"Just your gas gadget and tin hat. You never wear a revolver except in the front line, and then you shove it in your pocket."

Dusk was falling as they crossed the Bray-Albert road by a big dump of engineers' stores and took a narrow road running up the slope eastwards. Behind them a line of trees was fretted against the after-sunset glow. "Red at night is the shepherd's delight," quoted Stokes. "I really believe we shall have a fine day for tomorrow."

On either hand was the rank jungle grass that flourished over all the forward area, and the yellow weed that grew profusely in the shell-holes seemed to glow in the fast failing light. A long range shell waddled lazily across the sky and died away. And then a dull, distant crunch told that it had landed far back behind the lines. The hill crest ahead was outlined fitfully against the greenish glow of Verey lights, and occasionally a light itself rose above the crest like some new and splendid planet, sank slowly, and expired.

A sudden explosion close beside him in the darkness startled Eastwell, and instantly the unsuspected gun beneath its canopy of netting sprinkled with leaves leapt out of the dark, vivid in every detail like theatrical scenery, and was gone again.

Stokes pointed to a shattered roof that loomed darkly against the sky. "That's Bronfay Farm," he said. "And that's the trench. We use it only in daylight."

Eastwell peered at the low irregular bank of chalk that zigzagged away from the road, and he was conscious of a feeling of slight disappointment in his first view of a real trench.

Limber and G. S. wagons passed up the road, dark, slowly moving shapes except for the glow of a cigarette or a spark from a descending hoof. Guns banged to right and left, and their flashes danced like summer lightning among the hills. A sudden paroxysm of sound accompanied by vivid flashes came from the left.

"There, do you hear that?" cried Stokes. "That's a battery of French seventy-fives. I was watching 'em at it this morning. Potty looking little cannon they are, but they deliver the goods all right."

A line of trees lifted slowly above the dark crest ahead and stood out black and clear cut against the greenish glow that waxed and waned.

A steel-hatted officer wearing staff badges appeared suddenly beside them. "Hullo, Stokes!"

"Hullo, sir. Going to be fine, I believe."

"Looks like it. If so, we will put it across 'em tomorrow."

"I say, sir, could you give Eastwell a lift back to Sapper Corner?"

"If he does not mind waiting a bit."

"Not he. He wants to see the war. He has only just come out."

"Well, he can come along with me if he likes; I'm just going down into

Carnoy."

"I'll leave you to it then. Cheerio, sir. Cheerio, Eastwell." And Stokes' form was swallowed up in the darkness.

Eastwell and the staff officer walked on and reached a tree-bordered road littered with twigs that crackled underfoot. One fallen giant lay darkly across the straight pale ribbon, and its shivered stump showed like a broken tooth in the gap in the line of trees whose branches were etched upon the night sky.

They descended a steep, pot-holed track into the darkness of a little valley and found themselves in a hive of industry. Wagons were being unloaded with feverish speed. As soon as one wagon was emptied of its rations or ammunition, it jolted off and another took its place. Long files of men were passing field-gun ammunition from hand to hand in the dark; others were staggering under the weight of the big toffee-apples which were the projectiles of the heavy trench mortars; and a party of men, encouraged by long drawn "heaves," were hauling a howitzer into position, and the cautiously used flashlight of an officer revealed their bare, dripping backs and straining arms.

All this purposeful coming and going in the darkness held a suggestion of big things afoot that set the pulses galloping, and the thunder of the bombardment which went on ceaselessly seemed a fitting accompaniment to the ant-like activity. All too soon for Eastwell, Stockton turned and said: "Well, young fellow, we must be getting back, I suppose. Up bright and early tomorrow."

IV

Eastwell was awake early, and his first thought was the weather. Jervis, in shirt-sleeves, was shaving in the grey light of dawn before a cracked mirror propped on a box. A smell of wood smoke drifted up from the gypsy town of huts below. Eastward, the hills were hidden beneath wrappers of mist, but already the sky was growing rosy.

Jervis waved his safety razor at Eastwell's tousled head appearing from the Stevenson hut. "Hullo, young fellow! Topping morning. The mist will all be gone in an hour or two. Hark at the guns tuning up for the last lap! Poor old Jerry, he's for it today."

From behind the mists eastwards came a rapid undercurrent of sound as though thousands of wooden hammers were beating on balks of timber.

"I'm going up to Maricourt," continued Jervis; "and you are to report to Kennedy—he's the R.A.M.C. wallah who's running the dressing station and aid posts on our bit. You will find him in some shelters at the bottom of the road you went up last night."

Eastwell found the shelters and reported. "I would just cruise up and down the road if I were you and see what is going on," said Colonel Kennedy. "If I want you, I will send a runner." He glanced at his watch again. "Another five minutes now and they go over. I am going to ring up headquarters presently and get the news."

Eastwell walked slowly up the road. One or two orderlies wearing new red cross armlets hung about expectantly in the bright morning sunshine; otherwise the road was almost deserted. It seemed peculiarly peaceful in spite of the rumble of the barrage.

Eastwell glanced at his watch for the twentieth time. "They are going over now," he told himself breathlessly, and gazed eagerly eastwards where the road disappeared over the crest of the hill. But there was nothing to be seen except a half limber jogging slowly towards him.

He walked on, and only when the broken roof of Bronfay Farm lifted above the crest did he turn reluctantly and retrace his steps. He longed to go on and see something of the battle that must now be raging beyond that peaceful hill crest, but it would not do to go too far. He might be wanted.

Back at the dressing station Colonel Kennedy was standing on the roadside. "I have rung up headquarters," he said. "We went over ten minutes ago, and all is going well."

Eastwell wandered off again. Some twenty yards to the right of the road a French howitzer was in action. He stopped to watch the gun numbers at work. The heavy breech was swung open and the shell and charge pushed home. The short ugly nose of the weapon rose. Then came a spurt of flame, a slobber of smoke, and a detonation that smacked the ear-drums like a blow as the barrel slid back on its recoil buffers. He heard the shell sizzling away into the distance, and discovered that by watching along the line of fire he could even see the shell itself as a tiny black receding dot high up in the sky.

He went off again up the road, and this time he ventured further. He reached the farm. The yard was stacked with shells and stores. Some of the shells stood nearly four feet in height and were painted yellow. Two motor ambulances stood in the lee of the wall. On the left, by the outer wall, the communicating trench with its bordering mounds of excavated earth zigzagged away over the crest. A steel-hatted sentry with fixed bayonet stood on guard at the end of it. Away to the right was a small wood in which concealed field-guns were booming, but ahead nothing was visible except the trees on the twig-strewn road he had crossed the night before.

Three men were coming down the road towards him. Something odd about them held his attention. Their arms were about each other's shoulders, and the sound of their voices raised in a lusty chorus came fitfully between the booming of the barrage. They carried neither rifle nor equipment, and as they drew near he saw that they were wounded. Their tunics were open at the neck, and a little white label dangled from the third button of each. The middle man had one leg of his breeches cut away just above the puttee, revealing a broad white bandage bound round the thigh. The man on his right had one sleeve of his tunic ripped off and a field dressing bound round the upper arm. The third man had no puttee on one leg, and the bandage round the shin had a dark red stain in front. They hobbled cheerfully along, singing at the top of their voices.

Two men in fatigue dress strolled from the farm to speak to them, and

Eastwell joined the little group. He tried to avoid looking at the bandages, but they fascinated him. There was nothing shocking about them, however, and the men themselves seemed careless of their injuries.

"How are we getting on up there, boys?" asked one of the men in fatigue dress.

"Old Jerry's getting it in the bleedin' neck," replied one of the wounded.

"Got a fag, chum?" asked he of the bandaged arm.

Eastwell fumbled for his cigarette case and passed it round.

These men had passed the supreme test; they had been "over the top," and he basked in the reflected glory.

"'Ow far 'ave we got?" demanded the other man in fatigue dress.

"I copped this packet on Jerry's parapet," answered he of the bandaged thigh, puffing luxuriously at his cigarette. "We're in their second line now and going fine. Kaiser Bill won't 'arf be vexed."

"'O says we're Fred Karno's army?" demanded the third.

"Come on, me lucky lads, where's this dressin' station?"

Eastwell eagerly pointed out the way.

"Are we down'earted? No," they roared. "Is Jerry down'earted? Yes." And they hobbled off singing lustily.

More walking wounded appeared in twos and threes. One man wore a German pickelhaube on his bandaged head, and strutted along in imitation of the goose step whenever he passed a knot of onlookers. Men in fatigue dress came from their burrows and shacks and sat on the banks at the roadside to watch, and much good-natured chaff passed between the wounded and the onlookers.

The road became busy with traffic. Lorries and limber wagons passed up it; ambulances came slowly down. Then came the first batch of prisoners, half a dozen men in faded field grey and black, shin-high boots, shepherded by a jaunty Tommy, cigarette in mouth, bayoneted rifle slung over one shoulder, and an inexhaustible fund of back chat to the chaff of the onlookers.

Eastwell gazed at them much as he would have gazed at exhibits in a menagerie. These were the Germans who had turned the world upside down, the exponents of blood and iron, whose atrocities had sent a shudder through Europe. He had never seen a German soldier in the flesh, though he had seen countless sketches and caricatures of the spike-helmeted blonde beast with a machine-gun. But these men looked harmless enough. They looked like very poor and rather stupid country labourers. They were so much less imposing than he had imagined they would be. With their ill-fitting, dirt-stained clothes, narrow chests, and shuffling walk, they did not even look like soldiers. If they were all we were up against, then the whole thing was a vast bluff.

And an officer prisoner, whom he saw later, did not agree with his preconceived idea of the ruthless, efficient Prussian. He was a little squit of a fellow in an absurd tight-waisted top coat with plum colored facings. He wore a cap with an enormous shiny black peak that made him look like a bird under an extinguisher, and he gazed about him through his ridiculous monocle with such an air of affectation that Eastwell wanted to pick him up and spank him.

He went back to the camp in the valley for lunch, but Jervis had not returned. The cage on the opposite slope was nearly full of prisoners. A green-tabbed intelligence officer was questioning some of them, and others stood with hands raised above their close cropped heads while a sergeant-major searched them. A crowd of Tommies in grey shirt-sleeves lounged outside the wire and looked on.

Later in the afternoon he met the contents of the cage winding in a long, slowly moving column out of the valley, shepherded by half a dozen cavalrymen with drawn swords; and he was very amused when the cavalry officer in front shouted some order in German and the dreary column of field grey goose-stepped a dozen yards and eyes righted to an English Colonel who was passing.

V

After dusk the traffic on the road increased. It seemed as though the whole British Army was moving forward that night. Limbers, G. S. wagons, Maltese carts, gun wagons, water carts, and guns crowded up the road, the horses with their noses over the tailboards of the wagon in front; ambulances, lorries, and tenders coming down had difficulty in passing. Mounted military police rode here and there striving to keep the mass of vehicles on the move. Occasionally the stream was dammed to allow a long barrelled sixty-pounder gun with its team of eight huge, straining hairies to pull off the road. Caterpillar tractors rattled and clanked, dragging behind them six-inch howitzers or the huge steel mountings and squat barrels of nine-point-twos. By the wood to the right some sixty-pounders were in action, and at each salvo the night was lit as though a bonfire had been uncovered.

Beyond the farm stood Stockton, the A.P.M., pipe in mouth, steel helmet tilted over one eye, watching one of his men controlling the stream of traffic at the cross roads. He recognized Eastwell by the light of the sixty-pounder flashes.

"Bit of a scrum, sir," said Eastwell.

Stockton nodded. "Rather like the Mansion House—what! But that fellow is used to this sort of thing. He's a City policeman," he said, with a nod towards the traffic control man, who was manipulating the stream of vehicles with professional skill. "Fortunately, the Boche is too busy getting his own batteries back to worry about us, or he might have made it very unpleasant."

"News still good, sir?"

"I believe so. We were hung up at Fricourt this morning. But there is a rumor that we got into it after dark. We will go along to brigade headquarters here in a moment and get the latest news."

Fifty yards back along the road the lights of an aid post twinkled in the darkness, and, nearby, the red lamp of a brigade headquarters was propped on a mound of chalk. Stockton climbed over the tumbled earth and rank grass, and led the way down the dozen odd steps of a timber revetted shaft that led underground. It was Eastwell's first visit to a dug-out, and this one fulfilled his rather romantic expectations. The narrow pit-propped passage at the foot of the sloping shaft gave entrance to three or four compartments. From those on the left came the click of a typewriter and the hum of a buzzer, but that facing him was crowded with officers. The smoke of many pipes drifted in wreaths about the electric bulbs that hung from colored cables on the roof timbers. Regardless of the laughter and buzz of voices about him, the red-tabbed Brigade Major was at work at a table piled with papers; the Brigadier was talking to a group of officers in the centre of the dug-out. He caught sight of Stockton in the doorway, and called: "Hullo, Stockton! Come in."

Stockton saluted and went in, followed by Eastwell. The Brigadier took his long-stemmed pipe from his mouth and said with a grin: "Get him a drink somebody; he looks positively overworked."

Stockton grinned and said: "Thank you, sir."

The Brigadier tilted his gold-laced cap over his eyes and assumed an expression of mock ferocity. "Do you know, one of your damned fellows turned Everett back on the Peronne Road tonight," he growled.

"Did he, sir?" said Stockton with a smile.

"Did he!" echoed the General, giving a hitch to the gas respirator that hung over one shoulder. "You damn well know he did."

"Well, we are rushing up guns and ammunition chiefly, sir. And the corps heavies—"

The Brigadier clapped Stockton on the shoulder. "Oh, I dare say. Meantime Everett took nearly an hour to get to Maricourt."

Stockton took the glass handed to him and said: "Cheerio, sir. How is the war going?"

"Bon! My fellows are well up on the western edge of Montauban and full of buck. They are all out to give Master Jerry another shove in the face tomorrow. They have just reported some people moving across their front. We are not sure whether they are Boches retiring or our own fellows moving east from Fricourt. We are just ringing up division to find out."

Eastwell was rather awed by the presence of a General, but the prevailing spirit of optimism and good-fellowship put him at his ease. He sipped the whisky-and-soda that was put into his hands and took stock of his surroundings. It was rather like a scene on a stage, he thought. The confusing buzz of conversation, the uniforms, the scarlet and gold of the General's gorgets, and the bright electric bulbs shining on the heavy timbers of the low roof and the expanding metal revetment of the earth walls, were all a trifle theatrical and unreal. He must try to describe it all in his first letter home—that and the guns and limbers streaming through the night outside and the ghostly Verey lights rising and falling among the low hills.

A hand dug him suddenly in the ribs, and he turned to find Stokes behind him. "Finish that up and come out," said Stokes with a jerk of his head towards the door; and before Eastwell could ask why he was gone. Eastwell gulped down his drink and followed.

Out in the narrow timbered passage at the foot of the shaft Stokes stood with two other young officers. "We are going over to the old Boche front line," he whispered. "I want one of those German bivouac gadgets. And there's any amount of stuff in their dug-outs—field-glasses, helmets, Mauser pistols...Are you game?"

Eastwell was very much game.

"Right-o, then. Got a flash-lamp?"

"No."

"I'll borrow one for you."

Stokes went back into the crowded brigade dug-out and returned a few moments later with an electric torch. He thrust it into Eastwell's hands. "Come on, and not a word."

They climbed the steps into the night and stumbled along over the rough earth parallel with the road. Presently the now familiar line of trees loomed ahead. The stream of traffic had stopped. Horses tapped the road impatiently with their feet, and cigarettes glowed in the darkness. At the cross roads they saw the cause of the blockage. One of the tall trees lay across the road, and the dark figures of a party of men sweating to remove the obstacle could he seen against the glow of a fire in some distant village.

They crossed the obstacle and descended into the darkness of the little Carnoy valley. Here, as on the previous night, all was movement and hustle. The narrow road was badly pot-holed. Hummocks of jagged masonry and brickwork on either side proclaimed that they were passing through the village, and they overtook files of dark, trudging figures bearing strange-shaped burdens on their shoulders. The Verey lights came again into view as they ascended the slope, and Stokes led the way off the road. The going was rough. Unseen shell-holes were everywhere in the darkness, and their feet clattered old tins and became entangled in rusty wire. Occasionally Eastwell heard that thrilling aerial whistle, followed by a bump and the sound as of a sack of coals being tipped down a chute.

They fell into single file along a narrow track through the rank grass and wire. They crossed two or three trenches by narrow plank bridges, and Eastwell, peering curiously down at the slit of darkness he was crossing, found there was nothing to be seen except the sandbags of the parapet and the rusty tangles of wire and knife rests among the rank grass beyond. Not far distantly he heard the crack of a rifle and the clack-clack-clack of a machine-gun. That first letter home would be a long one, he thought.

"You are now in the old No Man's Land," Stokes told him.

They seemed to be in a shallow valley, for the Verey lights ahead revealed a near dark horizon behind which they rose and fell. Underfoot were the same rank grass, uneven ground, old tins, and scraps of wire. One of Stokes' companions stumbled and recovered himself with a muttered "damn." He flashed his torch behind him, and Eastwell saw a pair of upturned boots and puttees in the brief bright circle of light. "One of our fellows," said Stokes, and they went on.

Half right a pale grey line glimmered faintly. They turned towards it and found a breast-high barrier of chalk. Eastwell followed Stokes up the slippery incline of loose rubble and drew back precipitately at the top. Beyond it there was nothing. The grey chalk sloped steeply to a vast funnel-shaped pit, so deep that the tumbled chalky boulders at the bottom glimmered but faintly in the almost exhausted beam of the torch.

"Mine crater," announced Stokes, and switched off the light.

They skirted the curving bank of chalk that marked the perimeter of the mine crater and reached a lower bank of trampled earth. Stokes directed the beam of his torch downwards. At his feet was a broad, deep trench cut in the chalk, the bottom duck-boarded and littered with scraps of equipment, clothing, and chalky rubble.

"Here we are," he said, and dropped lightly down to the firestep. The others followed. They turned and leaned against the parapet, looking out across the darkness of the old No Man's Land.

"Queer, isn't it!" exclaimed one of Stokes' companions after a short silence.

Stokes grunted. "To think of the number of times we've looked out from across there and wondered what Jerry was doing over here; and now—here we are!"

It was very dark and quiet there in the trench. The direct rays of the Verey lights were cut off by the slope behind them, and only a faint greenish, moonlight-like glow told when they rose and fell. Faintly they could hear the clink of tins from a carrying party moving along a track away to their left, and the clank of a caterpillar tractor came distantly from the dark ridge facing them. On the same dark ridge a brief, lightning-like flash was followed by the bang of a gun, and they heard the shell sailing mournfully over their heads to detonate grumpily in the distance. The long, muffled cr-r-r-ump of a German five-nine far away to the right served only to accentuate the silence.

"Well, let's get on with the washing," cried Stokes, as he dropped from the fire-step. He rounded a traverse bulking hugely against the sky and threw the beam of his torch down the black-timbered shaft of a dug-out. "See how Jerry had built his dug-outs facing his rear so that our shells can't possibly land in the shaft as his sometimes do in ours!" he exclaimed. He started down the steps. "Come on, you fellows, but bags I the first bivvy sheet we see."

In single file they stumbled down the steep narrow shaft.

"Much the same as ours," commented one of Stokes' companions as the four torch beams moved over the earthen walls of the burrow below.

"Only a damn sight deeper and better built," growled Stokes. "Trust old Jerry! Look at that post. You might blow the top of the shaft in, but the biggest stuff would never touch this." He began rummaging with his foot among some broken boxes and rubbish beside a wire-netting bunk. He stopped suddenly and picked up something.

"What is it?" asked Eastwell, staring at the round grey object.

"Hark at him! What is it? Why, a pickelhaube, you fool."

"But I thought—" began Eastwell.

"This is the canvas cover they keep 'em in," said Stokes. He turned the helmet round to show the green cloth numbers stitched on the front. "I'll show you." He stripped off the cover and revealed a shiny black leather helmet decorated in front with the Imperial eagle.

"But where is the spike?" asked one of his companions.

"Lying about somewhere, I expect," said Stokes. "Look for it, you slackers. It fits into this notch arrangement on top."

They found it after a short search, and Stokes put on the German helmet and goose-stepped up and down the dug-out with a ten centimes stuck in his eye for a monocle. They found a round German gas-mask, which one of the other two appropriated, and a smutty German postcard.

"Come on, there's nothing more here. Let's try the next," said Stokes.

They tramped up the steps back into the trench and went on to the next shaft. Eastwell was coveting the pickelhaube. What a souvenir to send home with that letter describing his adventures! But if Stokes went down first each time he would get all the plums.

In the next dug-out one of the other officers appropriated a German pioneer saw bayonet, and Stokes got his bivouac sheet. There was nothing else there except lousy blankets and a few grey linen bandoleers of small arms ammunition.

Eastwell was determined to get something. He was first out of the dug-out and led the way along the trench to the next shaft.

"Bags I the next," he said over his shoulder.

"Right-o," agreed Stokes good humoredly. "You and Green take the next dug-out; Anderson and I will go on to the one after that."

Eastwell flashed his torch down the next shaft and started to descend. Stokes and Anderson passed on along the trench. Stokes halted suddenly and called back: "I say, Green, chuck me one of those cigarettes of yours."

Green turned on the second step and went up again into the trench. "Right-o. But give me a fill of baccy."

Eastwell hurried on down the steps. He would make sure of anything here for himself.

He reached the bottom of the shaft and swung the light round the dug-out. It was a large one, but there did not seem to be much there . Four or five bunks in tiers on the side nearest the shaft, a roughly carpentered table overturned on the floor, and the other timbered walls bare except for a nail or two on which hung a greatcoat and one of the round grey German caps. It was very quiet down there underground, and the place had a stale, pungent, garlicky smell like the lair of a wild beast.

He appropriated the little grey cap with its gay red band, and swung the light round on one last inspection. It was then that he noticed in the end wall to his right a low, timbered opening. Two steps led down from it, evidently to a small burrow beyond. Stooping in the low entrance, he inspected it with his torch. The circle of light slid slowly along the damp clay wall, rested a moment on a rough shelf containing a candle end and a jagged meat tin, and moved on to the corner and along the opposite wall. It reached the other corner, and remained like a circle of yellow paper pinned on a black screen.

The head and shoulders of a man were in the centre of the circle—a man with short, earth-encrusted hair and pale, dirt-stained face. His fixed eyeballs glittered in the strong light. Upon the lower edge of the circle, across the faded grey uniform, projected a hand clutching a short glittering trench dagger. The figure was motionless like a bust modelled in wax; only the tautness of the lean face and the madness of fear and desperation in the eyes showed that it was alive and, like a trapped animal, waited to spring.

Eastwell's trembling finger released its pressure on the button. The light wavered and went out. Seconds passed. He recovered himself sufficiently to draw back a pace from the low archway. His heart was pounding against his ribs, and in that intense silence, as he held his breath, he heard the watch ticking on his wrist. He pressed it against the back of his leg to muffle the sound. He pictured that terrifying figure creeping silently up the steps and springing upon him.

He held his breath and took another cautious step sideways. If he went straight back across the dug-out he would bump into that overturned table. Thank God, the walls on one side were clear of obstructions.

He put out his hand and touched the wall. He took another pace back. Still no sound. His heart was pounding so hard that he could hear it, and he was half suffocated with the effort to keep his breathing noiseless. He held the torch by the very end; he was terrified lest he should touch the button and give a tell-tale flash of light.

His back touched a wall behind him: he had reached the corner. Inch by inch in an agony of silence he started back along the long wall that faced the shaft. To his right distantly he discerned a slight lessening of the intense darkness. That must be the bottom of the shaft in the opposite wall. But he dared not cross to it. That paleness, faint though it was, would betray him. He was crouching. He would have a better chance when the man sprang upon him suddenly from the wall of darkness ahead, though he knew that when that happened he would scream and drop without resistance.

Faintly he heard a voice in the trench above. It was remote; it came from another world. He was like a diver in the dark, silent depths of the ocean.

Another long agony of suspended breathing and silent movement brought his back against the wall. He had reached the second corner. Then suddenly he knew what he would do. He would move in the same silent fashion along this wall to the third corner, and so along the next wall till he stood by the foot of the shaft. Then a deep breath and a dash up the steps before the trapped madman could spring upon him.

He went along this wall sideways, with his back to it, keeping his face towards the length of the dug-out and that opening in the far wall. He heard no sound, but he knew that the other had left the burrow and was not far from him. Inch by inch he moved along and reached the third corner. Crouching low, he moved on again with the tips of his fingers hovering over the wall to his right.

His fingers touched the post, the big post at the foot of the shaft, and he paused. After eons of silence it was not easy to break it now with that frantic rush up the steps. But it had to be done. He nerved himself for the effort. He would go when he had counted three. He began to count.

A faint sound from the shaft arrested him. It was a high-pitched drone, as though up there in the trench above a circular saw was cutting through timber. The drone rose to a scream and then rapidly expanded to a roar, as though an express train were coming down the shaft. A vivid orange flame slit the darkness; and as Eastwell's eyes went blind, he saw facing him on the other side of the shaft that pale, earth-stained mask and staring, desperate eyes. Then one side of the face went suddenly dark and shapeless; the grey form lifted like a dancer and curved through the air to the floor. Some great force swept up Eastwell also and hurled him to the ground. There came a crashing roar that shook the dug-out like an earthquake, and then darkness and silence, broken only by the tinkle of stones and earth down the steps.

He lay dazed and motionless. Then something soft beneath him twitched once convulsively and was still. He leapt wildly to his feet and rushed like a madman through the choking fumes and smoke up the steps. He tumbled panting into the trench at the top as two dark figures came round the traverse beside him.

"Hullo, young fellow!" cried the voice of Stokes. "Did that one put the breeze up you!"

Eastwell leaned panting against the wall of the trench, his eyes closed against the glare of Anderson's torch.

"Come on, pull yourself together," said Stokes. "That's nothing. You wait till you get mixed up in a proper strafe or have to hare backwards and forwards round a traverse all day dodging minnies."

"Hullo, he's stopped a bit!" exclaimed Anderson, as the lowered beam of his torch glistened on two thick trickles of blood on Eastwell's hand.

Stokes gently raised the wrist, and then for the first time Eastwell became aware that his shoulder burned as though it had been branded. Stokes produced a knife and neatly slit the seam of the sleeve. "Hold the light here—that's right." He slit the khaki shirt. "Umm! Get his dressing out, Andy."

Anderson ripped the first field dressing from the skirt of Eastwell's tunic. Another figure appeared round the traverse. "Hullo, anybody stopped one?" asked the voice of Green.

"Eastwell. Got a nice little knock on the shoulder. No serious damage as far as I can see."

"Cheer up, old son," cried Anderson. "You'll be in Blighty in a couple of days. They are bunging everyone right through to England, I'm told. Where's the nearest aid post?"

"There's one up an old Boche communicating trench on the right here. I'll take him along," volunteered Green.

Stokes lit a cigarette as the two figures moved off round the traverse. "That's quick work," he growled. "A Blighty one on his first day out! And here have I been dodging 'em for eighteen months.

"They will put him on to lecturing on the fighting on the Western front, I expect," said Anderson with a grin.

"But think of it, Andy: a Blighty one on his first day! He's never been in the line, and he's never even seen a Boche—except a tame one in a cage."

"Some people have all the luck," agreed Anderson.

Stokes bent down and picked up something from the floor of the trench. "And, damn it," he cried, "he's bust that torch I lent him."

The Watch on the Rhine

Ared White

As the first scattering notes of the division's lately improvised marching song rose from tired throats up near the head of the trudging column, Corporal McGee reached instinctively for the big silver watch that hung on a heavy link chain in the upper bellows pocket of his blouse just under his bright new Croix de Guerre. He consulted the faded dial of the ancient timepiece ostentatiously.

"Seven o'clock by Heinie's watch," he announced in a voice loud enough to be heard by the seven sullen members of his squad. "Seven o'clock. Another hour 'n' a half yet to hike!"

There was a groan as of protest at this needless reminder of the hour.

"Ah, perk up and take the gaff smilin'," he bantered them. "Ain't you gettin' the Rhine for a Christmas present? Another ten days by Heinie's watch and you'll be in soft billets eatin' Boche poison with your Christmas pork 'n' beans."

"Wish you'd throw Heinie's watch in the Rhine!" muttered someone disgustedly.

The song up ahead began to gather form. Dragging feet that sloshed through thin mud and scraped over rough cobblestones along the endless course of sinuous grey kilometres that led to the Rhine lifted a bit less heavily as the rollicking refrain swept through the ranks. Battalion and company officers smiled wearily or pretended not to hear. Anything had warrant enough that would bring spirit back into their leg-weary men.

> The General got the Croix de Guerre,
> *Parlez vous*,
> The General got the Croix de Guerre,
> *Parlez vous*,
> The General got the Croix de Guerre,
> The son of a gun was never there,
> Hinky, dinky, *parlez vous*!

It rose, like a wind at sea, from an eddying swirl among a few squads to a rhythmic storm hurled into the grey dreariness of the dying day by the strong lungs of six thousand men. Feet began dragging in cadence to the music. Shoulders that had drooped nearly to the waist under the heavy full field packs began rising higher. A bugler who a moment before had been all but staggering in exhaustion found strength to trumpet a crude accompaniment, using the five tones of his bugle scale to catch a chord here and there. Another bugler picked it up, and another. The march to the Rhine suddenly became, for the moment, all but a blithesome promenade.

Presently taut arms arose fully extended above the heads of the Majors who sagged wearily in saddles at the heads of battalions. It was the signal for the hourly halt. Barely half an hour had passed since the last halt; but dusk was gathering swiftly and who could know for certain that the new divisional commander himself might not dash back along the line at any moment in his military limousine to note the progress of this record hike of forty kilometres today. The song died out as suddenly as it had commenced as the men fell gratefully in their tracks at the sides of the road for ten minutes' surcease from the day's gruelling advance. Regimental commanders breathed easier. It was one thing to have one of this fighting division's allotment of French war crosses given to the new divisional commander, who had joined them from some imposing staff assignment after the Armistice had been duly signed.

It might prove another thing should that new divisional commander, in the course of the division's march to the Rhine, learn the men's opinion of the transaction as perpetuated in song. The music might be well enough for the men's marching morale; but then it might not, at the same time, stir the General's fancy in a way that would be good for the morale of the brigade, regimental and battalion commanders, anon, when they were part of the American watch on the Rhine.

Corporal McGee, sitting on his unslung pack while his men lay motionless about him, got out the big silver watch again and held it before him as the hands ticked swiftly toward that instant when he must get them back in column again. He invariably found some excuse for bringing the timepiece into use when the song was in the air. To him the watch was his alibi—a reminder to his squad that his own Croix de Guerre had not been issued to him with the ration or passed to him by some obsequious staff person.

"Five minutes more to go, by Heinie's watch!" he announced with forced airiness, heroically putting aside an impulse to cast himself alongside his men on the wet ground and pass into slumber.

"Wish you'd left that Boche clock where you got it from," grumbled a private, without raising his weary head from the ground. "It's allus takin' the joy out o' life."

"One minute left to go—get ready!" the corporal cautioned them, taking his own place manfully in the road, ready for the gruff chorus of "fall in" that presently would come from the officers.

He put the big silver watch carefully back in the bellows pocket of his coat under the Croix de Guerre. The watch had validated his war cross again. It had shielded his own decoration from the devilish innuendo of that song. Since the appearance, and instant popularity, of the musical satire on the General's cross, Corporal McGee had found the silver watch a source of comfort and gratification, as well as of utility. It was a grim token of the manner in which he had served, one whose mortal glory no mere song might dim. It was symbolical of that breathless moment in the crimson Argonne when he had gone ahead of his platoon to engage a German machine-gun crew hand-to-hand, vanquishing them with the bayonet in a desperate encounter against odds.

On one of his antagonists—the one he had vowed was the size of two ordinary men—he had found the ancient silver timepiece. Its owner had the watch chained to his belt, apparently for ready consultation against the moment when he need hold his position no longer and might retire to a place of greater security following the retreating German riflemen. Now the watch could not have been slow. It kept excellent time. Corporal McGee, in the momentary frenzy of battle that sometimes seizes individuals and endows them with the courage of a dozen men, simply had been ahead of schedule.

The corporal had cleaned his bayonet in the mud and slipped the watch remorselessly into his pocket. He was robbing no one. The German would have no further use for it. The corporal took it as one imbued with the common practices of the battlefield might take a spiked helmet or a Luger pistol or a sawtooth bayonet. Thoughts of its one-time owner and his untimely end haunted the corporal as little as a rabbit's foot or sealskin sacque might fret its possessor. War begets its own peculiar conscience in such matters. And this silver watch, with the name engraved in German script inside the heavy hunting case, was a souvenir such as only a first-class fighting man might hope to possess by means other than purchase. Non-combatants, denizens of deep command dug-outs, might win the Croix de Guerre by rank or favour—but how were they to validate their crosses in the eyes of the combatant men?

"Snap into it—keep movin' there!" Corporal McGee fumed, as the members of his squad took their places beside him in the long sluggish column that moved off grudgingly in that eternal sloshing and scraping of heavy feet that were moving toward the Rhine.

"Are they goin' to hike us clean on to Berlin without stoppin' for sleep?" a private of his squad demanded querulously.

"Another two hours by Heinie's watch and you'll all be tucked away in a nice Boche feather bed-sleepin' with one eye open to keep Heinie's wife from stickin' a knife in between your ribs," he cheered them.

"Two hours more o' this an' I'll be lyin' dead 'longside the road," groaned another member of the squad.

Corporal McGee felt his first concern that one or two of his squad might give up the hike and join the footsore and weak of will who made up the ambulance and truck-riding slackers. Not a single member of his company had so disgraced himself. The corporal shuddered at the thought of such dishonour coming to his own squad.

"Ah, you birds just think you're gettin' tired out," he bantered them. "You ain't even had good leg exercise yet today!"

His own feet came out of the thin mud heavily, each of them seeming to weigh more than the sixty-pound pack on his back; and he all but winced every time one of his raw feet struck a submerged cobblestone in the muddy road.

But sense of responsibility fed his sinews and strengthened him in carrying his own fatigue while laughing at the others. And it fed his strength, this laughing at the others, and cheering them on; attesting his own superiority of moral and physical fibre which a leader must have.

"Bet I could talk you buddies into hikin' all night an' all tomorrow an' the only kick you'd make was when I asked you to stop to rest or eat!" he challenged them whimsically, intent on keeping the thought fixed in their minds that they really were far from exhausted.

"I'll bet ye another five kilometres and ye'll need a ambulance fer the second squad," came a vacant threat from the ranks.

"But supposin'," chuckled the corporal, "supposin' I'd jus' give the order 'squads right about' and informed you the Watch on the Rhine was all off an' we was startin' back to Brest to catch a Christmas boat home, what'd happen?"

"It'd take a darned fast horse to keep up with me," announced one of the squad.

"You said somethin', buddy," came a voice from the squad in rear. "I could do it to Brest in nothin' flat if they'd only turn me loose and gimme the road."

"That's different. Course we could do that," echoed someone in his own squad.

"You all agree?" Corporal McGee asked them.

"It wouldn't be a march, it'd be a stampede," another averred feelingly. The others muttered their assent.

Corporal McGee chuckled triumphantly. There had been method in his queries.

"Then it all goes to prove you birds ain't as tired as you might be," he charged them. "It's mostly homesickness just like you had it last year at Christmas time when you'd nothin' to do but lay around billets. Now cut out your dream stuff and quit laggin'. Come on now, snap into it. Ain't you gettin' the Rhine for Christmas—an' maybe a slit throat!"

Corporal McGee's diagnosis which he had emphasized thus to his own advantage as squad leader, was flawless. The War was over. In the minds of the men who fought it, the conflict ended November 11. Up to the hour of eleven o'clock of that greatest of days in human experience they had been sombre supermen, baiting a death-dealing Frankenstein in its lair with little thought of what life might hold for them when this desperate mission were ended—if it should ever end. Life was too insecure, and the demands of duty too sacred, to reckon deeply with the future. And at fifteen minutes after the hour of eleven they were so many homesick men and boys with their thoughts upon home, and Christmas; reckoning the chances of getting to the base ports and back home in civvies again for Christmas Day. What a Christmas present!

The unfailing grape-vine, greatest of army communications, had brought their home-bound orders to the—the Division every day after the Armistice until that dismal hour when the crushing official orders actually arrived with the calamitous information that they were crossing the Rhine, rather than the

Atlantic, for Christmas Day of 1918.

General and Colonels—and an occasional Major—might find a thrill in the thought that "Die Wacht Am Rhine" was going to have a new set of works— American works; even in the leading of a victorious army on past Coblenz to Berlin itself, or around the world for that matter. But for the butcher boys, clerks, farm hands, students, brokers, artists, and artisans who made up the ranks a more dismal disaster could not come into their lives at Christmas time.

Fifteen miles a day they had marched in the early stages of the advance—an easy hike, readily completed before noon. With the four other veteran combat divisions that had been taken from the flower of the brilliant Liggett's fighting First Army to make up the invading Third Army, their advance was by "bounds," which is to say that they marched three days or so and rested an equal period in cities along the route, billeting with the natives in accordance with carefully wrought military plans. In France, and throughout that borderland where France and Germany merged into an area whose populace had cultivated the art of enthusiastic welcome for conqueror, whoever he might be, their march was one triumphal procession, noisy throngs packing the streets and countryside waving flags and cheering *Vive les Américaines* or *Vive les Allies.*

Now they had entered into the true Rhineland whose allegiance to the Kaiser had paid its full toll of sons and gold into the Prussian cause, and the olive drabbed columns were met with a sodden, almost sullen indifference. Sober faces peered discreetly from behind closed windows. Conquered were looking with dire forebodings, if not with smouldering venom, upon conqueror. The advance guard was reinforced. Strong connecting groups were put out to maintain liaison with other allied columns marching on parallel routes to the north and south in readiness for instant deployment. The security measures were those of an advance in the face of the enemy. Occasional glimpses were to be had of the shattered German war machine as its jaded rearguards faded sullenly into the grey distance barely ahead of the American advance parties. Anything might happen.

Only an occasional old man appeared on a street corner in the villages to watch the Americans parade by at rigid attention; flags flying at the head of regiments in the main column behind the advance guards, bands blaring American march music. Old men, and the ubiquitous small boy, the latter drawn to the bands in small droves as by a magnet and trooping fearlessly along, bigeyed and beaming; stirred by the thrumming drums and throbbing brass, thrilling innocently to the compelling rhythm of "Stars and Stripes Forever" quite as if it had been some Teuton martial quickstep proclaiming "*Deutschland Über Alles!*"

Today's historic march of forty kilometres had begun at day break. It would bring the division late at night through the final stage of the long hike. Tomorrow and the next day, and perhaps the day after that, the men would rest in billets near the west bank of the Rhine, replace worn-out uniforms, shoes, and impedimenta, and then sweep on across to the east shore of the haughty river into the heart of Rhenish Prussia, a spic-and-span bit of fighting mechanism bent on seeing to it that the Kaiser's hosts made good the hard terms of the Armistice they had signed.

Heinie's watch, which Corporal McGee found occasional vindication in quoting, had ticked off two heavy hours before the fatigue-driven column tumbled into German billets at the end of the final "bound." And its stocky little hour hand had completed six revolutions of the ancient dial before the column, now rested and fully outfitted, found the proud old Rhine rolling humbly under their democratic American feet as they trod, route step, toward the beckoning spires of Coblenz in that moment of pulsating magnificence when the Stars and Stripes rose suddenly over stern old Ehrenbreitstein, replacing the Prussian red, white, and black and all that those colors symbolized by way of evil omen to the world.

"The thing ain't as wide as the Hudson," announced someone disparagingly.

If the men in the ranks had been fired for the moment by the portentous significance of their arrival at the Rhine, their sense of the dramatic moment which thrilled a continent at home quickly gave way to the spirit of badinage which the now humble stream itself aroused. It had been forbidden them that they scoff at persons and things along the route of march. Not that the feelings of their broken foemen mattered—but such a show is not of a well-disciplined army. The river, however, was an inanimate thing even though it did seem to echo of the one-time splendour of the vaunted Hohenzollerns.

"It's a crick 'longside the Miss'sippi," another soldier proclaimed.

"I wouldn't trade a quart of the muddy ol' Missouri fer the whole thing," another insisted with feeling.

"Gimme the Columbia fer mine," chorused a soldier from the far West; and the rivers of America followed in quick succession.

A warning order came snapping down the column and brought them back to the serious business at hand. The moment was at hand when they would cross into the great Prussian city itself. The new division commander would add to the import of the occasion, and to his own martial traditions, by personally reviewing this division as it set foot east of the Rhine. His large red command flag with its two white stars could be seen unfurled in the distance, just beyond the bridge-approach on the Coblenz side. The men began checking their accoutrement and blouse-buttons. A few lapsed into a gentle humming of the division marching song, brought to their vagrant minds by proximity of the new division commander; but officers quickly suppressed them with sharp words of reprimand or caution. This was no time for such foolishness.

Corporal McGee, at the first humming notes, instinctively reached for the big silver watch that hung on a heavy link chain in the upper bellows pocket of his blouse, in full vindication of his own bright new Croix de Guerre.

"Right on time, fellows," he announced plausibly. "Right here to the dot. An' say, fellows, ever stop to think that Heinie's watch's back on the Rhine—with me carryin' it? Let 'em write a song about that if they want to!"

The division snapped into its best military stride as it swept from the bridge with a magnificent "eyes right" for the stern visaged new division commander who stood reviewing them with arms folded and a brooding martial air that hinted of "Napoleon at Friedland"; then on through the principal business section of Coblenz with every man putting himself into the business of presenting a proud and lasting spectacle of armed superiority before the awed eyes of a conquered host. The Germans had laughed a year ago, had they? Well, let them take a close-up of these despised American volunteers and see what it was that had amused them so. Let them laugh now if there was humor left in their souls! The thought was expressed in the demeanour of every marcher as feet rose and fell with perfect unison, shoulders dipped with a splendidly coordinated rhythm and eyes looked hard and fast straight to the front in those files that covered off as perfectly as if they had been laid by field transit.

The streets were all but empty except for the inevitable old folks and the everlasting small boys; but the invaders sensed the thousands of eyes that were observing them carefully, and estimating them anxiously, from behind windows and curtains. Let all such form their own opinion as to whether such men might be temporized with; whether isolated treachery, poison in food and knife-thrusts in the dark might be indulged in with impunity!

At the end of an interminable parade, when the populace must have been duly impressed, the columns broke into regiments, then into battalions, companies, and finally on down into squads as the elaborate billeting plans unfolded; and such men as had been selected for duty within the city itself marched off to present themselves at the homes which were to receive and shelter them.

Corporal McGee brought his own squad to an impressive halt, late in the afternoon, in front of a plain-appearing stone house in the residential district. It was one of an endless row of houses, all alike, of the kind occupied by the better middle class, two stories and attic, distinctive only in the possession of steep slate roof and green shutters. Before presenting his billeting ticket, the corporal faced his men impressively and gave them their final instructions. "Remember, fellows, no fraternisin' with the enemy. Get that! That's one thing the Cap'n won't stand for. Remember we're dealin' with the enemy. What's more, we're conquerors an' we got to act our part. The Cap'n says we're to keep our hats on in the house even when wimmin folks is present. You ain't to say 'thanks' for nothin' they try to do for you. Wear sidearms all the time an' if any of 'em tries to knife you—well, you knows what to do without bein' told. Now then, in we goes!"

He strode firmly to the door and rapped decisively.

A middle-aged woman, thin, grey, and with a cold reserve in her careworn face, answered the summons. She reached in a dignified, detached way for the billeting ticket that Corporal McGee held out to her; then paused suddenly, hand extended without taking the ticket, the while she stood staring at the members of the squad who were assembled in wide-eyed expectancy about the door stoop.

Her expression changed to one of startled surprise as she looked slowly from one to the other as if she had been suddenly confronted by some unbelievable phantom.

"What's matter, marm—don't you like the looks o' my crew?" broke in the corporal nervously, turning to look at the squad as if to learn what caused her sudden change of humor. "Not a bad bunch o' lads if they ain't ruffled."

She turned with a start to the corporal, looking at him with wide puzzled eyes, then took the billeting ticket without looking at it.

"Why, you are just a few liddle boys, no different much as mein Heinrich," she exclaimed in a voice that reflected her perplexity and seemed to carry a measure of sudden and unexpected approval of them.

She threw the door wide open confusedly, still staring from one to the other, and led them silently to their sleeping-places on the second floor. Three rooms, the billeting ticket called for—and there were three comfortable rooms with two large feather beds in each room, rug carpets on the floor, a few pictures on the walls and other evidences of homelike luxury such as belonged to a cherished but dimly remembered past existence. While they laid out their meagre possessions from their packs and prepared to make themselves comfortable in their temporary German domicile, she bustled back and forth dragging large rocking-chairs into the rooms and adding bits of bric-a-brac as if under a sudden impulse to minister further to their comfort.

"Is it you haf hunger?" she asked them suddenly when they were settled and she had finished rearranging their rooms.

The suggestion found instant response.

"Hungry's right—hungry enough to eat a slab o' raw salt pork," exclaimed Corporal McGee spontaneously.

"I haf some nice cakes und some tea should make if you will wish for it," she tempted them, with a friendly smile.

"Cakes!" exclaimed one of the squad. "Is they any such thing in the world! If they is lead me to 'em. It's sure be a life-saver, Mrs.—"

"Fenstermacher—Frau Fenstermacher," she supplied the name. She bustled out of the room and downstairs; and members of the squad could hear distinctly the exquisite music of clattering chinaware as the spread was being made ready for them. It was late afternoon. The noon meal had consisted of two heavy sandwiches, designed to carry them through the last brief hike across the Rhine and tide their stomachs over until the company messes were set up to ladle out hot food late that evening. As for cake, it had vanished entirely from their lives that same day the Statue of Liberty sank into the hazy skyline behind them. Cake and war had remained persistent strangers throughout the length and breadth of France.

"Think of real cake and tea," Corporal McGee fairly gloated, betrayed for the moment by his treacherous appetite; for in common with the other youngsters of twenty-two and under who made up the bulk of the fighting forces, and all of Corporal McGee's squad, his stomach had found few moments of actual delight in this thing of war. The veneer of discipline swept him suddenly and rescued him from his peril. He jumped to his feet and faced his squad sternly, remembering his duty.

"Put on you hats, you birds—what did I tell you about how you was to act!" he ordered them, covering his own head abruptly by way of example.

"Your cake und tea it is ready—and I have found some cold poultry," came the inviting voice of Mrs. Fenstermacher from below.

Corporal McGee held the others in the room with an abrupt warning order of his hand. Then he marched manfully and with true martial stride out into the hall, downstairs, and faced Mrs. Fenstermacher, hat in hand again.

"Where are der oder liddle boys?" she smiled lightly. Her kindly face and the sight of cakes and viands on the table nearly swept the corporal from his course.

"Thank you—thank you, Mrs. Fenstermacher—but we can't put you to a lot of fuss over us," he stammered. "Besides, it ain't—"

"It's not any troubles," she said earnestly. "It will gif me pleasure to see you liddle boys eat. Come, die tea it will cold get."

The corporal, recovering himself in his habit of obeying orders, dashed his recalcitrant hat back on to his head and blurted out the worst.

"We ain't allowed to fraternise with the enemy," he said thickly, and turned quickly back upstairs as if in search of a refuge, leaving Frau Fenstermacher to look after him in pained wonderment.

"Now you fellows pretty near stubbed your toe first rattle," he cautioned his squad once he had assembled them in his own room and closed the door.

"If it's agin orders to eat a piece of cake with a nice old German lady, then this is goin' to be a fine Christmas package they handed us," protested one of the squad.

"And I'll bet she sure can make cake," spoke up another of the disgusted seven. "She looks just like Sergeant Billie Walters' mother back home and she made the best cakes in the world next to my own mother."

"Yes, an' for all you knows the old lady'd slip a few pinches of rat poison in the tea and then where'd we all be? The Cap'n 'd know right away we hadn't followed orders and we wouldn't even get a decent military funeral. We got to remember that these folks is our enemy and we can't mix with 'em," the corporal warned them.

But if Frau Fenstermacher's cake and tea went untouched that afternoon; if the corporal and his squad wore their hats and their sidearms about the place when they were there during the off-duty hours of the next few days, the end of a week found these precautionary habits laid aside almost entirely; and Mrs. Fenstermacher's cake had a habit of disappearing as quickly as it was baked.

Not only in Corporal McGee's squad, but among squads wherever billeted, the nightly relations became more those of host and guest. Neither conquered nor conqueror measured up to previous expectations of one another. Living under the same roof seemed to bring the amazing discovery to them that all were mere human beings, moved by similar impulses and attributes. The Americans, strangely enough, neither pillaged, plundered, nor pushed people arrogantly off the sidewalks into the streets. Moreover, they were a cheerful, kindly lot among whom women and children were quite safe. Why, their own Teuton troops had not behaved themselves so much as gentlemen and been such tolerant and tractable billet guests!

"These Americans are not savage beasts as we had been led to expect," was the word that went around among the civilian populace at the end of a week of nervous observation.

"These Heinies are not going to stick knives in our backs while we're asleep—they're a mighty hospitable lot and don't rob us the way the French did," was the American estimate that passed from mouth to mouth in the billets at the end of the week of watchful observation.

"Propaganda!" cautioned the French high command sharply, bringing pointedly to the attention of the American high command the reports of French liaison officers that a spirit of flagrant, if not open, fraternisation with the enemy was springing up between the German populace and American soldiers.

"Those artful Huns are laying it on thick trying to win the hearts of the American soldiers and gain favour at the peace table," shouted the British War Office, urging that the practice be wiped out summarily.

New and rigid orders came out forthwith against fraternising with the enemy. They were emphasised at officers' assemblies and passed on down through every channel of command to the squad leaders themselves, who carried them to the men in the billets.

Corporal McGee carried his orders to his own squad with righteous indignation at their derelictions, reflecting the spirit that had come on down to him from the higher command with unerring precision and spirit, as becomes a squad leader. He saw the thing in its proper light now that it had been made clear to him. Chevrons had come to him within a month after he left his job as an apprentice brickmaker to help win the war, and he always had taken his responsibility seriously, carrying out his orders without fear or maudlin sympathy for those who were wont to complain of military exactitude.

"Let me warn you birds again," he admonished them, "this fraternisin' with the enemy has got to stop right now."

"Seems to me you've been eating your share of the enemy's cake," retorted Private Jones, the most outspoken of the squad, whose first year at college, interrupted by the War, had given him critical propensities.

"New orders has come today and I want this fraternisin' cut out," the corporal asserted himself. "We got to remember we're conquerors and not get too gay with the natives."

"Don't being conquerors rank us a piece of cake and cup of tea once in a while," persisted Private Jones, encouraged to debate the matter by the sympathetic attitude of his buddies and the past culpability of his corporal. "'Specially when the enemy's a nice old mother who says she's adopted us and wants us to be happy while we're at her house."

"It's Boche propaganda," affirmed Corporal McGee. "The Cap'n told us all about it. He got it straight from the Colonel, who got it right from the General himself."

"Stuff!" sneered the squad spokesman.

"It's not stuff neither," Corporal McGee affirmed. "I been thinkin' it over on the way up here and it is kinda odd the way these Heinies are treatin' us. What should this old lady want to make us a lot of cakes and feed us all the time if she didn't have some motive? She's got her orders from the Kaiser direct if we only knew the truth. The Cap'n said as much about all of 'em. He says we can't make friends out of our enemies and get away with it."

"Stuff!" persisted the obdurate Jones. "Don't we know what's got under the feelings of Mrs. Fenstermacher. The only thing that's puzzlin' us is that she don't want to put rat poison in the cake."

"What you mean?"

"Didn't she get confidential with us the other night," Private Jones narrated feelingly, "and tell us she had three boys of her own in this War—and that none of 'em came back—an' that they were all just kids–an' the last of 'em killed in the Argonne fracas! And wasn't there tears come into her eyes when she tells us that she was expecting a lot of long-bearded cut-throats and—when she saw us come up she said that except for the uniform we might've been her own boys coming back home. And she says to us—she likes to imagine we are her boys back in the house again and she wants to take care of us until we go back where we'll have our own mothers. That may sound like propaganda to the Cap'n or it may sound like mush to you, Corporal McGee, but not to us that was there and heard her say it."

Corporal McGee swallowed hard and sat in wide-eyed reflection for some minutes, debating Private Jones' disclosure against the Captain's stern warning. Mothers were really baffling creatures. He never had been able to fathom the strange feelings akin to awe that they had awakened back in the training camps when they had revealed themselves to him as hallowed beings who alone seemed to sound the depths of tragedy and scale the heights of courage that went into this sombre business of sending an army of their boys away to battle. There came into his memory the grim pathos of a brave smile he had seen, time and again, following some lad from his mother's face until the troop train was lost in the distance. Then see her break and fall! The memory of mothers he had seen at the troop trains had come up before him suddenly to haunt him in battle when youngsters he had known fell.

He put the picture out of his mind suddenly. What had that to do with fraternising with the enemy? he demanded of himself. Why permit his squad to be taken in further by organised propaganda intended to disarm their suspicions and gain their favour for no good purpose? There was no craftiness of which these Germans were not capable. He had his orders and he would assert them.

"You birds talk like you ain't growed up," he charged them. "If you're a growed-up sample then I never want to be one," retorted Private Jones.

"All I got to say," the corporal replied stubbornly, sensing the unsympathetic attitude of his squad, "you'd better not let me catch you fraternisin' with the enemy. Take your own chances if you quit bein' soldiers-an' if you get in the hoosegow don't ask for no sympathy from yours trooly. I can't be here every second to watch you—but after this watch your step when I'm around!"

"Then all I got to say to the corporal is that you're kiddin' yourself out of a mighty fine Christmas dinner right here in this billet," Private Jones asserted disgustedly.

The Christmas spirit had been in the air for a week. Everyone sensed it without realising very definitely just what it was until the day was hard upon them. Christmas was a day to reckon with this year, for the bounty of peace was hung in the world's stocking. Christmas was no longer a hollow mockery, even though it brought sad memories and heavy hearts in its wake. It held at least a glad portent for Christmas days to come, Christmas days when the gaping wounds and blinding hurts of war were as nearly healed as the miracle of time can heal them. The spirit of Christmas must have been at bottom of this fraternisation that winked covertly at stern orders; the spirit that nurtured goodwill among men along with the peace that now had come in just ahead of the Yuletide.

Corporal McGee's squad, less Corporal McGee, decided to make it a day. Frau Fenstermacher herself had invited them to a Christmas dinner, to be held in the evening behind closed doors, after they had returned from their own company mess. Private Jones had suggested a Christmas tree. The others had fallen in with the spirit of the enterprise avidly. It would help drive away the ominous blue devils of gloom that had invaded their division at Christmas time a year ago and gnawed at the entrails of strong men and boys. These same haunting blue devils were in the offing now and they could be counted upon to haunt the camps at Christmastide until those camps were a thing of black memory.

Corporal McGee scoffed at the idea and flatly refused to have anything to do with such an affair. He shut the squad off from telling him too much of their plans. What he did not know would not hurt his conscience as corporal. If they were intent on making fools of themselves behind his back—it was their affair. He could not remain eternally at the billet and spy upon their every move. And he was not the kind to report his whole squad in to the Captain.

"I'm goin' up to Bonn for the Christmas ball-game and root for our bunch while they clean up on the Canucks," he told them gruffly. "I'm gettin' back home here about ten o'clock and leavin' it to you not to do nothin' you shouldn't do!"

"Don't be a saphead," Private Jones badgered him. "We're having a real Christmas tomorrow. Ma Fenstermacher's having in a few little kids that's minus dads as a result of this War, and we're giving 'em some chocolate tins from the commissary and we got some dolls and sleds and skates for 'em. Then Ma Fenstermacher's going to—"

"You can't get away with that stuff—that's fraternisin' with the enemy." Corporal McGee answered warmly. "What'd the Cap'n say if he—"

"Cap'n shucks," laughed Private Smith, the youngest member of the squad, a red-faced cherub of sixteen. "He's in about the same fix you'se in on this fraternisin' business, I guess."

"What do you mean?" demanded the corporal.

"Didn't me and Jonesey run into him this afternoon? We goes into a store to buy some dolls and skates. We just git started when in waltzes the Cap'n. We hid out fast behind a counter—and what does the Cap'n do but buy a half-dozen dolls and some skates, tin soldiers and a lot of truck, lookin' around nervous like at the door every minute. Then he has 'em wrapped up and carries 'em out in the company mailbag actin' just like he was pullin' off a bank stick-up. What's that but fraternising? Or maybe you think he was gettin' them dolls for his dear little pet corp'rals and sergeants."

"If he bought them things it was to send to his own kids at home," protested Corporal McGee loyally. "You wouldn't catch the Cap'n fraternisin' with the enemy after the way he laid it out to us about these Dutch."

"You're right that no one'll catch him," asserted Private Smith acridly. "Leave that to him. But just the same the Cap'n's goin' to fraternise—and German kids 'll be playin' with that sackful o' toys before Christmas is over."

"Well, anyhow," retorted Corporal McGee bluntly, "you ain't goin' to see me taken in by none of this Boche propaganda and rewardin' these Dutch for killin' off our buddies by given' 'em a nice Christmas present. And you birds better be in your feather beds when I get in from Bonn at ten o'clock."

He stalked from the room with an air of washing his hands of the whole affair and leaving them alone to their perilous and treasonable folly.

From a Third Army truck driver who made the long supply haul up the Rhine to regiments billeted in the Rhenish hill lands the squad secured a small fir-tree for five marks. They smuggled it into their billet late at night, hidden in shelter halves and ponchos lest their premeditated plan of fraternising with the enemy awaken the ready suspicions of the military police.

"Nice Christmas spirit," grumbled Private Jones when the tree was safely inside. "Nice Christmas spirit when you got to sneak around about it like robbin' somebody's watermelon patch."

But the Christmas spirit lost nothing of its zest for all its perils; and it was with something akin to bubbling youthful enthusiasm that the seven temporarily transplanted youngsters strung popcorn and devised colored paper ornaments for the tree under Frau Fenstermacher's skilful instructions. No blue devils should haunt them this Christmas. It was really not such a bad Christmas after all. They would put nothing on the tree for one another. The monthly war wage of privates, after the allotments for Liberty bonds and what-not had been deducted, put a strain upon their combined resources in buying dolls and trinkets for the youngsters that Frau Fenstermacher was to have in for the evening. And besides, they had bought for her a Christmas surprise—a warm new cape of real cloth, not cheap ersatz material, at the staggering cost of seventy marks.

"I was just thinkin'," ruminated Private Smith when their Christmas arrangements had been completed and they were assembled upstairs in their billet ready for bed on Christmas Eve, "I was just thinkin' that I'm gettin' more kick outa this Christmas than if the tree was goin' to be loaded with things for me alone, like it used to be back home. And none of us gettin' a thing either."

"Don't be too sure none of us ain't getting a thing," Private Jones rejoined cynically. "If they catch us romping around that tree with that old lady and these kids the whole bunch of us is likely to get about six months in the hoosegow for fraternisin' with the enemy."

When Corporal McGee approached his billet, glum and blue from a dismal, cheerless Christmas which not even the drubbing his buddies gave the Canadians at Bonn served to dispel, his ears were greeted by the unmistakable sound of revelry. The squad was trying to sing a discordant ensemble that served nevertheless to herald their high spirits. It enraged him that they not only had ignored taps but were cavorting thus noisily at ten o'clock on Christmas night in open fraternisation with the enemy. As he entered the hall of the billet in high wrath and firm purpose, he found that the door to the living-room shut off the merriment. He pounded officiously on the door. Mutual disgrace could only come of such conduct should the noise come to the attention of the military police. He would assert his authority at once.

Frau Fenstermacher had answered the door and seized him irresistibly by the arm before he could announce his stern humor. She bustled him quickly inside to the table that was littered with the remnants of cakes and tempting viands, and upon which stood two half-empty bottles of Rhine wine which she had served up after the custom of the country. His squad gathered about him on the instant in noisy and effusive greeting. Corporal McGee remained inflexible.

"I thought I told you birds to be in bed by ten o'clock," he raged, ignoring Frau Fenstermacher's tender of a chair. He left his hat on his head, set at an arrogant angle.

"The children's gone with their dolls 'n' things but you shoulda seen 'em— eyes big as saucers and they had the time o' their lives," effused Private Smith, unaffected by the corporal's martial austerity. "Say 'n' you ought to see what we give Ma Fenstermacher!"

Another member of the squad brought the cape gaily from a chair in the corner of the room and had her put it on for inspection.

The corporal did not look.

"Nice bunch—fraternisin' with the enemy an' me up to Bonn rootin' for our buddies while they clean up the Canucks!" he sneered unyieldingly.

Frau Fenstermacher took him in hand firmly, removing his hat and seating him in spite of himself at the table before an uncut layer cake and a glass of wine with an expertness that bespoke long practice and expert knowledge in the art of handling stubborn striplings. In a few moments his overcoat was off and his grumbling silenced for the moment. She led him off into a discussion of the game at Bonn and clapped her hands with delight at the news that the Americans had won over their Canadian allies. In the finesse of her skill in bringing him into something of the spirit of the merry squad she chanced presently to inspect his Croix de Guerre with an intimate and friendly interest.

"Und that pretty medal is for being a goot soldier in der wars?" she asked him guilelessly.

Private Jones leaped from his seat on the instant and raised his hand to the members of the squad.

"All together fellows," he announced hilariously. "All together—the division song. Sing!" As he led off the others picked up the air and words and carried the song through waggishly as if in answer to Frau Fenstermacher's inquiry.

> The General got the Croix de Guerre,
> *Parlez vous*,
> The General got the Croix de Guerre,
> *Parlez vous*,
> The General got the Croix de Guerre,
> The son of a gun was never there,
> Hinky, dinky, *parlez vous*!

Corporal McGee reddened as he arose and reached instinctively for the big silver watch that hung on a heavy link chain in the upper bellows pocket of his blouse just under his bright new Croix de Guerre. As they ended the song with a jeering laugh he drew the watch forth and consulted the faded dial of the ancient timepiece ominously.

"That'll be all for you birds this night," he muttered decisively. "It's ten-fifteen by Heinie's watch-time for bad boys to be tucked in bed. All upstairs, you birds. Snap into it!"

The sight of Frau Fenstermacher, suddenly frozen to a stark staring statue, her face white as death, swept upon them in the next instant. Her eyes were fixed upon the ancient timepiece that Corporal McGee held in his hand; and as he made to put it back in his pocket she laid her hand upon his wrist.

"Where did you came by it?" she asked in a low voice that trembled with some strong emotion.

"What—you mean that clock?" said the corporal airily. "I took it off a bull elephant of a—"

He stopped speaking suddenly, his voice arrested by an intuition that Frau Fenstermacher's tragic manner aroused. He turned quickly to another explanation.

"Why, I—I got that there watch from—from one o' them big French pawnbrokers—down there at Nancy—for ten francs," he stammered. "Why?"

"It was mein liddle Heinrich's," Frau Fenstermacher whispered simply, taking the watch and pressing it pathetically to her lips.

She opened the hunting case and held it up before them.

"See," she whispered, pointing to the inscription in German script. "It is der name of his fadder also. Heinrich. He haf it at Sedan und he gif it to liddle Heinrich, to bring him safe back from der wars like it did for his fadder. But no, it was not so for mein liddle Heinrich. Some low Frencher kilt mein Heinrich und took his watch."

The Christmas gaiety in the German billet was replaced by the noisy ticking of the clock over the mantel. Corporal McGee stood gaping in the throes of a sudden rending revelation. Frau Fenstermacher no longer puzzled him. She was disclosed—the mother of a soldier.

"Maybe," he said when he could direct a voice that seemed intent on choking him, "maybe you'll—let me give it back to you—for a Christmas present."

Acknowledgments

The Publishers wish to thank the following for use of previously printed material in this collection.

The Estate of Richard Aldington and Chatto and Windus for "Introduction to the Trenches" from *Death of a Hero* by Richard Aldington.
"In Another Country" from *Men Without Women* by Ernest Hemingway, copyright© Ernest Hemingway, reproduced by permission of the Curtis Brown Group Ltd, London.
"Among the Trumpets" by Leonard Nason, copyright©1927 , reprinted by permission of *The Saturday Evening Post.*
William Heinemann Ltd for "The Traitor" from *Ashenden* by W. Somerset Maugham, used by permission.
"One Hundred Per Cent" by Leo V. Jacks is reprinted with the permission of Charles Scribner's Sons, an imprint of Macmillan Publishing Company, from Scribner's Magazine.
Every effort has been made to trace the owners of the copyright material in this book. In the case of any question arising as to the use of any such material, the Publisher would be pleased to receive notification of this.

For the endpaper image: The Daily Telegraph map of the world, showing events of World War I, including insets showing Belgian, Dutch, French, Italian, Portuguese and United States possessions. Published by Geographia, London, 1918. Credit: Library of Congress.
For the spine image credit: Created by NAS from the Noun Project